Believers

Believers

FAITH IN HUMAN NATURE

Melvin Konner, MD

W. W. NORTON & COMPANY

Independent Publishers Since 1923

For information about permission to reproduce selections from
this book, write to Permissions, W. W. Norton & Company, Inc.,
500 Fifth Avenue, New York, NY 10110

For information about special discounts for bulk purchases, please contact
W. W. Norton Special Sales at specialsales@wwnorton.com or 800-233-4830

Manufacturing by Lake Book Manufacturing
Book design by Fearn Cutler de Vicq
Production manager: Beth Steidle

ISBN 978-0-393-65186-7

W. W. Norton & Company, Inc., 500 Fifth Avenue, New York, N.Y. 10110
www.wwnorton.com

W. W. Norton & Company Ltd., 15 Carlisle Street, London W1D 3BS

1 2 3 4 5 6 7 8 9 0

To

Rabbi Emanuel Feldman,

The Reverend Dr. James M. Gustafson,

and

Professor Ann Cale Kruger,

believers

Religious suffering is, at one and the same time, the expression of real suffering and a protest against real suffering. Religion is the sigh of the oppressed creature, the heart of a heartless world, and the soul of soulless conditions. It is the opium of the people. The abolition of religion as the illusory happiness of the people is the demand for their real happiness. To call on them to give up their illusions about their condition is to call on them to give up a condition that requires illusions. The criticism of religion is, therefore, in embryo, the criticism of that vale of tears of which religion is the halo.

—*Karl Marx, introduction to* A Contribution to the Critique of Hegel's Philosophy of Right, *1844*

I had no intention to write atheistically. But I own that I cannot see, as plainly as others do, & as I sh^d wish to do, evidence of design & beneficence on all sides of us. There seems to me too much misery in the world . . . On the other hand I cannot anyhow be contented to view this wonderful universe & especially the nature of man, & to conclude that everything is the result of brute force. I am inclined to look at everything as resulting from designed laws, with the details, whether good or bad, left to the working out of what we may call chance. Not that this notion at all satisfies me. I feel most deeply that the whole subject is too profound for the human intellect. A dog might as well speculate on the mind of Newton.—Let each man hope & believe what he can.

—*Charles Darwin, letter to Rev. Asa Gray,*
May 22, 1860

The human religious impulse does seem very difficult to wipe out, which causes me a certain amount of grief. Clearly religion has extreme tenacity.

—*Richard Dawkins, BBC Two* Horizon *program,*
April 17, 2005

Contents

Introduction

Tragedies dominate the news, often man-made, enough to fill our lives if we look. But for most people, tragedy finds *them*. Even in the developed world, tragedy seems to visit more now than it once did. And often, the men who bring it home to us say they are motivated by faith.

Some use faith as an excuse, but for now let's take them at their word: faith is one of their motives. In Africa, Muslims and Christians build rogue armies that murder and rape on a large scale; in the Middle East, fanatical Jews desecrate Muslims' graves and burn down homes with families inside; in the United States, violent Christians murder doctors who perform abortions; in Burma, Buddhists brutalize Muslims; in India, Hindus torment Muslims; and in many countries, Muslims murder "unbelievers" in God's name.

But most "unbelievers" believe; they share the same God with their attackers. They must die not only because they are, say, Christians or Muslims but because they cross themselves with a different number of fingers or keep the feast of a different ancient imam. Theologians may say all of humankind is one, but extremists split hairs and murder "infidels," thinking they are doing right. They pray for wider war between faiths—as soon as enough deluded moderates see the light.

None of this is new. In fact, killing in the name of faith is less common today, when you consider human numbers. For much of our past, it was the rule, not the exception. It is how major religions became major—a long clash of "civilizations," war after war between armies moved by the conviction that their beliefs were solely true. But of all the different kinds of mutually exclusive belief, only one can be true—at most. Most people of faith accept the fact that billions don't share their most important commitments. Each of the largest religions is a fraction of humanity. Most adapt.

> Too bad, you won't find salvation in Christ.
> Sorry, you won't be reborn as a higher being or escape the cycle of rebirth.
> Pity you won't be absolved of your sins before you die and are punished forever.
> You won't get credit for following God's 613 commandments.
> You'll never know the precious sound of one hand clapping.
> I can help you get the truth, and it will save you; if you don't get it, too bad for you.

Not,

> If you don't, I'll kill you.

This letting people be is not just part of civilization; it's the heart of it: freedom of thought includes freedom of faith, an ability to practice one's observances, or none—a cosmopolitan acceptance. As an adjective, "cosmopolitan" means "open to those who are different"; as a noun, "a citizen of the world." Cosmopolitan civilization—humanity's greatest invention—is higher because it is wider. "Clash of civilizations" is an oxymoron. What we face is a clash between civilization and something else. Something that hates and fears civilization. Something that we can be confident—for the first time in history—will lose its futile battle against the future, against our vast humane majority.

But most of that majority are people of faith—people whose faith leads them to build, not destroy; help, not hurt; thank, not rage. People who are uncertain about the future, but whose faith helps them to go forward: to raise their children; to come to each other's aid; to wake up every morning and embrace, or at least face, a new day. Yet people with no religious faith are growing in numbers, and that's fine. In northern Europe, conventional religion is now a minority culture, although spirituality is not. Russia and China, whose generations of Communism repressed religious adherence, still have religion, although conventional believers are probably a minority. Even the US, long the most religious advanced country, is starting to catch up to Europe.

The rise of the "Nones"—those who check "none of the above" when asked about religion—is the strongest trend in American religious life. A generation ago, millions of dropouts from conventional faith ended up in spanking-new evangelical megachurches; today's dropouts end up in sports arenas and coffee shops, gyms and health food stores, clubs and psychologists' offices, surfing the waves or the internet, religion the last thing on their minds. Spiritual? Many say there is more out there than material reality. But keep the beliefs and practices of prior generations? No thanks.

Is it a worrisome trend? No. As countries modernize, become wealthier, reduce child mortality, and live longer, they grow less religious. Let's put off the explanation for now and just grant that fact. The most religious countries are the least developed ones. It's no accident that Pope Francis came from the developing world—a first for the Vatican. Both the Catholic Church in Rome and the Church of England in Canterbury now have strong second centers of gravity south of the equator. But as the planet's South modernizes, it will follow the path blazed by developed countries, toward less conventional spirituality and more Nones. Some say religion will fade away.

In fact, some very smart people *want* it to fade away and are sure it will, as indicated by the titles of certain popular books: *The End of*

Faith, The God Delusion, Breaking the Spell, God Is Not Great. I agree with many of their criticisms of religion, and I am not a believer, but I don't like their attacks on other people's faith. I don't think faith will fade away, nor do I think it should. I want to understand faith—its basis in brain function and genes, its growth in childhood, its deep evolutionary background, its countless cultural and historical varieties, its ties to morality, and its many roles in human life. I think faith can be explained, but not explained away.

We are rapidly leaving behind—and good riddance to it—a world in which religion could coerce not only heretics (those with a new interpretation or faith) but also those with no faith at all. In many places, religions have that power today. But take the long view. Our great-grandchildren will live in a world where religion is on the defensive, and many of us already do. It's hard to watch the news and believe this, but here we will not be looking at the headlines; we will be looking at the evolution and history of faith in all its varieties, the grand sweep of good and evil, the aspirational and tragic displays of a human inclination grounded in biology.

I think faith will persist in a large minority, and in some form perhaps a majority, permanently. It has always manifested itself in different ways—some revelatory and comforting; some kind and good; some ecumenical and cosmopolitan; some bigoted, coercive, and violent. But the future will both produce more Nones and incline the religious among us to reject bigotry, coercion, and violence.

As for murderous fanaticism, it is not solely grounded in religion. Europe's gas chambers murdered millions, but not in God's name; the Nazis—despite the *Gott mit uns* motto on their belts—were a political, not a religious, movement. Stalinism and Maoism, each of which killed scores of millions, were *anti*religious tyrannies. Later, mass murders in Indonesia, Cambodia, and Rwanda had nothing to do with religion. The frequent terrorism of the early and middle twentieth century owed more to leftist politics than to faith. The 1995 Oklahoma

City bombing and the 2011 mass murder of teens at a Norway summer camp stemmed from right-wing politics, and most American terrorists are right-wing, *non*religious zealots. Religion as the root of all evil does not fit the facts.

Belligerent atheists attack faith because—not being true cosmopolitans—they are intolerant of the idea that our actions can be legitimately motivated at times by something other than pure reason. Soon people will be asking not, "Do I have a right to disbelieve?" but "Do I have a right to faith?" Atheism, for all its rationality, has taken a fundamentalist turn, seeking to exclude all other forms of belief. It is the mirror image of the exclusionary fanaticisms of faith. So, this book is not only a scientific attempt to understand religion—including its toxic infusion with violence—but an a-theistic defense of it as a part of human nature, for many. People of faith have the inclination, and should have the right, to believe things for which there is no evidence.

I was raised as an Orthodox Jew and remained so until age 17. I have now been a nonbeliever for over half a century. I understand those two traditions—Judaism and nonbelief—very well. I lived for two years among a people commonly called Bushmen, hunter-gatherers in Botswana, and was for a time an apprentice in their trance-dance religion, so (with the help of others who have studied it) I know about that faith too. I live in a Christian country, know the role of Christianity in the history of the West, and have had important friendships with Christian clergy and laity—not least of all my wife, whom I would describe as a mildly believing Presbyterian. You might say I cut my eyeteeth on the contrasts between Judaism and Christianity—often, in the past, ominous for Jews—so I have been thinking about varieties of faith all my life.

In various ways—as an anthropologist, traveler, teacher, and friend—I have encountered Tibetan Buddhism, Hinduism, Islam, and other faiths, always with respect and openness to learning about their commonalities and differences. I have spent many years studying and teaching about culture, brain function, evolution, child development, and other ways of knowing how religion relates to our brains and bodies.

Believers is about the *nature* of faith: an evolved, biologically grounded, psychologically intimate, socially strong set of inclinations and ideas that are not universal but are so widespread and deeply ingrained that, in my view, faith will never go away. I also think that it *should* never go away—a value judgment I will try to justify. But let's acknowledge those who think it should and will. Their twenty-first-century movement defends an old philosophy in vehement, persuasive ways: *religion is irrational, does great harm, and therefore should and will disappear from human experience.* Notice that there are four different propositions in these few italicized words. I will argue that the first two are partly true, but the last two are not evidence based. So, the movement against religion is also a faith.

The movement has had brilliant leaders, among them evolutionary biologist Richard Dawkins, philosopher Daniel Dennett, neuroscientist Sam Harris, and essayist Christopher Hitchens. They've been called the "Four Horsemen of the Apocalypse," "Ditchkins," and other unfriendly names, but I'll just call them "the Quartet." Their books are worth reading. Dawkins is and Hitchens was as eloquent in speech as in writing. The last months of Hitchens's life, when he was dying of cancer, did not much curtail his work; he was exemplary in poise and courage. Rabbi David Wolpe, who debated Hitchens publicly six times, was an admirer. To paraphrase the comedian W. C. Fields, also a proud atheist, Hitchens died without knuckling under.

I am not the first to criticize their views or to try to defend religion from them, not even the first nonbeliever. (My credentials for that label are sound; I am on an online list of celebrity atheists—between actress Keira Knightley and graphic artist Frank Kozik—and at times have been on an honor roll called *Who's Who in Hell.*) I don't plan to rebut them in detail here, any more than I plan to describe Buddhism or Judaism in detail. What matters for me about religions is that they have noticed something about human nature and tried in varied ways to give it form, expression, and meaning. What matters about the critics is that they have mostly missed it.

I have nothing against nonbelievers; I have been one for over half a century. I know that atheistic writings, speeches, debates, and websites comfort people who are struggling to feel that nonbelief is okay. Some are surrounded by believers who find them odd and bad. I am not being facetious when I say that Dawkins, Dennett, Harris, and Hitchens are pastors to those people, who need and deserve care and moral support. But gratuitous and ignorant bashing of religion does not just give comfort to harried atheists; it attempts, with all verbal guns blazing, to cause pain to believers. I will offer my opinion on whether and how much religion is irrational, harmful, and deserving of elimination from human life. However, it is the last of the four claims of the recent critics of religion, that it *will* disappear, that inspires my main argument.

There is another way to say that. My friend Robert Hamerton-Kelly was an eloquent, charismatic Methodist minister and philosopher, for many years the chaplain of Stanford University. I asked him whether he was worried about the New Atheism. He raised a white eyebrow under a thick shock of hair and, with a twinkle in his eye, after a careful professional pause, said in his basso profundo, "God can handle it."

———

Sir Francis Crick, codiscoverer of the structure of DNA, described himself as an agnostic, leaning toward atheism, but he had a lifelong contempt for religion. In 1963, a year after winning a Nobel Prize, he contributed £100 toward a prize for the best essay on the subject "What Can Be Done with the College Chapels?" The winning entry proposed that they be turned into swimming pools. In an essay of his own entitled "Why I Am a Humanist," Crick wrote, "The simple fables of the religions of the world have come to seem like tales told to children." When another biologist wrote a response to his essay, Crick replied, "I should perhaps emphasize this point, since it is good manners to pretend the opposite. I do not respect Christian beliefs. I think they are ridiculous."

Many scientists and philosophers have been inspired by Crick's view, but not all are as committed. Astrophysicist Neil deGrasse Tyson has separated himself from some:

> Atheists I know who proudly wear the badge are *active atheists*, they're, like, in-your-face atheists, and they want to change policies, and they're having debates! I don't have the time, the interest, the energy. . . . I'm a scientist, I'm an educator, my goal is to get people thinking straight in the first place, to get you to be curious about the natural world, that's what I'm about. . . . It's odd that the word "atheist" even exists. I don't play golf. Is there a word for non-golf-players? Do non-golf-players gather and strategize? Do non-skiers have a word, and come together and talk about the fact that they don't ski?

Another nemesis of religion, Steven Weinberg, a Nobel laureate in physics, detaches himself from certain scientists—Stephen Jay Gould, E. O. Wilson, and others—who see the possibility of détente or even an alliance (on environmental protection, for instance) between science and religion: "I'm not having it. . . . The world needs to wake up from its long nightmare of religious belief. Anything that we scientists can do to weaken the hold of religion should be done, and may in fact in the end be our greatest contribution to civilization."

But Weinberg also raises a concern: "If not religion, what?"

Certainly I'm not one of those who would rhapsodically say, "Oh, science. That's all we need, to understand the world, and look at pictures of the Eagle Nebula, and it'll fill us with such joy we won't miss religion. I think we will miss it. I see religion somewhat as a crazy old aunt. You know, she tells lies, and she stirs up all sorts of mischief and she's getting on, and she may not have that much life left in her, but she was beautiful once, and when she's gone, we may miss her."

Dawkins, when he heard this, was adamant: "I won't miss her at all. Not one scrap. Not one smidgen. I am utterly fed up with the respect that we, all of us . . . have been brainwashed into bestowing on religion." Weinberg has impeccable antireligious credentials, yet he has a subtlety that is missing from the Quartet's discourse. If they are a brass quartet, Weinberg is off to the side playing a plaintive solo violin. They are all humanists, true and faithful, but Weinberg is a tragic humanist, and even when they are standing shoulder to shoulder on the barricades, there is a difference.

I am one of those secular people "brainwashed" into showing respect for religion. I came by this brainwashing honestly, having been raised as a Modern Orthodox Jew. But I believe religion is a part of human nature. That doesn't mean it's a part of every person's makeup; it just means it's very persistent and will never go away.

Western Europe has experienced a large decline in religion in modern times, and the US is catching up. This is true by any measure, from church attendance to declarations of faith. These are natural declines, not government-enforced ones as in China or the Soviet Union. Is this what the world will look like when all of it is as prosperous, educated, and healthy as Europe is now? Perhaps, but at present, in the less developed countries, population growth among the religious makes for a stronger countervailing trend. We may end up with something like a steady state. Some see a transition that will end with the end of faith. I don't agree. I argue that religion's future depends on competing trends in biological and cultural evolution, and I think they will end in equilibrium. As physician-anthropologist Wulf Schiefenhövel has said, "We are, by our very nature, *Homo religiosus.*"

So, what about us atheists? Dennett, in *Breaking the Spell*, says we should be called "Brights," but for some reason this term has not caught on. I prefer the term that sociologists of religion use: "Nones" (because they check the "none of the above" box when asked about religion). It's not ideal, but it is catching on. The rise of the Nones is a common theme among scholars of religion, clergy, and theologians, and it is making a lot of people nervous about the human future. It needn't.

Nones have compassion, thankfulness, love, sometimes even a sense of oneness with other beings. We have feelings, hopes, dreams, responsibilities, ethics, rules, and rights. We have existed and been persecuted since the start of human time. Only recently, and so far only in a few parts of the planet, have we begun to be able to hold our heads high, be open about our beliefs (or lack of them), conduct our lives and raise our children as we wish. We don't deserve to be looked down on because we stay away from the church, mosque, shrine, synagogue, or temple. We don't want to be ostracized because we decline to prostrate ourselves, curtsy before a cross, burn incense at a statue, or wear a fringed garment during prayer. Some of us find it painful to see our children pledge allegiance to a nation "under God," or our parents buried with rites and sacraments that they might not have cared for, for the sake of someone else's idea of decorum. We have often been subject to such pressures.

We have also felt isolated. Nones, like gays, often appear in families and communities where they may not know anyone else like themselves. I have a friend in this situation. For many years, she and her father, a deeply believing Christian, argued warmly and frequently about his faith and her nonbelief. Both gave up on having the other come around, but they never stopped talking. Then, after becoming disabled in his seventies, her father took his own life. My friend was bereft but unwavering, and Richard Dawkins's writings against religion helped her cope. In fact, she resented me for thinking and writing otherwise and for what she saw as my equivocation and inconstancy. Nones, like gays, need to find and defend each other.

I apologized, and I tried to avoid causing her further pain, but the fact that Dawkins and others comfort those without belief does not license them to afflict all who are otherwise comforted. Not everyone lives by bread alone, or even bread and circuses and symphonies and science. Many want or need more. A geneticist who was a Dominican priest before he lost his faith and became a scientist said, "There are six billion people in the world, and if we feel that we are going to persuade them to lead a rational life, based on scientific knowledge, we are not only dreaming . . . it's such an illusion, it would be like believing in the fairy godmother. . . . People need to find meaning and purpose in life . . . and they find meaning and purpose in religion." He accused aggressive atheists of their own worst sin: "believing in the fairy godmother." God may be a delusion, but atheists' confidence in the imminent end of faith is a delusion too.

Consider their claims. You are not religious unless you have been indoctrinated in childhood, and your religiosity is proportional to the strength of your indoctrination. Intelligence is the key to overcoming the indoctrination, given the right arguments. Finally, religion is a vice, harmful, and in fact evil.

But there are a few problems. For one thing, parents of all religious inclinations, including atheists, often find that their children grow up to believe things quite different from what they were taught, and are sometimes more devout than their parents. Second, while doubts of philosophers, scientists, and others are as old as the oldest major religions, some of the brightest people in the world have been aware of those arguments and have rejected them in favor of belief. Among these are Aristotle, Isaac Newton, Michael Faraday, James Clerk Maxwell, Robert Boyle, William Harvey, Louis Pasteur, Gregor Mendel, Max Planck, Ronald Fisher, David Lack, Theodosius Dobzhansky, Freeman Dyson, and Francis Collins. Also included are about 40 percent of scientists and about 7 or 8 percent of the US National Academy of Sciences. The number of believing scientists has declined, but they still refute the claim that intelligence, even scientific intelligence, is incompatible with religion, or that faith precludes scientific achievement.

As for religion being a vice—well, if you were going to act like a scientist, you might start with an open digital document and divide it into two columns. At the top of one you would key in, "Harm Done by Religion"; at the top of the other, "Good Done by Religion." You would gather empirical evidence on both sides, then compare them. I don't say this would be easy or precise, but some truth might be gained. What you would not do, if you wanted to be a scientist, is have only one column. Yet this is what many critics do. The litany of religious tyranny, wars, terrorism, logical errors, and opposition to science are these critics' meat and potatoes, but religion's most insidious harm is that it dupes innocent people into believing a pack of lies.

I will not challenge the litany, except the last item, and that only partly. We will explore the possibility that religion does some good, that this good is to some extent observable and measurable, and that it might just outweigh the evil that religion also does. That tipping toward good will likely be more true in the future, as the most tyrannical, violent, and exclusivist forms of faith are supplanted by tolerant ones, and as those who walk away from faith can do that without prejudice.

As for being duped into believing a pack of lies, let's rephrase that a bit. People are led, often beginning in childhood, into following their religious inclinations (if any) and expressing them with rituals, practices, ideas, symbols, and narratives traditional to the culture they come from. Most of these forms have no basis in evidence and never will, except that they feel right to the person involved with them. In other words, the "evidence" is subjective, not scientific.

Joan Roughgarden is a leading evolutionary ecologist at Stanford University who is also a believing Christian and the author of *Evolution and Christian Faith*, which Roughgarden herself has said is not a work of science, but a religious book. She criticizes science for being arrogant and often wrong. She disputes the claim that scientists don't have prophets, saying that Darwin is treated as such, and she uses his theory of sexual selection as an example. She rejects intelligent design but believes that, in view of the frequent and persistent errors of science, "the credibility of the Bible rises."

I disagree with her about sexual selection, which has received overwhelming empirical support—foreseen by Darwin not because he was a prophet but because he was a smart observer. I agree that the discourse around it sometimes has a locker room odor. As for errors in science, they persist beyond their time, but usually not by much; the whole point of science is to replace bad ideas with better ones. That process happens in religion, but religion takes much more on authority.

However, I agree with Roughgarden that "it's not irrational for someone to relatively emphasize the status of the Bible," although it is nonrational. And I agree more strongly when she asks, "Is rational thought all that correct? What about our emotions? Do we actually require a rational argument for God?" My answer to that is no, argument is irrelevant. I also appreciate Roughgarden's observation that communion is a symbol of community, the latter being to my mind one of religion's most valuable assets. As for our thoughts, feelings, and experiences, many argue that they are completely based in brain function. I accept this claim; I have written and taught it for a lifetime. Every day we find more support for it. But however strong it is, it is not the last word on whether faith should make sense to believers.

Read the criticisms of faith; they will sharpen and may persuade you. But you may not meet up with much you haven't heard before. Here is a partial list, with some of their past proponents:

There is no reason to think that a supernatural being intervenes in nature, history, or everyday life. (Aristotle)

The God of the Old Testament is punitive, misogynistic, brutal, unforgiving, obsessional, and at times an ethnic cleanser. (many ancient rabbis, including Jesus)

Religions have often caused or worsened devastating wars. (Herodotus)

The Bible contains contradictions and far-fetched tales. (Maimonides, Spinoza)

The Qur'an seems to condone violence to spread Islam. (Javed Ahmad Ghamidi)

Nothing supernatural is needed to explain the human mind. (David Hume)

Jesus cannot have been the son of God. (Thomas Jefferson)

The history of life, including human life, is a natural process. (Charles Darwin)

Religion discourages people from bettering their real lives. (Karl Marx)

God is a mental holdover from our experience with our parents. (Sigmund Freud)

Religion results from childhood reward and punishment. (B. F. Skinner)

No scientific evidence exists to confirm belief in reincarnation. (the Dalai Lama)

Some terrorism results from religious fanaticism. (Bill Clinton, George W. Bush)

It is best not to believe in things for which there is no evidence. (Bertrand Russell)

If life has so far sheltered you from these arguments, then you have a lot to learn from recent atheistic writings. Even if you've heard them, the arguments are ably made in these works. But if you are not aware that some of the most religious people, including leaders and thinkers in all faiths, have acknowledged almost all these claims and found ways to deal with them *without* abandoning their faith, or even while embracing it more strongly, you will not learn that fact from recent critiques, which hold that believers are as ignorant of doubt as the atheists themselves are of faith.

In fact, these authors do not know the first thing about faith, which is that faith is *the conviction of things unseen.* They ignore or belittle the key phrase describing this realm of human experience: *the leap of faith*—a metaphor for what believers must daily do in the absence of evidence. Faith is *supposed* to be a struggle, a striving toward belief; a difficult overcoming, not a denial, of doubt. The history of faith is one of people trying to find God, spirituality, or unity in a way that adds meaning and mystery to a purely material world. I long ago gave up that struggle for other quests that *I* found meaningful. But I let people who are still engaged in it find their own way; I don't belittle them or try to block their chosen path, and I hope they do the same for me.

This book is, in part, a personal story of religious and irreligious encounters. I like the tension and drama of electric, sometimes bitter conversations among people with different views of life. But there is new research on the neuroscience, psychology, childhood development, evolution, anthropology, and sociology of religion. And there is the dynamic reality of faith and practice throughout the world. In what I hope is a colorful weave of words, facts, and thoughts, I will try to represent both.

Believers

Encounters

Brooklyn is the Borough of Churches, and it made me nervous as a child to walk past some of them, although I was roughed up only a few times, at the cost of my pride and a handful of coins. The immediate wake of World War II was a tense time for Jews.

But it wasn't just about threats, past or present; I was steeped in Judaism and Jewishness. My earliest memories are of my grandfather swaying in the sunlit parlor of our apartment, wrapped in a prayer shawl, his left arm and forehead adorned with the black leather straps and boxes that observant Jewish men put on for weekday morning prayers. My initial religious inspiration came from him. He sat me in his lap and taught me Hebrew letters from the headlines of the left-leaning, Yiddish-language daily the *Forvertz*. He was a retired hardware store owner, not a socialist; the *Forvertz* was just the leading daily in his native tongue. But his faith was a constant, and I was in awe of it. I prayed long and hard for him in his last illness, yet when he died I did not lose faith; like most people whose prayers are not answered (at least not simply), my response was different.

A year earlier my grandfather had enrolled me in after-school Hebrew classes at the local Orthodox synagogue. I was there every day between ages 8 and 17. I became *more* religious than my parents and most of my friends. But at 17, I lost my faith. I started college that fall, but there were other things going on in my life and in the world. In

August, still 16 by two days and not yet quite a college boy, I defied my parents and boarded a bus to Washington, where I heard the Reverend Dr. Martin Luther King Jr. deliver the speech that would change America and the world. His stunning oration ended with an imagined future cry that would unite liberation and faith: *Free at last, free at last, thank God almighty, we're free at last!* For him and me, God was there.

White as I was, King's dream was mine too. While still in high school, I was active in that struggle, as well as the one to avert nuclear war, a constant threat. I still went to synagogue on Saturday, and I knew Dr. King's speech and much other discourse on integration drew its metaphors and phrasing from the Bible I had studied, but my rabbi did not say the things I hoped to hear.

That fall, in one class at Brooklyn College, the professor came in, sat cross-legged on the desk, lit his pipe, and began "doing philosophy"—which meant, among other things, undermining faith. Still an Orthodox Jew, I had little use for this, and I often whispered with the young woman next to me. Halfway through the semester, the professor quite properly asked us to sit separately. I sulked, stopped coming, and got a D+. But his message sank in. After synagogue on Friday nights, I walked—keeping the Sabbath—to that young woman's house, almost an hour each way. By winter I no longer believed.

It wasn't just because of the philosophy class. My generation and I were in turmoil—politically, sexually, artistically, and musically, as well as religiously—and it is likely I would have changed without the philosopher's challenges. But the analytic language he taught me was a bridge. I turned to anthropology to get a new take on religion and a new account of the deep human past. Like many Jewish boys, I was pre-med, but I went to graduate school in physical anthropology and studied the biology of behavior—the embodiment of mind.

I lived for two years in Africa, doing research among hunter-gatherers in the Kalahari. I taught about human nature for five years, but then went to medical school after all. *Nothing human is alien to me,* a favorite saying, now meant not just the lives of hunter-gatherers but also mental and physical illness. I saw people give birth (I delivered thirty-six babies) and face death (rarely peaceful), with or without religion. It didn't seem crucial. But if a patient was religious, I was the one who called a chaplain. After medical school I taught again. Africa, medicine, and fatherhood remade me, but I began another thirty-five years of teaching evolution, human biology, and brain science. If students are religious, I help them reconcile evolution with faith; if they are doubting, I help with that too.

My childhood and adolescence were steeped in conventional faith. But what is the logic of my half century of *non*belief—what some would call my healthy resistance to rubbish; others, my tragic inability to embrace some of life's most meaningful experiences? I almost failed philosophy, but it helped give me the framework I needed to understand a painful personal experience: the loss of faith. Philosophy alone could not have caused the loss or maintained it all my life, but it mattered to me at the time, and it still matters now. The professor, Martin Lean, was an analytic philosopher; he closely examined words and sentences, with the goal of clarifying discourse. The following simplification may help.

The modern analytic tradition begins with David Hume, goes through John Stuart Mill, and embraces Bertrand Russell, Ludwig Wittgenstein, and many others. I fell in with some of Lean's smart and funny graduate students. They covered a door in their apartment with an evolutionary tree of philosophers, their faves and bêtes noires drawn as ancestors and descendants. The phrase "The Qua Being" was prominently scrawled in one corner, an evolutionary side trunk of bad philosophers. The Qua Being culminated in the mid-twentieth century with thinkers like Martin Heidegger, who wrote, "Nothing nothings itself" and, "To think Being itself explicitly requires disregarding Being to the extent that it is only grounded and interpreted in terms of beings and for beings as their ground"; Jean-Paul Sartre, who wrote, "If the being of phenomena is not resolved in a phenomenon of being and if nevertheless we can not say anything about being without considering this phenomenon of being, then the exact relation which unites the phenomenon of being to the being of the phenomenon must be established first of all"; and Edmund Husserl, who wrote, "Phenomenology as the science of all conceivable transcendental phenomena and especially the synthetic total structures in which alone they are concretely possible—those of the transcendental single subjects is *eo ipso* the a priori science of all conceivable beings."

Now if you're thinking, "He's taking these quotes out of context; they can't routinely write so incomprehensibly," consider another Heidegger quote: "To make itself understandable is suicide for philosophy." You might be in a better position if you are a native German speaker (he reportedly said that the German language speaks Being, while all other languages only speak *of* Being) or a pagan ("Only a god can save us"), but if you read these philosophers, you get the impression that they are impenetrable on purpose. Some experts say that if you spend a couple of decades studying these texts, you begin to understand. I'll take their word for it, although in that case I'm guessing that "understand" will be a word I no longer understand as I understand it now.

Analytic philosophers can be difficult to read, and they require study. But they are aiming to clarify discourse, while some philosophers are, sometimes explicitly, trying to muddy it. Analytic philosophers would say that making itself intelligible is the guiding light of philosophy, while suicide would be a growing and lasting unintelligibility. Although the Qua Being chart ended in 1964, I am pretty sure that much of postmodern philosophy would have found its way into my friends' genealogy as offspring of the trio of mystification. It certainly found that place in mine.

The analytic approach grew its own branches, but it has always been closely allied with science. This close relationship applies to the philosophy of science, but also to other subjects, like perception, knowledge, language, ethics, and metaphysics. This last term is a catchall label for subjects beyond physics in Aristotle's works, and an age-old war has pitted his (skeptical) followers against those of his elder colleague Plato, who taught that the world consists of shadows of real forms we can't see. You could say that Aristotle, being a scientist as well as a philosopher, was his era's leading skeptic of metaphysics, although for analytic philosophers he was not skeptical enough. Unfortunately, Aristotle, like Hippocrates and Galen in medicine, was canonized, so for over a thousand years these gifted observers of nature had their *writings* proclaimed as scientific gospel, instead of their *methods* (observation, induction, deduction, hypothesis, theory, challenge, modification), which were far more important.

Francis Bacon revived awareness of the methods in the early 1600s, and his philosophical work was a banner that an army of scientists could rally to. Vesalius and Fabricius did anatomical dissections that challenged Galen. William Harvey discovered how the heart really works (the blood doesn't slosh out and get consumed, but rather circulates). Copernicus, Kepler, and Galileo made observations that put the sun, not the Earth, at the heart of the heavenly spheres—decentering the church, the world, and the human race. And countless inventors used the scientific method to create labor-sparing machines, tools of navigation, medicines, and weapons that proved the method's value every day.

Meanwhile, Europe's religious leaders, while often tolerant of practical inventions, strongly opposed changes in the ancient view of the heavens or of the human body, and they held back early modern science. Later they did the same with vaccination, evolution, and many other truths. Scientists were first known as "natural philosophers," which is why they are still called doctors of philosophy, even if they earn the degree by inventing a new drug or discovering a new species or noticing a new galaxy. Metaphysics continued to mediate between science and faith, including attempts to prove the existence of God, the soul, an afterlife, and other intangible entities. John Locke and René Descartes engaged in such efforts, and even David Hume composed a debate between a voice claiming that God's existence could be proved and an opposing voice. But philosophy drove theology into retreat.

In fairness to what my old friends called the Qua Being, existential and postmodern philosophers are usually as antitheological as analytic ones are. Theology and metaphysics thrive in some circles, but they have lost their age-old wars of conquest. They influence, but they no longer rule. So I came to that freshman philosophy class with strong religious faith and left with none. Most people think, as I did at the time, that there are three basic answers to the question "Does God exist?"

1. "I believe that God exists."
2. "I don't believe that God exists."
3. "I can't tell for sure whether God exists."

Roughly parallel positions can be held by the hundreds of millions of Buddhists who were brought up to deny the existence of God (or, officially at least, gods) but to believe in reincarnation in a karmic cycle. The equivalents for them would be "I believe in a karmic cycle," "I don't believe in a karmic cycle," and "I'm not sure whether a karmic cycle exists."

But there is actually a fourth answer to these questions, which is, basically, "*Huh?*" This is shorthand for "I don't understand you" or "I don't get it." Some of us feel we can't really make any of the previous three statements about the existence of God because we don't understand what the word "God" (or "karma") means. Of course, you might define God as in the biblical book of Ezekiel (1:26–28): "And on top, upon this semblance of a throne, there was the semblance of a human form. From what appeared as his loins up, I saw a gleam as of amber—

what looked like a fire encased in a frame; and from what appeared as his loins down, I saw what looked like fire. There was a radiance all about him." If you say something like that, I can say, "Oh, that; no, I don't believe that."

Likewise, I don't believe that God appeared to Moses in a burning bush, or that God took a human form and lived a life in which he was both God and man, or that Shiva, the Hindu god of destruction, can appear in a carved abstraction of his phallus, or that I might have had a previous incarnation as an insect, or that bringing water and burning incense to a statue of the Buddha will affect my next life. To these things so defined I can say clearly no, I don't believe in them.

But many religious people say vaguer things. Baruch Spinoza said there is only one substance called God or nature, and many who believe this (sometimes called deists, and including some founders of the United States) also say they believe in God. If you ask me whether I think that *that* God exists, that's when I say, "Huh? I don't get it." If I am in the mood for a conversation, I may go on to say, "It's nature; why are you calling it God?" And the same goes for people who say things like, "God is life—the special quality of living things," or "God is the laws of physics," or "God is the love in all our hearts." I don't get it. "I don't get it" describes my position better than "agnostic" or "atheist," but "atheist" is close enough, given what most people mean by it; I don't believe, and I'm not in doubt. By the time I started my freshman philosophy course, I had probably become something like a deist (although still observing Jewish law), but by the end I could not hear myself describe my own position without saying "Huh?" to myself, so I stopped trying.

Many other things were going on in my life: I was disappointed in love, I was depressed, I was getting more involved in political movements, I was leaving my adolescence behind. Here I am trying to describe the intellectual framework that I built on the ruins of my faith, rising ever since. Yet the intellectual currents were much more complex. Mill's father taught him "that the question, Who made me? cannot be answered . . . since the question immediately presents itself, Who made God?" Bertrand Russell, in his 1927 essay "Why I Am Not a Christian," says that reading this statement made him realize there could be no argument from First Cause, a staple of theology. Russell goes on: "If there can be anything without a cause, it can just as well be the world as God. . . . There is no reason to suppose that the world had a beginning."

Now, personally—and probably luckily, all in all—I did not have a dad like Mill's. Mine never finished high school and would never talk philosophy. But from my physics teacher, I learned that energy and matter are interconvertible—otherwise, no atom bomb—so the laws of conservation of mass and conservation of energy were not true. But the law of conservation of mass-energy was probably true; mass-energy could not be destroyed. So I wondered, why should the amount of mass-energy in the universe ever have been different from what it is now? Why should it ever be different in the future? If there is anything eternal, why can't it just as well be mass-energy as God?

I also took a seminar in modern intellectual history—not as rigorous as analytic philosophy, but new to me, exciting, and no friendlier to God. We read Søren Kierkegaard's *Fear and Trembling* and *The Sickness unto Death*, which did not suggest that this theologian-philosopher, the founder of existentialism, had solved the problems of even his own existence; Friedrich Nietzsche, whose fiery brilliance led him to pronounce God dead; Karl Marx, who called religion the opium of the people; Sigmund Freud, who described the deceptive psychological sources of faith; and books by Herbert Marcuse and Norman O. Brown, who blended Marx and Freud and, like their mentors, saw religion as an irrational diversion. The trend of modern thought was away from faith. It was not all the thinkers' fault, but Marx spawned Stalin, Nietzsche enchanted Hitler, and Freud's intellectual empire was about to crumble under withering criticism and the power of scientific psychiatry. Godlessness was not working for everyone, nor had it rippled out to engulf the human species. Religion, in fact, was about to experience a resurgence throughout the world.

But not in my world. Changes that matter in a human life happen on many levels in a kind of parallel processing. (The brain is itself a massively parallel processor both within and among its systems, which is why purely cognitive explanations of religion cannot be right.) I was having my mind changed and my life changed too. I was studying evolution, and the temporary compromise I had arrived at—that the first chapters of Genesis were a précis of a process that took billions of years—seemed less and less meaningful. The variety of the world's religions, which a few years earlier had led me to deem my own the best, now looked like evidence that no faith could claim the truth. And what I had always called the soul increasingly struck me as the interactions of brain circuits, bodily ebbs and flows, and the vicissitudes of life.

Anthropology, I decided, would help. First, it would give me a new, progressively truer origin story. Second, it would supply a material basis for the soul in all its cultural variety, as well as a set of tools for thinking about how that *material* soul came to be. Evolution made human nature, but cultures bent it through human development. Third, anthropology would help explain history, which I saw as a material encounter between human needs—physical, social, ethical, and aesthetic—and a less than benign world. Finally, it would help me understand religion itself.

Atheists argue among themselves. Steven Weinberg, for all his condemnation of faith, is criticized by people who condemn religion more strongly than he does. They find very annoying his crystal clear statement: "The one thing that science cannot do . . . —any more than religion can—is to justify itself. . . . It's a moral choice . . . and one that I think cannot be argued about rationally." In contrast, the Quartet is firm about the immorality of religion and the morality of science, arguing rationally for the corruption and foolishness of the one and the superiority of the other. They fully concede that science can be corrupt, wrong, and sometimes tyrannical, but they argue that the whole thrust of science is to correct and right itself from such deviations, and that this gyroscope is the essence of science, while religion is, inescapably, in the grip of authority and dogma.

I agree. However, the philosophers who laid the intellectual groundwork for a world without religion were closer to Weinberg's view.

———

PERHAPS RUSSELL'S MOST famous contribution to skepticism is a parable sometimes called the "celestial teapot" (or "cosmic teapot"). He wrote about it in an article, "Is There a God?" unpublished in his lifetime but an item of atheist folk tradition. Russell said,

> If I were to suggest that between the Earth and Mars there is a china teapot revolving about the sun in an elliptical orbit, nobody would be able to disprove my assertion provided I were careful to add that the teapot is too small to be revealed even by our most powerful telescopes. But if I were to go on to say that, since my assertion cannot be disproved, it is intolerable presumption on the part of human reason to doubt it, I should rightly be thought to be talking nonsense. If, however, the existence of such a teapot were affirmed in ancient books, taught as the sacred truth every Sunday, and instilled into the minds of children at school, hesitation to believe in its existence would become a mark of eccentricity and entitle the doubter to the attentions of the psychiatrist in an enlightened age or of the Inquisitor in an earlier time.

Russell's point is that it should not be up to the person who doubts the existence of the teapot to prove that it does not exist; rather, those who insist on the teapot's existence should have the entire burden of proof, and everyone else should feel free to ignore them. Carolyn Porco, the astrophysicist in charge of the Saturn flyby mission, has pointed out hilariously that she could in fact *prove* that not one but perhaps as many as a billion teapots are in orbit around the sun, with the proviso that they are all on planet Earth. Or, an ironic astronaut might have secretly put a teapot into orbit during a spacewalk, thus making the denial of Russell's parable more questionable. Otherwise, Russell is right.

What was wrong was to think that this has anything to do with the faiths that move billions of people on that planet. It is not the teapot denier who would be referred to a psychiatrist but the one who preaches about it on the street corner. This is because the best the poor psychiatrist can do is to use something like the formal definition of delusion, which in the end is based on being in an extremely small minority when you insist on your idea. Sometimes this rule will lead you far astray, as when Galileo was placed under house arrest for promoting a sun-centered planetary system. In retrospect we say he was visionary, not psychotic, because time has confirmed his sanity and not that of our hypothetical street-corner prophet of teapots.

But Russell, in popular articles and debates with religious leaders, fielded better analogies. For instance, he liked to point out that no one he knew would object to his denying the existence of Zeus and Hera, the troubled couple heading up the ancient Greek pantheon. But for centuries, millions did believe in them, and others (Jews for instance) were persecuted for rejecting this loved and feared celestial duo. Russell, in answering the question of whether he was an atheist or an agnostic, said that, strictly speaking, he was agnostic, because he could not prove that the Christian God does not exist. But then he also couldn't prove that Zeus and Hera don't exist, yet no one had a problem with his saying they don't. So, he was an atheist in common parlance.

Zeus and Hera are more interesting than the cosmic teapot; once, most people in the West believed in them, and now almost no one does. So they're not ridiculous, and they should make us ask, Is it just historical change that has made Zeus and Hera seem silly, or at least inappropriate as objects of faith? Do we approach religious truth more closely over time? Did events—a voice in a burning bush, a virgin birth, a dictation from an angel—reveal new religious truths? Or is it just that the passage of time has left the Greek gods in the dust of some great worldwide fashion show of otherworldly beings?

It gets more challenging. In India, hundreds of millions of people believe in Shiva, Brahma, Vishnu, Lakshmi, and other gods and goddesses whose physical representations are sacrificed to, bowed to, and asked for help throughout the land. Some Hindus insist that their religion is no more polytheistic than the Christianity of the three-personed God or the Judaism of the God with thirteen attributes. Reading the Vedas gives the sense of one god, although the Bhagavad Gita and other Hindu texts offer a complex pantheon.

It gets harder with Buddhists, who don't believe in many gods, one god, or three in one. They believe, with Bertrand Russell, me, and many others, that the world has always been here; if God can be eternal, why can't the world? The difference between us and Buddhists is that they believe with all their hearts and minds that the world—the universe—has profound meaning. Each person (or any other sentient being) has had lives upon lives, as far back as time, which has no beginning and will go forward without end.

Moreover, the life you live now accumulates positive or negative "karma," a quantity in a cosmic bookkeeping scheme that determines how you are reborn after you die. If you are human now, you have been good in your past lives; if born a Buddhist, you are even luckier, since you can study the Buddha's teachings and accumulate more merit that may put you on your path to exiting the cycle—liberation, which some call "nirvana." When you ask *what* is reborn, what passes from this life to the next, there is no clear answer. It can't be the soul, because Buddhists don't believe in the soul. With rare exceptions, we completely forget past lives. But if there is no soul to be reborn in another form, what *is* reborn? It's hard to say. What *can* be said is that all sentient beings deserve our compassion.

The monks that my colleagues and I met and taught during a stay in Dharamsala are good, gentle, highly intelligent people who look up to those who teach them—including us Westerners—as gurus, and who sometimes write us in anguish because they have read of a massacre or a war somewhere in the world and are, for a time, despairing over our species' hopes for a decent future. I can't separate their compassion for sentient beings from their belief in the karmic cycle of life. But Russell, too, was renowned for compassion, and he had no such beliefs.

Tibetan Buddhists strive to grasp *nonexistence*. Lecturing on "Self and the Brain," I declared that I feared bringing that subject to the world's experts on the self and our efforts to suppress it. But one advanced monk, a *geshe*—a sort of PhD of Buddhism—came up afterward to explain my error. Buddhists cannot be trying to *suppress* the self, because the self does not exist; they are trying to grasp its nonexistence. The self's nonexistence is part of the nonexistence of everything. These are difficult concepts, even for those who have been studying Buddhist texts and meditating for decades. Yet we must face them to progress toward liberation.

I have to say that (while I would never foist this view on a monk unless invited), my basic reaction to these ideas and claims is like my response to deism or the idea that God is love: *Huh?* I am not saying that "reincarnation" and "karma" are meaningless words because the monks can't give me a prediction about them that could be falsified. I know they have meaning; I just can't understand it.

But the monks say they do understand it, or at least that they keep getting closer to understanding. And for reasons that have to do with my almost-instinctive anthropological "nothing human is alien" stance, I respect their claim. In fact, if you were to show me—on a remote Greek island, say, or in a commune in Oregon made up of former classics students—a heartfelt revived or ongoing faith in Zeus, Hera, Aphrodite, Athena, Apollo, Poseidon, and Dionysus, complete with rituals and supplications, I would respect their claims too, as long as they were sincere and weren't trying put up a statue of Zeus in the town square or Methodist church. But I will never have to make the same decision about a cult of the cosmic teapot, because such a religion will never exist. It has none of the features that all faiths have shared.

Varieties

An early attempt at a science of religion was *The Varieties of Religious Experience*, published in 1902 by the founder of modern psychology, William James. It's a work of eloquence and wisdom, which ran in his family, his siblings Henry and Alice both being gifted writers. The book is based on William's Gifford Lectures, a still-ongoing annual series on religion at the University of Edinburgh. The book quickly became a part of the canon of psychology and philosophy, and has been in print ever since.

Not that it didn't have critics. For one thing, James declined to consider organized religion, offending many who belong to one. He defined religion as "the feelings, acts and experiences of individual men in their solitude, so far as they apprehend themselves to stand in relation to whatever they may consider the divine." He *ruled out* formalities like churches. As the *New York Times* said on the hundredth anniversary of the book's publication, "theologies, philosophies, orthodoxies of all sorts, religious rituals, rules and fellowship—James considered 'secondhand' religion at best, hypocrisy and tyranny at worst. His view recalls the current catch phrase 'spiritual, not religious.'"

Charles Taylor, a Catholic philosopher, points to the drawbacks of this individual focus. He says,

Let us imagine that we think of religion (also) as living out . . . the ways we are called upon to follow by some higher source. . . . Imagine further that these ways are in some respect inherently social: say, that we are called upon to live together in brotherly love, and to radiate outward such love as a community. Then the locus of the relation with God is (also) through the community.

This "is the way that the life of the Christian church has been conceived . . . and also the way Israel and the Islamic *umma* have been conceived." As we will see with the Bushman trance dance, a faith does not need a church to be essentially social. Very adept healers can enter trance alone, but their training and power rests on communal ritual.

Community matters to most religious people. So, James's ultra-individual approach did not endear him to major religions, with their congregations, social orders, and professionals. But he also drew strong critiques from the other end of the scale, because although James was a philosopher, a leading psychological experimenter, and something of a skeptic, he was oddly religious: spiritual, but open-minded. He did not rule out multiple supernatural beings or communication with the dead.

James was trying to create a science of religion *while believing*. His approach to faith was pragmatic, which in his philosophy meant that it has real consequences: "The world of our present consciousness is only one out of many worlds of consciousness that exist," and although they are usually separate, "yet the two become continuous at certain points, and higher energies filter in. By being faithful in my poor measure to this over-belief, I seem to myself to keep more sane and true."

Keeping himself "more sane and true" is the real-world outcome that, for a pragmatist philosopher, was the ultimate test of an idea: "I *can*, of course, put myself into the sectarian scientist's attitude, and imagine vividly that the world of sensations and scientific laws and objects may be all. But whenever I do this, I hear that inward monitor . . . whispering the word 'bosh!' Humbug is humbug, even though it bear the scientific name, and the total expression of human experience, as I view it objectively, invincibly urges me beyond the narrow 'scientific' bounds."

I cannot say "Humbug!" either to the scientist's denial, which James denounces, or to his own position, which leads him to describe what is subjective—however many people report it—as objective. It *is* evidence of some people's *internal* states, but no account of those states can provide evidence of "other worlds" of consciousness outside their network of brains. So, to James's assertions, too, I do not say, "Humbug!"; I say, "Huh?"

Yet I share James's interest in a science of religion. He believes that "an impartial science of religions might sift out from . . . their discrepancies a common body of doctrine" which we could adopt as "a reconciling hypothesis, and recommend it for general belief." When he adds that by using the word "hypothesis" he "renounces the ambition to be coercive in his arguments," I applaud. But he concludes that he can "offer something that may fit the facts so easily that your scientific logic will find no plausible pretext for vetoing your impulse to welcome it as true." I have to reply that my pretext for vetoing it would simply be that nothing that happens only inside my head (or only inside yours and mine, or inside a billion heads nodding together across the globe) can dictate the facts.

I respect his right to think otherwise, but his logic is not science. We agree that human beings do not live by logic alone, and that the religious stance has much in common with love, joy, fear, anger, grief, and other feeling states. Love can be illogical, joy inexplicable, fear inchoate, anger against injustice counterproductive, and grief too much to bear, but we aren't about to ignore them because we can't fully support them with evidence in the world. One person's grief over the loss of a beloved dog may strike another as excessive, but the grief is no less real to the one feeling it. Sometimes our internal states have consequences that affect others adversely, and we need a reality check.

But we don't go around preaching logic to besotted lovers, dampening joyful abandon, brushing fears aside, scolding enthusiastic reformers, or belittling extremes of grief, unless they cross a line to doing serious damage.

You have a right to prostrate yourself a thousand times circling a sacred mountain, fast on certain days, dance yourself delirious, talk in tongues, sing hallelujah, weep under a cross, wear a cap to cover your head or a shawl to hide your hair, make arduous pilgrimages, parade statues of gods through the thoroughfares, meditate for years on end, burn incense for your ancestors' souls, or give away large sums of money to buy handwritten holy scrolls or stained glass or prayer rugs for your place of worship—as long as you do it within the bounds of law and respect for others, not coercing anyone.

Yet James saw what philosophers often forget: religion is about feeling as well as thought, passion as well as belief, body as well as mind. That is why he focuses on private experience, especially emotional and transcendent conversion or "rebirth." He is candid about their origins: "The *subconscious self* is nowadays a well-recognized psychological entity. . . . Apart from all religious considerations, there is actually and literally more life in our total soul than we are at any time aware of." That includes "imperfect memories, silly jingles, inhibitive timidities. . . . But in it many of the performances of genius seem also to have their origin; and in our study of conversion, of mystical experiences, and of prayer, we have seen how striking a part invasions from this region play in the religious life. . . . The control is felt as 'higher' . . . the sense of union with the power beyond us is a sense of something . . . literally true."

The ideas conveyed in this quote resemble what Freud believed about religion, except that the same reasoning led Freud to call it an illusion, albeit one with a future. For James, as for many religious people, there is no contradiction; if the unconscious is our way of accessing powers beyond us, so be it; those powers are still real. Recall James's definition of religion: "*the feelings, acts and experiences of individual men in their solitude . . . in relation to whatever they may consider the divine.*" But, he continues, "since the relation may be either moral, physical, or ritual . . . out of religion [so defined] theologies, philosophies, and ecclesiastical organizations may secondarily grow." So it's not fair to say that James willfully ignores religion beyond the individual. But to "moral, physical, or ritual," he doesn't add communal, or for that matter emotional, cognitive, or symbolic. Yet faith is all these, engaging many human tendencies. It is also why statements like "religion is simply . . ." or "religion is really . . ." or, worst of all, "religion is nothing but . . ." fail.

James admits he is not a theologian, historian, or anthropologist; he is a physician by training and a scientific psychologist by practice. But he realizes that religious sentiment is not a single entity. One person

> allies it to the feeling of dependence; one makes it a derivative from fear; others connect it with the sexual life; others still identify it with the feeling of the infinite. . . . There is religious fear, religious love, religious awe, religious joy. . . . But religious love is only man's natural emotion of love directed to a religious object; religious fear is only . . . the common quaking of the human breast, in so far as the notion of divine retribution may arouse it; religious awe is the same organic thrill which we feel in a forest at twilight, or in a mountain gorge; only this time . . . at the thought of our supernatural relations.

James casts his net widely. He knows that Buddhists do not believe in a god (although popularly, the Buddha seems like one). He cites Ralph Waldo Emerson as proposing another godless religion: "Modern transcendental idealism . . . also seems to let God evaporate into abstract Ideality. Not a deity . . . not a superhuman person, but the immanent divinity in things, the essentially spiritual structure of the universe."

James saw the "frank expression of this worship of mere abstract laws," contained in Emerson's famed address to the class of 1838 at the Harvard Divinity College, as creating "the scandal of the performance." He quotes it at length, but I'll quote a different part first:

> Through the transparent darkness the stars pour their almost spiritual rays. Man under them seems a young child, and his huge globe a toy. The cool night bathes the world as with a river, and prepares his eyes again for the crimson dawn. . . . One is constrained to respect the perfection of this world. . . . In its fruitful soils; in its navigable sea; in its mountains of metal and stone; in its forests of all woods; in its animals; in its chemical ingredients; in the powers and path of light, heat, attraction, and life, it is well worth the pith and heart of great men to subdue and enjoy it. . . . But when the mind opens, and reveals the laws which traverse the universe, and make things what they are, then shrinks the great world at once into a mere illustration and fable of this mind.

Emerson means by "fable" the laws of natural science. Yet he also says, "The child amidst his baubles, is learning the action of light, motion, gravity, muscular force; and in the game of human life, love, fear, justice, appetite, man, and God, interact. These laws refuse to be adequately stated. They will not be written out on paper, or spoken by the tongue. They elude our persevering thought; yet we read them hourly in each other's faces, in each other's actions, in our own remorse."

Emerson means "the laws of the soul," and he says, "These laws execute themselves." The relevant sentiments are virtue, purity, and piety. As a Christian minister speaking to young men about to assume that role, Emerson added, "This thought dwelled always deepest in the minds of men in the devout and contemplative East; not alone in Palestine . . . but in Egypt, in Persia, in India, in China. Europe has always owed to oriental genius, its divine impulses. What these holy bards said, all sane men found agreeable and true. And the unique impression of Jesus upon mankind, whose name is not so much written as ploughed into the history of this world, is proof of the subtle virtue of this infusion."

"Such," James comments, "is the Emersonian religion," and he includes it in his definition just as he does Buddhism. We will return to the question that Emerson thinks he has answered by saying that human nature makes virtue its own reward—which comes down to whether ethics is a product of evolution. We know that there are people without remorse; nevertheless, there is truth in Emerson's words.

What about piety? My friend James Gustafson, a Lutheran minister and professor of theological ethics, has an exceptional grasp of science and a keen interest in human nature. He says that piety in human nature came first and led to a search for God or a perception of the sacred. In *A Sense of the Divine*, Gustafson calls it "natural piety" and attributes it to all those, secular or religious, who have cared enough to devote themselves to the conservation of nature. "What is finally indisputable . . . is that human and other forms of life are dependent on forces we do not create and cannot fully control, forces that bring us into being and sustain us and life around us, but forces that also limit and destroy us. . . . This dependence . . . evokes a sense of the sublime, or for some of us a sense of the divine." This view shares something with Emerson's transcendentalism, and also with E. O. Wilson's "biophilia"—love of the living world. But a sense of the sublime can lead to thankfulness (not necessarily *toward* anyone or any thing), a desire to preserve and protect, and piety in the sense of respect and wanting to do right.

Recently I asked another friend, Rabbi Emanuel Feldman, now long retired from four decades as the leading Orthodox rabbi in Atlanta, and one of the most passionately religious people I know—he also loves baseball and has a legendary sense of humor—"What is the essence of religion?" He answered in one word: "Awe—the sense that there is something bigger and more important than we are." If you have that sense about the living world, or about the world of human beings, or even about the lawfulness and power of the universe in its trajectory starting from Lumina (the Big Bang)—and if the awe includes heightened awareness tinged with fear, you are probably in some sense religious. Gustafson always insisted that I was, despite my denials.

But James's first lecture, "Religion and Neurology," left definitions for the second. Here he uses medical language to put to rest the idea that physiology can explain religion away. "A religious life . . . does tend to make the person exceptional and eccentric. I speak not now of your ordinary religious believer, who follows the conventional observances of his country. . . . His religion has been made for him by others, communicated to him by tradition, determined to fixed forms by imitation, and retained by habit. It would profit us little to study this second-hand religious life." I disagree; ordinary religious minds are interesting; they must differ from those of nonbelievers, and I want to understand individual differences. But I agree we should search for

the pattern-setters . . . individuals for whom religion exists not as a dull habit, but as an acute fever . . . "geniuses" in the religious line; and like many other geniuses [they] have often shown symptoms of nervous instability . . . led a discordant inner life, and had melancholy during a part of their career. They have . . . been liable to obsessions and voices, seen visions, and presented all sorts of peculiarities which are ordinarily classed as pathological.

In other words, religious leaders in history would, without hindsight, be called pathological in James's time or ours. Yet this trained physician rejects "medical materialism," saying, "Few of us are not in some way infirm, or even diseased; and our very infirmities help us unexpectedly." Such deeply religious, disturbed temperaments "have the emotionality which is the *sine qua non* [the 'without which nothing'] of moral perception." James mocks the "robust Philistine type of nervous system, forever offering its biceps to be felt, thumping its breast, and thanking heaven that it hasn't a morbid fiber in its composition."

As with most traits, this is a continuum, and followers may have related insights. James cites a 49-year-old man who wrote,

> God is more real to me than any thought or thing or person. I feel his presence positively, and the more as I live in closer harmony with his laws as written in my body and mind. I feel him in the sunshine or rain; and awe mingled with a delicious restfulness most nearly describes my feelings. . . .
>
> I talk to him as to a companion in prayer and praise, and our communion is delightful. He answers me again and again, often in words so clearly spoken that it seems my outer ear must have carried the tone. . . . Usually a text of Scripture, unfolding some new view of him and his love for me . . . I could give hundreds of instances, in school matters, social problems, financial difficulties, etc. That he is mine and I am his never leaves me, it is an abiding joy. Without it life would be a blank, a desert, a shoreless, trackless waste.

James says, "thousands . . . would write an almost identical account."

This, I find, is a central fact of religious life often missed by opponents and explainers alike: companionship, communion. But James also recounts hallucinations, out-of-body experiences, mystical sensations. Some, contradicting his individualism, happen in church—one, during the ritual of wafer and wine. James places himself squarely among those "once-born." The twice-born speak of their "rebirth."

They range from Saint Paul, who had a dramatic conversion after a blinding vision of light, perhaps a seizure, on the road to Damascus; to the emperor Constantine, who saw a sword in the form of a cross in the sky the night before a battle, and the words *In hoc signo, vinces* ("In this sign, conquer"), and after he did, made Rome Christian; to ordinary men and women whose lives are suddenly changed.

James was fascinated by saints, and he saw "a composite photograph of universal saintliness, the same in all religions," including

- "the feeling of being in a wider life than that of this world's selfish little interests"
- "a sense of the friendly continuity of the ideal power with our own life, and a willing self-surrender to its control"
- "an immense elation and freedom"
- "a shifting of the emotional center towards loving and harmonious affections, towards 'yes, yes,' and away from 'no'"

These mental states may lead to asceticism (including self-mortification, which doesn't seem like "yes, yes"), strength of soul (the dropping away of fears), purity, and charity.

Humility is key: "Francis of Assisi kisses his lepers"; other saints "are said to have cleansed the sores of their patients with their . . . tongues; and the lives of such saints as Elizabeth of Hungary and Madame de Chantal are full of a sort of reveling in hospital purulence . . . which makes us admire and shudder at the same time." Also key is poverty: "Hindu fakirs, Buddhist monks, and Mohammedan dervishes unite with Jesuits and Franciscans in idealizing poverty."

As for "cosmic or mystic consciousness . . . Hindus, Buddhists, Mohammedans, and Christians all have cultivated it methodically." One Hindu method is yoga, "the experimental union . . . with the divine. . . . The diet, posture, breathing, intellectual concentration, and moral discipline vary," but they aim to help the yogi overcome his lower nature and enter into "samadhi," a state of consciousness beyond reason or instinct. The feeling of an *I* is gone, but the mind, free of desire or restlessness, bodiless, knows ourselves "for what we truly are, free, immortal, omnipotent, loosed from the finite, and its contrasts of good and evil." After samadhi, a man remains "enlightened, a sage, a prophet, a saint, his whole character changed . . . illumined."

James describes similar states in Buddhists, and we know now from brain research that altered consciousness, achieved through meditation, is real. From the Islamic world, he quotes Al-Ghazali, an eleventh-century Persian philosopher and theologian: "The Science of the Sufis . . . aims at detaching the heart from all that is not God, and at giving to it for sole occupation the meditation of the divine being." Al-Ghazali recounts the discipline of solitude and abstinence leading to "transport," and "the prophetic faculty." Some Sufis whirl in ceremonial dress. The adept's arms are held out, the right hand pointing toward the sky, the left toward the earth. The whirling is controlled and dignified, to bring about union with God.

For James, then, religion is about personal altered states, emotions like fear, love, awe, and joy, insight of an intense and overwhelming sort, commitment to purity and service, transcendence, assurance that life has meaning and purpose beyond physical law, and union with God, with the spirit of all beings, or with some expression of the divine. Its *pragmatic* result, he believes, is a more hopeful, joyful, and positive life—or at least one that enables us to "keep more sane and true."

Thus the psychology of religion, circa 1902. But another physician-psychologist, a younger contemporary of James, had at least as much influence. Where James was systematic, scientific, academic, and careful, Sigmund Freud was bold, creative, sure of himself, iconoclastic, and nonconformist. James pursued scientific psychology through experiment. Freud had followers; his movement was in some ways a cult, clinically oriented and based on the statements of patients, mostly interpreted by Freud himself.

Yet for all his errors, Freud had an indelible impact. It is hard to imagine the culture of psychotherapy, the sexual revolution, the unconscious, the repressed, or our ideas about childhood experience without him. He considered himself an outsider; Hannibal, the African conqueror of Rome who came over the Alps with elephants, was his hero. But Freud's impact was on the empire of thought.

James, a different kind of thinker, was open-minded about the Viennese wunderkind—sex, dreams, and all—welcoming Freud on an American lecture tour a year or so before his own death. Freud, also a physician, was struck by James's calm during an angina attack while they strolled together. But the elder kept his distance; he disliked Freud's hostility to religion. He put his arm around one of Freud's disciples and said, "The future of psychology belongs to your work," but he also suspected Freud, "with his dream theory, of being a regular *halluciné*." Soon after, James wrote to a Swiss colleague with doubts about Freud's "fixed ideas," but stating his hope that, "Freud and his pupils will push their ideas to their utmost limits. . . . They can't fail to throw light on human nature."

James preferred Freud's intellectual son Carl Jung, who was open to religion and more skeptical about sexual determinism. These differences would soon lead to a break. But for the time being, the two were corresponding, and in January 1910 Freud confided to Jung that he was exploring "infantile helplessness" as the source of faith. This would be his core idea about religion: the sense of oneness with the world or God was a holdover of the "oceanic" feeling of the newborn infant dissolving its own boundaries, merging with the mother and the world. Dependency and fear left a wish for parental love and a guilty fear of retribution. Religion offered parental care, comfort, and threat writ large.

Jung took a different path. Freud was the neurologist and brain scientist who invented psychoanalysis, becoming a psychotherapist and theoretical psychologist. Jung was a psychiatrist, attending very ill patients in a mental asylum in Switzerland. He understood constitution and temperament, and he did not derive all of psychology from childhood. Jung used Freud's method but adapted it to his patients, who tended to be older, some previously psychoanalyzed. They focused more on the meaning of their lives than on childhood harms.

Jung's approach to dreams involved archetypes—symbols or themes that recur in human life. Fire had meaning, but it was not necessarily sexual, and when certain symbols—the circular mandala for example—occurred widely across religions, Jung explained them as rooted in deep history. He viewed religion as part of a search for meaning; he had no interest in explaining it away. Like James, he was too soft on religion for the taste of later behavioral science, which turned from emotion, altered states, and archetypal symbols to thought, not feeling. Yet Freud—in *The Future of an Illusion*—prefigured the cognitive approach, citing

> the earth, which quakes and is torn apart and buries all human life and its works; water, which deluges and drowns everything in a turmoil; storms, which blow everything before them; . . . diseases, which we have only recently recognized as attacks by other organisms; and . . . the painful riddle of death, against which no medicine has yet been found. . . . With these forces nature rises up against us, majestic, cruel, and inexorable; she brings to mind . . . our weakness and helplessness, which we thought to escape through the work of civilization.

Our answer to this crisis of helplessness, this continual return to the bewilderment of infancy, is "the humanization of nature."

> Impersonal forces and destinies . . . remain eternally remote. But if the elements have passions that rage . . . in our own souls, if death itself is not something spontaneous but the violent act of an evil Will, if everywhere in nature there are Beings

around us of a kind that we know in our own society, then we can breathe freely, can feel at home in the uncanny and can deal ... with our senseless anxiety. We ... are no longer helplessly paralyzed; we can at least react. Perhaps ... we are not even defenseless. We can apply the same methods against these violent supermen outside that we employ in our own society; we can try to adjure them, to appease them, to bribe them, and ... we may rob them of a part of their power.

Since gods may not respond, other ideas arise: fates the gods can't control, rivalries that pit them against each other on a field of human suffering, punishments not negated by any amount of pleading or repentance. Yet in Freud's idea of faith, "Life in this world serves a higher purpose; no doubt it is not easy to guess what that purpose is," but everything results from "an intelligence superior to us, which ... orders everything for the best. ... Death itself is not an extinction ... but the beginning of a new kind of existence."

These general ideas are found in Hinduism, Shinto, and countless animistic religions in addition to the Abrahamic traditions. Buddhists would have no problem with Freud's generalizations about purpose, perfection, and a different existence after death. Despite their emphasis on philosophy and ethics, Confucianism and Taoism originated and persist—together with indigenous Asian religions—in beliefs and rituals involving gods and spirits, cherished by common people even when leaders reject them. Freud noticed that "pious America laid claim to being 'God's own Country,'" a version of chosen peoplehood; today the country that helped pioneer democracy and cherished individualism remains the most religious advanced nation.

Freud points out the different standard for religious beliefs. We convince ourselves of the Earth's roundness by sailing around it. But when we ask what religious belief is founded on, "we are met with three answers. ... Firstly, these teachings deserve to be believed because they were believed by our primal ancestors; secondly, we possess proofs which have been handed down to us from those same primeval times; and thirdly, it is forbidden to raise the question of their authentication at all. . . . This third point rouses our suspicions. After all, a prohibition like this can only be for one reason—that society is . . . aware of the insecurity of the claim." As for the beliefs from ancient times, "They are full of contradictions, revisions, and falsifications," and the claim of divine revelation doesn't help, because "no proposition can be a proof of itself."

Freud mentions the long history of doubt, dating back to those who bequeathed us all religious legacies. There were equivalents of the Gospel's doubting Thomas long before his qualms about Christian revelation; doubts go back as far as religious claims do. There was never uniform belief, although society suppressed misgivings. The very transformations that mark the births of new faiths entail doubts about prior claims. Freud cites two "desperate efforts" to "evade the problem." The first is *Credo quia absurdum*—"I believe it because it is absurd"—a paraphrase of the second-century church father Tertullian, who said of religious doctrines, "Their truth must be felt inwardly, and they need not be comprehended." But he asks, "Am I . . . to believe every absurdity? And if not, why this one in particular?" Bertrand Russell's cosmic teapot comes to mind.

In the second evasion, we hear an echo of James's pragmatism, although Freud calls it "the philosophy of 'As if.'" This asserts that our thought-activity includes a great number of . . . 'fictions,' but for a variety of practical reasons we have to behave 'as if' we believed in these fictions . . . because of their incomparable importance for . . . human society." But Freud claims implausibly that only someone swayed by "philosophy" would buy the "as if" argument. For others, "the admission that something is absurd or contrary to reason leaves no more to be said." Here he ignores the beliefs of hundreds of millions.

He recalls one of his children asking if a fairy tale was true and disdaining it after hearing it was not. We will return to children's beliefs and doubts and how they grow, but for now, consider Freud's ambitious inference from his son's rejection: "We may expect that people will soon behave in the same way towards the fairy tales of religion." It hadn't happened then, and a century later it still hasn't.

Whether you call religious beliefs illusions or delusions, the source of false belief is wish fulfillment; it must be true because we so want it to be. Religion is "the universal obsessional neurosis of humanity; like the obsessional neurosis of children, it arose out of the Oedipus complex, out of the relation to the father." Today, psychologists see no such role for fathers. But one claim about religion as neurosis may be real: "devout believers are safeguarded . . . against the risk of certain neurotic illnesses; their acceptance of the universal neurosis spares them the task of constructing a personal one."

Freud assumes his critics' voices, gives them good arguments, and rebuts them. One says, " 'Man has imperative needs of another sort, which can never be satisfied by cold science; and it is very strange—indeed, it is the height of inconsistency—that a psychologist who has always insisted on what a minor part is played in human affairs by the intelligence as compared with . . . the instincts—that such a psychologist should now try to rob mankind of a precious wish-fulfillment and . . . propose to compensate . . . with intellectual nourishment.' " Freud could be "quoting" James, who decades earlier fully acknowledged the instinctual and unconscious sources of faith, yet continued believing.

Freud's answer? "Men cannot remain children for ever; they must in the end go out into 'hostile life.' We may call this 'education to reality.' . . . The sole purpose of my book is to point out the necessity for this forward step." And "the voice of the intellect is a soft one, but it does not rest until it has gained a hearing. . . . The primacy of the intellect lies . . . in a distant, distant future, but probably not in an *infinitely* distant one."

Another of Freud's imagined critics asks, " 'Have you learned nothing from history? Once before an attempt of this kind was made to substitute reason for religion, officially and in the grand manner. Surely you remember the French Revolution and Robespierre? And you must also remember how short-lived and miserably ineffectual the experiment was? The same experiment is being repeated in Russia at the present time, and we need not feel curious as to its outcome.' " He compares trying to eliminate religion by fiat to Prohibition, the American attempt at the time "to deprive people of all stimulants, intoxicants, and other pleasure-producing substances . . . another experiment as to whose outcome we need not feel curious."

Freud raised the same objections to religion that we have heard more recently. But he saw how attached human beings are to faith and had a more respectful way of weaning them away. By analogy to the psychoanalytic treatment of neurosis—itself a long, hard process—he proposed that our species may someday overcome its religious bent, but acknowledged that this hope may itself be an illusion. He wanted to see a generation of children raised without religious indoctrination. His hypothesis? They would be mentally healthy unbelievers. He did not urge this path on everyone, and he saw it as a scientist would: an experiment that was worth trying, but that might prove him wrong.

Six years after *The Future of an Illusion*, Jung published *Modern Man in Search of a Soul*. It includes (despite Freud's dismissal of him) a spirited defense of his onetime mentor:

Psychology has profited greatly from Freud's pioneer work; it has learned that human nature has also a black side, and that not man alone possesses this side, but his works, his institutions, and his convictions. . . . Even our purest and holiest beliefs can be traced to the crudest origins. . . . It is painful . . . to interpret radiant things from the shadow-side, and thus in a measure to reduce them to their origins in dreary filth. But it seems to me to be an imperfection in things of beauty, and a weakness in man, if an explanation from the shadow-side has a destructive effect. The horror . . . we feel for Freudian interpretations is entirely due to our . . . childish naïveté. . . . Our mistake would lie in supposing that what is radiant no longer exists because it has been explained from the shadow-side.

Here we have James's acceptance of the source of religious sentiment, acknowledging the "dreary filth" of the unconscious, without negating religion. "This is a regrettable error into which Freud himself has fallen." Jung's analytic psychology was more inclusive than Freud's, and recognized other unconscious motives besides erotic pleasure (the will to power, for one). But Jung, like Freud, believed in helping people explore the unconscious to open "the way to a normally disillusioned life."

"Normally disillusioned" is a delicious phrase. Jung cites his successes in guiding people through that change but says he learned more from his failures. These tended to be patients over 40, and in the end he saw they were very different, "that the elements of the psyche undergo in the course of life a very marked change. . . . We may distinguish between a psychology of the morning of life and a psychology of its afternoon." As a physician, he finds the change "hygienic . . . a goal towards which one can strive; and that shrinking away from it is something unhealthy and abnormal which robs the second half of life of its purpose." A third of Jung's patients, he says, "are suffering from no clinically definable neurosis, but from the senselessness and emptiness of their lives. It seems to me . . . that this can be well described as the general neurosis of our time."

This is quite different from seeing *religion* as the general neurosis. These middle-aged patients were "stuck," and he did not know how to help them. He turned to dreams, but not Freud's "system" for interpreting them. Anthropology, mythology, and comparative religion recognize symbols that people have used throughout history, a balm to those who had focused their lives on the personal and the rational but later were unsatisfied. For them, symbols meant that "the matter-of-fact and the commonplace come to wear an altered countenance, and can even acquire a new glamour. . . . The least of things with a meaning is worth more in life than the greatest of things without it."

Although Jung knew that some would say he was indulging in fantasy, he says, "Truth to tell, I have a very high opinion of fantasy. . . . All the works of man have their origin in creative fantasy . . . the imagination frees man from his bondage to the 'nothing but' and liberates in him the spirit of play." But here is where Jung and Freud truly part: "Experience shows that many neuroses are caused by the fact that people blind themselves to their own religious promptings because of a childish passion for rational enlightenment."

For Freud, the neurosis of the human race *is* religion; for Jung, the neurosis may be worsened by *denying* it. For Freud, religion is childish, while for Jung, what is childish is too much passion for reason. For Freud, religion is repression, wishful thinking, and guilt; for Jung, it can be freedom to play. Like James, Jung equivocated about whether the spiritual was inside the psyche or outside the body. "To the psychologist there is nothing more stupid than the standpoint of the missionary who pronounces the gods of the 'poor heathen' to be illusions . . . as if what we call the real were not equally full of illusion." He attributes "a positive value to all religions. . . . Ceremonial, ritual, initiation rites and ascetic practices, in all their forms and variations, interest me profoundly. . . . I likewise attribute a positive value to biology . . . in which I see a herculean attempt to understand the human psyche by approaching it from the outer world."

Freud stressed the instincts and believed that reason must control them; Jung said, let religion channel them for some, as it always has, while science lights the way for others. Accused of mysticism, Jung said it was not his fault "that man has, everywhere and always, spontaneously developed religious forms of expression. . . . Whoever cannot see this aspect of the human psyche is blind, and whoever chooses to explain it away, or to 'enlighten' it away, has no sense of reality. . . . It is easy enough to drive the spirit out of the door, but when we have done so the salt of life grows flat."

"Primitive" people, lacking science, attribute many events to imps, demons, witchcraft, sorcerers, and spirits. But modern folk also want answers that science can't give—for things that are either so wonderful or terrible that the laws seem inadequate. Some of us make ourselves draw a line in the sand: *Here is what I can explain, here is what I can't; that's how it is.* But most people who have ever lived yearn to cross the line. We will try to understand what it is about the brain, as a product of evolution, that has made this so. We will also consider attempts, such as existentialism, to find meaning in life without being religious. We will even take seriously the idea that for many people, science will suffice, that our own insignificance in the vastness of the cosmos is in itself enlightening and comforting. But first we drill down further into the varieties.

Elementary Forms

I n his *Elementary Forms of the Religious Life*, Émile Durkheim chose Australian aborigine totems as key to religion's origins. His view of totemism was simplistic, but he was right to want to look at hunter-gatherers, the simplest human societies and the first.

In the 1970s, I lived for two years among the San in northwestern Botswana, on the margins of the Kalahari Desert. Commonly known as Bushmen, they call themselves *Jun/twasi*, meaning roughly "the real people." I was not there to study ritual, but no one could be there that long and ignore their most dramatic rite, the trance dance—at once the culture's way of facing and dealing with illness and its central religious experience. After seeing the ritual and often being "healed," I became an apprentice. Consider the scene.

Dusk is closing. The Kalahari horizon makes a distant, perfect circle, broken only by scrub brush and a few acacia trees. The sounds of the evening meal are heard throughout the village camp, a rough ring of small grass shelters with a fire and a family in front of each. For one reason or another, on this night there is excitement. There is fresh meat, or just the round moon rising. Someone is ill. Or maybe no one is; what is about to happen will benefit the well as much as the sick.

The women talk and decide to try. Men may have prodded them; they may have tested the men's interest with questions, or decided on their own. They clap in complex rhythms and sing in a yodeling style that bridges octaves gracefully, creating mesmerizing sounds. Gradually, they circle around a fire. Emotionally and musically, they echo each other's enthusiasm. Someone stokes the fire as dusk turns to dark.

Two of the men sitting cross-legged in front of a hut poke each other and stir. "These women are really singing," says one, "but we men are worthless." They chuckle and then become more serious, although joking will continue as the night wears on. They strap dance rattles around their ankles and get the feel of the sound when their feet slap the ground. "Look," one woman says, smiling. "These things might become men tonight." Other men join in, tracing a circle around the singing women. The men's feet slam at the ground repetitively. That sound orchestrates with the women's clapping and singing, and the ripples of enthusiasm widen. A baby wakes, cries, and is adjusted in the sling at her mother's side. A toddler stumbles to his mother, leans on her, and stares, wide-eyed, at the dancers. A pretty young woman whispers something into the ear of the woman next to her; both of them glance at one of the men dancing and burst out laughing. The fire is stoked again; it burns more brightly.

A man falls to the ground. Because he is in late middle age, the naïve observer wants to rush to his aid, but his companions are unconcerned. He lies there for a time, moaning and trembling. Other men drift over and kneel. They rub him gently, then vigorously; one lifts the fallen man onto his lap. Finally, the man comes to a semblance of his senses and gets to his feet. Now he is in another state entirely, still trembling and moaning but walking, charged with energy. He bends over one of the women in the circle and places his hands on her shoulders. The trembling intensifies, taking on the rhythm of his breathing. With each breath, the amplitude of his voice and his arm tremor increase until the crescendo ends with a piercing shriek: "*Kow-hee-dee-dee!*" He relaxes momentarily, moves on, and repeats the ritual.

The circle of singers swells, more men join the dancing, and other villagers—mostly children, adolescents, and the elderly—form a spectators' circle. One onlooker is pregnant, with a fever. The man in trance lays hands on her, exerting himself intensely. At one point he pauses and stares out into the blackness, shouting: "You all! You all get out of here! You, all of you, get out of here!" His voice is directed into the empty night. He stares into the void beyond the spectators, before resuming the healing.

How does the healing trance come about? Does it truly have any power to heal? And if so, how? If Lorna Marshall, Richard Lee, and Richard Katz—three experts on this ritual—could surround you while you watched, they might say this: The trance and its power to heal are due largely to the energy of the group. If the women sing and clap well, the men dance well; if the sound of their ankle rattles is good and someone enters trance, the clapping and singing will rise to a new plane; if the men are sufficiently trusting of the women and each other, several may descend into deep trances, and their healing power may last until dawn.

The power itself, called *n/um*, is said to reside in the flanks of the abdomen, the pit of the stomach, or the base of the spine, and to boil up very painfully in trance. Healing power is not exactly the same as susceptibility to trances, but both are said to grow during early adulthood and diminish in old age. A young man may have all the courage and energy he needs to enter into trance but, lacking experience and control, may be useless as a healer; an elder may have the experience, but his energy is not what it was. As many as half of all men can heal— a brave act, since in trance the soul may leave the body forever. The trance itself is at once self-absorbed and selfless. The individual is elevated in a way that is almost unique in this egalitarian culture, yet his identity is dissolved; the trance dance is of, by, and for the community.

If the dancer is experienced, his soul can travel to the village of the spirits and talk with them about people's illnesses. Only the healer's skill and the ministrations of other healers control his wavering between life and death; their embracing him and rubbing him with their sweat are lifesaving acts. The power can be transferred from an older, "big" healer to a novice; the novice puts his life in the hands of the older man, who must protect the novice from dangers spiritual and material.

The music created by the combined instruments of voice, clapping, and dance rattles struck me as psychedelic. Its eerie beauty seemed to bore into my skull, loosening the moorings of my mind. The dancing delivered a shock wave to the base of my skull each time my heels hit the ground. My heels hit perhaps eighty times a minute for hours. The effects on my brain were direct and physical. Hyperventilation played a role; smoke inhalation too. The sustained exertion made me light-headed. And staring into the flames while dancing those monotonous steps around and around the circle had an effect all its own.

But more than any of these, what enabled me to enter into trance to the extent I did was trust. On a night that was followed by a morning full of compliments, especially from women, I had that "oceanic" feeling of oneness with the world, which Freud said echoes our blissful infant dependency. Whom did I trust? Everyone: the women, the other dancers and healers, the community. But most of all I trusted my teacher. He was not the most powerful healer, but he was strong enough to teach a novice like me. God, he said, had strengthened his healing power and given him his own dancing song in a dream, during a long illness. He was well respected, and he was my friend.

Over the two years we worked closely together, my regard for him became affection. He was sensitive, wise, loyal, witty, bright, vigorous, generous—the ideal father. That night I committed myself entirely into his hands, much as a suggestible person might do with a hypnotist. As I drifted into a mental world not quite like any other I have experienced, my mind focused on him. I felt sure he would take care of me. He left me to my own devices for hours, and then at last, when I most needed contact, he took my arms and draped me over his shoulders. We must have looked comical—a six-foot-tall white man slumped over a five-foot San hunter-gatherer—but to me it was one of the most important moments of my long and eventful stay in Africa.

All folk healing systems—and modern medicine too—are based on the relationship between the healer and the sufferer. The psychological features of this relationship—authority, trust, shared beliefs, teaching, nurturance, and kindness—significantly, sometimes dramatically, affect the course of illness. Counseling and psychotherapy speed recovery from surgery and heart attack and mitigate the suffering of patients getting cancer chemotherapy. A room with a view reduces the amount of pain medication requested by those recovering from surgery. Call it placebo, but the human touch has measurable effects. It may act directly, through the brain and hormones—messengers from mind to body. Meditation lowers heart rate and blood pressure, but psychological stress decreases the number of "natural killer cells," which seek and destroy tumors. Importantly, trust can improve the patient's compliance with medical advice—a domain where modern doctors have not excelled.

My all-encompassing trust did not last through the night. I drifted into a kind of delusion that something terrible was happening to my wife, who was back resting in our grass hut, a mile or so away. This idea arose from a largely irrational fear of the Kalahari and all its creatures, animal and human. I darted from the circle, jumped into our Jeep truck, and began to drive. The trance was broken by the sound of the Jeep lodging itself on a tree stump and its rear wheels spinning in the sand.

What was happening in my mind and brain? In that era I could only guess. My neocortex, one key to logical thought, was likely dulled, and probably some parts of my brain had heightened functioning. Because trance can superficially look like a seizure, and because of the powerful shifts in emotion, I guessed that the limbic system—the circuits between the brain stem and the neocortex that generate emotions—had to be involved. Finally, I thought that my trance—

to whatever extent I had entered one—must have involved the brain stem's reticular activating system, which regulates consciousness, ushering us from sleep to waking, concentration to reverie.

The San trance is very hard to study with the methods of brain science—intense movements make imaging almost impossible (although there are some approaches that might work)—but some new studies of other cultural forms of trance might shed light on what the San do, and we will look at them in the next chapter. But what of the San's own claim that their healing is effective? I will argue that the claim is probably valid, but it is too soon to conclude that San healing "works" according to scientific standards, or to adequately explain the trance itself. In the meantime, we can give the San credit for creating an insightful system of medical psychology, based on knowledge and methods as interesting as our own psychological interventions— and with far more symbolic power.

Consider a young mother feverish with malaria after her father's death. The healer entered a deep trance; his soul "left" his body. On the road to the spirit world, he met her father, who held the daughter in his arms. The healer persuaded the father that his daughter's responsibilities on Earth outweighed his own need for her and even his own grief, so the father returned her to the living. A few days later, her fever and chills were gone. Could the healer's report of his encounter with the father have influenced the daughter's parasitic illness? I don't know, but it is possible, and later in the book I will try to explain why.

———

LET'S STEP BACK and see what social scientists said about the *communal* side of faith before James, Freud, and Jung tried to parse the religious mind. Edward Tylor, a pioneer anthropologist, published *Primitive Culture* in 1871, and one of its two volumes focused on religion. His main subject was animism, the tendency of people everywhere to see life and action in nonliving things and events. This, for

Tylor, was the essence of all religion—"primitive" and "civilized," ancient and modern—and it anticipated the cognitive psychology of religion by more than a century.

His opening, "Doctrine of Soul's Existence after Death," discussed a baby's birth or an animal's appearance soon after a loved one's death: "A missionary heard a Chiriquane woman of Buenos Ayres say of a fox, 'May not that be the spirit of my dead daughter?' Among the Abipones we hear of certain little ducks which fly in flocks at night, uttering a mournful hiss, and which fancy associates with the souls of the dead; while in Popayan . . . doves were not killed, as inspired by departed souls." Tylor does not belittle these ideas, considering them "a portion of the wide doctrine of the soul's future existence." Thirty years before James, Tylor showed a deeper understanding of Buddhist traditions, and there is no excuse for Freud's speculations about primitive rites when such scholars long preceded him. Tylor knew the Egyptian Book of the Dead, kabbalistic Jewish mysticism, Manichean ideas of the transmigration of souls, and many other beliefs of humanity that were and are ignored by many theorists.

Tylor sought an evolutionary pattern: "As it seems that the first conception of souls may have been that of the souls of men, this being afterwards extended by analogy to the souls of animals, plants, etc., so it may seem that the original idea of transmigration was the straightforward and reasonable one of human souls being reborn in new human bodies, this notion being afterwards extended to take in rebirth in bodies of animals." San hunter-gatherers believed that animals descended from people and told hilarious stories about how ancient humans became transformed. Death itself came from an argument between Hare and Moon, which Moon—reborn every month—sadly lost.

Tylor does not spare "civilized" authors; he quotes critic Samuel Johnson on the spirits of the dead: "All argument is against it; but all belief is for it." But as much as any anthropologist since, Tylor took seriously the customs of countless cultures with regard to the dead. Worldwide, throughout history, the dead were treated with disgust, respect, and fear, and expected to be in a liminal—in-between—state for a time after passing. Death in every culture is a transition, not an end. Petitions to the recently dead, picnics and feasts in cemeteries, valuables buried with the deceased, skulls as relics or children's toys, detailed accounts of the soul's journey after death, visits to or from the dead, a "Zulu Dante" who traveled underground among them, "St. Patrick's Purgatory," the sun as "the bright dwelling of departed chiefs and braves" for the Natchez of Mississippi, and many other examples avow that death is not thought final. Recent observations confirm Tylor's general point and most details as well.

Yet all is not bright in the other world. For the Basuto, "shades wander about in silent calm, experiencing neither joy nor sorrow," and the Yoruba say that "a corner in this world is better than a corner in the world of spirits." These sayings recall what Achilles says to Odysseus, a rare live visitor to Hades: "I would rather follow the plough as thrall to another man . . . than be a king over all the perished dead." Death is in many faiths a passage to a worse, not a better world, and often not what you deserve, so the idea of religion as a comfort in the face of existential anxiety over death is simplified at best. If you are bored or in pain, at least you have not met oblivion.

From these same disappointed dead come countless annoyances for the living. "Patagonians lived in terror of the souls of their wizards, which become evil demons after death; Turanian tribes of North Asia fear their shamans even more when dead than when alive, for they become a special class of spirits who are the hurtfullest in all nature." On all continents, people fear and worship ancestors, and blur the boundary between human and animal spirits. Embodiment of and possession by spirits is common; so is the belief (as among the San) that illness can be blamed on the dead. "The cases in which disease-possession passes into oracle-possession are especially connected with hysterical, convulsive, and epileptic affections." Yet, with their normal trances, San healers see themselves not as embodiments of the dead but as defenders of the living.

Tylor describes the spirits in volcanoes, streams, trees, vampire bats, and other natural things—a very basic form of faith—and the worship of idols, often in the form of serpents, bulls, and other creatures—to him a higher form of religious belief than simple animism, spirit possession, and transmigration of souls. In every part of the world people try to persuade or cajole the spirits of streams, forests, and other natural things. Tylor claims that polytheism, too, is an advance, with its hierarchies of gods and goddesses.

He does not always find "modern" people rational. In southern India and Bulgaria, but also in Sweden and the Hebrides, people carried lighted fires around to protect newborn children. Tylor calls the rosary a "devotional calculating machine . . . of Asiatic origin" and the prayer wheel of Tibetan Buddhists a "still more extreme development of mechanical religion." Anticipating cognitive models, he says, "As prayer is a request made to a deity as if he were a man, so sacrifice is a gift made to a deity as if he were a man." The Jewish concept of prayer blends it with ancient sacrifice, using the same word, *avoda* ("service"), for both. Many rituals—fasting, smoking tobacco and other substances, dancing, whirling, meditating—are techniques of ecstasy.

We can doubt Tylor's theories but value the observations; he was closer to undisturbed traditions than we are: "In Tasmania, a native has been heard to ascribe his deliverance to the preserving care of his deceased father's spirit"; since there are no native Tasmanians left, we have only such records. Tylor's conclusion is that the historian and the ethnographer, not just the theologian and natural scientist, must be consulted, "for there seems no human thought so primitive as to have lost its bearing on our own thought, nor so ancient as to have broken its connection with our own life."

Modern anthropology rejected the hierarchical arrangement of cultures, wisely focusing on evaporating cultural variety. It relied not on reports by missionaries and colonists, but on a professionalized social science whose practitioners lived with people and, without trying to alter them, learned through participant observation as much as they could about them. Yet occasionally, they paused to think more generally about what they were seeing—not with grand historical schemes like Tylor's or flights of fancy like Freud's Oedipal anthropology, but with more modest overviews.

Even a dedicated ethnographer like Bronislaw Malinowski, famous for decades of research in the Trobriand Islands off New Guinea, allowed himself a bit of theorizing in a short, sensible book: *Magic, Science, and Religion*. Robert Redfield, another leading ethnologist of the era, responded in his introduction to the objection that Malinowski generalized too often from the one case he knew best: "The criticism . . . loses much of its force if the assumption may be admitted that there are a common human nature and a universal culture pattern." The search for such universals is our goal here.

4

The God Map

In 2005, the BBC did a little experiment on the air. Dr. Michael Persinger, using noninvasive brain stimulation, had already studied hundreds of people, tickling a part of their temporal lobes that some were calling the "God spot." (If you put your fingers between your temples and the tops of your ears, they'll be an inch or so away from it on either side.) The God spot was said to be in one of these, on the right.

Now, no one who understood brain science was going to take seriously the idea that religiosity was located in a spot. It might be located in a circuit linking many spots—something like the roads you would have to take if you wanted to visit, say, all the cathedrals in England; although most roads would be left out, there would be many roads and cathedrals in the circuit. But if you could choose a spot strategically and plunk down a lot of gas pumps, you might increase cathedral touring. That wouldn't mean you had found "the cathedral spot," but it might mean you had found a circuit and a good place to poke it. Now you could draw a diagram and call it "the cathedral map."

Persinger had been stimulating people's right temporal lobes for years, and he had claimed he could increase the traffic in religious, or at least spiritual, ideas. People said they felt a presence or oneness with the world, or had dreamlike experiences, or saw and heard ghosts or spirits, or became aware of a larger mystery of life. They also had physical sensations. Persinger thought he could get reactions in almost everyone. So, the BBC series *Horizon* "set Dr. Persinger's theories and his machine the ultimate test, to give a religious experience to one of the world's most strident atheists—Professor Richard Dawkins." Although Dawkins said his wife might leave him if he was "turned into a devout religious believer," he had always wanted to have a mystical experience. Suitably stimulated, he said he felt a bit dizzy, and as the 40-minute session went on, with Persinger adjusting the target and the intensity, Dawkins reported feeling "sort of a twitchiness in my breathing. I don't know what that is. My left leg is sort of moving, right leg is twitching."

Dawkins had hoped for more: "Unfortunately I didn't get the sensation of a presence." He did get sensations, "but I would be hard put to it to swear that those were not things that could happen to me any time on a dark night. I'm very disappointed. It would have been deeply interesting to me to have experienced something of what religious people do experience in the way of a mystical experience, a communion with the universe. I would have liked to have experienced that." But he talked for years afterward about his lack of response, and he seemed to think he had learned something about religion. Others disagreed. Persinger noted that people have different susceptibilities, and he thought Dawkins was one of the least susceptible ever. A bishop on the same show, Stephen Sykes of the University of Durham, also didn't feel much; he said that if he *had* felt spiritual under such stimulation, he wouldn't think it had to do with religion.

And a famous clinical neurologist, V. S. "Rama" Ramachandran, also on the show, said, "Just because there are circuits in your brain that predispose you to religious belief does not in any way negate the value of a religious belief. . . . Nothing our scientists are saying . . . about neural circuitry for religion in any way negates the existence of God, nor negates the value of religious experience for the person experiencing it." Dawkins expressed another disappointment: "The human religious impulse does seem very difficult to wipe out, which causes me a certain amount of grief. Clearly religion has extreme tenacity." He later said, "I was a failure—it did absolutely nothing for me at all." Rama, on the other hand, quoted the bishop of Oxford: "Well, so what? It just shows that when God made us, he put an antenna in our brains so we could find him, and it just happens to be in the temporal lobe."

We have much more research on how the brain generates, manages, and responds to religious and spiritual experiences; the details are fascinating, but the principles and the arguments are the same. In fact, they have been the same for centuries, since philosopher David Hume claimed that all human mental experiences have correlates in the brain—or really since Hippocrates, who said the same. Brain scientists want to trace just how the brain does every one of its functions, not explain the functions away.

So, how far have we come with regard to religion? We have long known that certain mental illnesses, including bipolar disorder and schizophrenia, involve delusions, and in some people these delusions take a religious form: I am God, God talks to me, an angel visited me during the night, the devil threatened me. Generally, ordinary religious people (including clergy) do not recognize these as true religious experiences, but there have been attempts to locate them in brain circuits. Certain neurological conditions also cause visual or auditory hallucinations, but since those who have them are not mentally ill, they typically discount them as symptoms without meaning.

While in medical school, I helped take care of a monk hospitalized for a manic break in a long bipolar illness. I interviewed this very religious and candid man about how his illness might be interacting with his faith. It didn't interact at all. He had been working in the monastery laundry, and he crouched down, cowering in a corner because the noise of the spinning machines suddenly felt ominous. Something in the tumultuous rumble was pursuing him, but there were neither devil nor demons in the grinding rotations, and neither angels nor God himself was present or even prayed to. He found the event meaning-less, as a bipolar atheist might—a sign of illness, not a sign from God.

But there are ways of giving legitimate diagnoses to people who have religious insights, visions, voices, trances, meditative states, the sense of being outside their bodies, or even faith itself. James began *The Varieties of Religious Experience* with "Religion and Neurology," saying, "Scientific theories are organically conditioned just as religious emotions are. . . . So of all our raptures and our drynesses, our long-ings and pantings, our questions and beliefs. They are equally organi-cally founded. . . . To plead the organic causation of a religious state of mind, then, in refutation of its claim to possess superior spiritual value, is quite illogical and arbitrary." This "illogic" James called "medical materialism," rejecting it as reductionist. Yet it remains interesting to ask how the brain generates religious or spiritual states.

Conditions sometimes tied to religiosity include not only psycho-sis, but intoxication, sleep deprivation, social isolation, anorexia, dis-sociative states, and epilepsy. James thought people with profound religious experiences, even founders of new faiths, had pathological brains, but he admired them as spiritually open. Some doctors have diagnosed epilepsy with religious features—retrospectively—in Joan of Arc, Saint Teresa of Aquila, Joseph Smith, Søren Kierkegaard, Fyo-dor Dostoyevsky, and others. All these diagnoses can be challenged. But Dostoyevsky wrote, "The air was filled with a big noise . . . it had engulfed me. I have really touched God. He came into me myself, yes, God exists, I cried, and I don't remember anything else." A type of epilepsy often linked with religious experiences is TLE (temporal lobe epilepsy). It usually involves changes in thought and feeling, not invol-untary movement. Religious experiences can occur during seizures, as part of the aura leading up to them, or immediately after; some tempo-ral lobe epileptics are more religious *between* seizures.

In a study of 11 patients who had "ecstatic" seizures, 5 had a reli-gious experience. One woman, an artist and agnostic, said, "I had an intense sensation in my stomach as if I were a teenager helplessly in love. Sometimes I heard voices, enjoyable and frightening at the same time." But her first, terrifying episode, was at the end of a church musical performance; she thought she heard God's voice. Another described her beloved grandfather walking toward her, offering a message she couldn't grasp, but she felt intensely happy and wished it would go on. A third heard symphonic music, with a delightful inebriation, floating, her mind leaving her body. A fourth, during her spells, heard "a strange musical theme" with "harsh and pungent taste and smell." She would meet a wise woman who would give her, without words, "the ultimate mission of her life . . . related to saving children." A man described erotic sensations and "a clairvoyant feeling of a 'telepathic contact with a divine power.'" Some patients can have seizures voluntarily, by concentrating, or sniffing a certain odor. People experiencing ecstasy may want to repeat it, and may interpret it as spiritual.

Conversion experiences can occur with TLE. A bus driver was depressed for a week, then, while collecting fares, "overcome with a feeling of bliss. He felt he was literally in Heaven. He collected the fares right, but told his passengers how pleased he was to be in Heaven. At home he did not recognize his wife" but gave her an "incoherent account of his celestial experience." Hospitalized, he laughed constantly and claimed that he had seen God, "and that his wife and family would soon join him in Heaven. . . . He remained in this state of exaltation, hearing divine and angelic voices, for two days." Discharged well, he stayed religious for two years. But then, after three days in a row of seizures, he said that his mind had cleared: "I used to believe in Heaven and Hell, but after this experience I do not believe there is a hereafter," or that Jesus was the son of God. This second sudden conversion also gave him a sense of well-being and clarity. It was a revelation, and he continued as an agnostic for at least eighteen seizure-free months.

The brain-imaging lab of David Silbersweig and Emily Stern has explored the underpinnings of hallucinations, religious or not. In 2012, Tracy Butler in their lab used PET scans (positron-emission tomography) to compare the hallucinations of patients with schizophrenia who either do or do not also have epilepsy. Deep brain structures, including limbic (emotional brain) circuits, were hyperactive in hallucinations, but the frontal lobes were muted—an imbalance between the restraining frontal lobes and the limbic system, including parts of the temporal lobes hyperactive in "religious" seizures.

This kind of evidence led Persinger to stimulate the right temporal lobe with very weak transcranial magnetic stimulation (TMS)—scary sounding but very mild, not even disturbing the scalp. It would seem magical if we didn't know that the brain responds to harmless magnetic waves. In fact, Persinger's stimulation is about a million times weaker than that routinely approved for other studies—which may be a problem. Persinger found, in response to these weak magnetic fields—buzz from "the God helmet"—the "sensed presence" of a deity, another consciousness, or "a Universal Sentience." But one double-blind study—neither subjects nor experimenters knew whether they were stimulated—showed no effects. Perhaps Persinger's subjects were merely suggestible? The dispute continues. But religion is not just a "sensed presence."

Brain imager Uffe Schjoedt suggests, "Experimental neuroscience must appreciate the diversity of religious thought and behavior analyzed by the comparative study of religion for more than 150 years." Schjoedt studies everyday prayer and ritual, finding that they recruit the same circuits that social cognition, interpersonal relationships, and rewarding habits use. He compared four conditions in a group of orthodox Lutherans in Denmark: the Lord's Prayer (formal and religious), personal prayer (improvised and religious), a nursery rhyme (formal and secular), and wishes to Santa Claus (improvised and secular). Personal prayer activated brain regions involved in personal relationships. Does this mean that personal prayer is just another relationship?

Schjoedt also found that the caudate nucleus, part of the reward circuit deep in the brain's core, is active in personal prayer and especially the Lord's Prayer, suggesting that formal-and-religious practices are rewarded by dopamine release. The caudate is also activated in studies of trust and romantic love. In another study, Schjoedt played the same prayers to three groups of religious Christians but told them one of three—randomly assigned—different things: that the person praying was (1) non-Christian, (2) an ordinary Christian, or (3) a Christian with healing powers. In believers told the latter, frontal lobe–centered "executive" circuits were *de*activated, as in hypnosis. Schjoedt interprets the deactivation as similar to what happens in a student-teacher or leader-follower relationship.

This makes sense, but states like hypnosis, romantic love, and profound trust capture more of the flavor of religious experience; we don't have to call praying or feeling healed supernatural to classify them with other human mysteries. Hypnosis, romantic love, and profound trust are not magical, but they are special mental states. Just as TLE can feel religious, so can taking certain drugs. The caudate is enlarged in cocaine users. And while brain imaging reveals circuits involved in religious thought and feeling, drugs can reveal much about the chemistry.

Neurophysiologist John Smythies has done this kind of research for a long lifetime—mainly with hallucinogens like LSD and mescaline. Mescaline, he says, produces "fantastic visual hallucinations ... described by those who experience them as being more beautiful than anything they've ever seen in normal art." Some have mystical experiences like communion with God. And all hallucinogens target the brain's serotonin 2A receptors. Serotonin cells originate in the brain stem but project to the cerebral cortex; they are involved in thought, normal or strange. Activating the 2A receptors stimulates thoughts and visions in ordinary secular people.

The other side of the coin is to look at the same brain cells in *religious* people *without* drugs. "One study . . . took a group of people who were not psychologically interested in religion and [compared them with a group] who were, and they measured the activation of the 1A receptors . . . people who were religiously inclined had a decreased binding to the 1A receptors," which naturally *inhibit* such thoughts. "So the 2A receptors are activated by drugs that produce religious experiences, and the people who have them normally"—without drugs—"have an underactive system which inhibits it." Less inhibition, more religious thoughts.

Mescaline, which stimulates the 2A receptors, is the drug in the peyote cactus, used ritually by Native Americans for millennia. Cultures throughout the world have used mind-altering plants for spiritual insight, meditative states, sacred visions, and closeness to gods. We now study the molecules in those plants and how they work on the brain, and this research sheds light on the chemistry of spirituality. If religious people have less active 1A receptors, then their serotonin cells are less inhibited, so *without* drugs they may be more inclined toward visual beauty, mystical experiences, and communion with God. Interestingly, the people who took mescaline did not hear things, while the temporal lobe epileptics sometimes did, including beautiful music.

We will look at the "plants of the gods," but for now let's consider another angle. If epilepsy gives us glimpses into what happens when certain circuits get too excited, what about conditions that shut part of the brain down? In Italy, Cosimo Urgesi and his colleagues studied 48 patients with brain tumors (gliomas), before and immediately after surgery, along with 20 who were studied months to years later and 20 more with tumors *on* rather than *in* the brain (meningiomas), which did *not* require the removal of brain tissue. Among the 68 people who had some brain removed, each subgroup was divided equally between those whose loss was in the frontal areas and those who lost parietal lobe tissue, farther back in the brain. The researchers measured "self-transcendence"—creative self-forgetfulness, transpersonal identification, and spiritual acceptance. Patients with *parietal lobe* losses experienced an increase in self-transcendence from before to after surgery; others did not. Months to years later they still had higher self-transcendence.

In two related studies in Missouri, Brick Johnstone and his colleagues examined people with moderate traumatic brain injury. The subjects were outpatients—not severely impaired—but almost all had lost consciousness, and most had some amnesia. The study used accepted measures of brain function and spiritual experience. Transcendence (agreement with statements like "I feel the presence of a higher power") was related to one psychological process, selflessness (blurring of the boundaries of the self), and both transcendence and selflessness were related to poor functioning of the right parietal lobe. This finding is consistent with the Italian brain tumor study, although in the Missouri study, *right*-sided injury mattered more.

As in other studies, these researchers found that *frontal* lobe functioning is *positively* related to religiosity, which overlaps with but is not the same as spirituality. They suggest that selflessness ranges from "connection with the beauty of nature/art/music (e.g., losing a sense of self while listening to a favorite piece of music), to romantic love . . . (e.g., becoming one with your soul mate), to an ultimate transcendence . . . a trance state that involves the complete breakdown between a sense of the self and a complete connection with God/the universe." Religious and cultural experience help determine when, where, and how the self is blurred, but frontal and parietal function matter.

Paul Butler's group in Boston studied people with Parkinson's disease, which damages circuits centered in a dark stripe of brain stem cells, the substantia nigra. They project dopamine to higher body control and reward systems, including the frontal lobes. A key symptom is hesitancy in movement; the Parkinson's patients I met in medical school felt trapped in their bodies. Drugs like L-dopa slow the disease but don't stop it, so there is gradual frontal lobe damage. Butler's group, knowing that patients often have the disease on one side of the body first, compared the patients' religiosity. Many Parkinson's patients had reduced religiosity by self-report and by the speed of their processing of religion-related words, but the left-side-onset patients were more affected, indicating that damage to the right frontal lobe had greater impact.

In the next study, the researchers told patients of various faiths brief stories designed to prime different degrees of religious thinking. A mother and child leave home in the morning to visit the father who works at a hospital. What follows is "the child's untimely death in an accident, the child appreciating an awe-inspiring view of the ocean from atop the hospital, the child observing a prayer ritual in the hospital chapel, [or] the child watching the hospital staff practice a drill." Each patient heard all stories in random order in different sessions over a two-week period and *after* hearing a reading about religion. They then rated their agreement with seventeen statements, including five about belief in God. They also got a standard measure of frontal lobe function.

The story in the Aesthetic condition of the study, in which the ocean view inspires the child, primed the most religious belief. But this priming occurred only with the right-side-onset patients, who had dopamine deficits in their left frontal lobes. The story in the Ritual condition prodded the two groups in opposite directions: belief *increased* for the patients with better *left* frontal lobes but *decreased* for those with better *right* frontal lobes. This finding confirmed that the left frontal lobe is involved in the *ritual* aspects of religion—which makes sense, given the left brain's usual dominance for symbols. Butler draws a lesson from the impact of the Aesthetic story on religiosity and the lack of (or even reverse) impact of the story in which the child dies; the results suggest that religion is *not* about fear of death.

There is other evidence about the frontal lobes. A study led by Erik Asp was inspired by Antonio Damasio's pathbreaking work on a type of frontal lobe damage. Damasio showed that injury to the ventromedial prefrontal cortex (vmPFC; if you touch the spot between your eyebrows you'll be close to it) results in personality change and big life mistakes because of poor judgment, even though, by almost all tests, reasoning is intact. Patients are literally disconnected from their gut feelings, which, it turns out, are essential for good judgment. "Gut decision" is no metaphor.

Because these patients tend to be gullible, the lab tested them on two dimensions of "doubt deficit": authoritarianism and religious fundamentalism. The participants were compared to people with other kinds of brain injury, to people with serious nonbrain illnesses, and to normal controls. All were rural Iowans, and almost all belonged to a moderate Christian church. Of all these groups, only the people with vmPFC damage showed high authoritarianism, as well as almost double the average religious fundamentalism. In addition, their religious beliefs were intensified more than those of the other seriously ill people. The husband of one saw her as a "new" person, now a "strong believer in God and Heaven" who felt "overwhelmed that God did so many miracles." They reported increased beliefs in ghosts, in the literality of the Bible, in having a special role in God's plan, and in heaven, and *strongly* increased beliefs in the idea that everything has a purpose, in life after death, and in God. The other patient groups—despite having brain damage or other serious illnesses—showed no increase in almost any of these beliefs.

But brain damage does not always take something *away*. Tony, a 42-year-old surgeon and former football player described by Oliver Sacks, was struck by lightning in a phone booth, had an out-of-body experience, and almost died. "I saw my own body on the ground. . . . I floated up the stairs. . . . Then I was surrounded by a bluish-white light . . . an enormous feeling of well-being and peace. The highest and lowest points of my life raced by me. No emotion . . . pure thought, pure ecstasy. . . . Then, as I was saying to myself, 'This is the most glorious feeling I've ever had'—SLAM! I was back."

This was not a tumor, stroke, or blow to the head; it was, as Sacks calls it, a bolt from the blue—or, since it was raining, from the gray. But as Tony healed, he had a new, intense desire to listen to piano music. Despite no musical training, he began composing in his head and soon taught himself to crudely write down his compositions. His head was filled with music. A decade later, his devotion to it was still strong. He got training and performed one of his own compositions along with classics at a concert for talented amateurs. He was not a world-class pianist, but he was highly praised, and he had started from scratch in his forties, after lightning struck.

Religious people, of course, might interpret this in a certain way. For a century, doctors have described cases of epilepsy triggered by music or intensifying musical experience. We saw several temporal lobe epileptics who heard music during seizure-related spiritual experiences. The nineteenth-century neurologist Hughlings Jackson called the phenomenon a doubling of consciousness. Sylvia, another Sacks patient, began having seizures in her thirties, some with only mental changes. She felt like a teenager in a dream state. The songs that had pervaded her Italian childhood became important and often triggered seizures. In one, "it was the future I saw. . . . I was up there, going to heaven. . . . My grandmother opened up the gates of heaven. 'It's not time,' she said—and then I came to." When removal of part of Sylvia's temporal lobe stopped her seizures, she was grateful—some were physical—but she also felt nostalgic for the mental ones.

Sacks describes cases of musical hallucinations in patients who *know* they are not real and find them annoying—the music without the delusions. These are quite different from the brain changes in schizophrenic patients who hear voices or music; they are "hallucinations in the sane." People may fear that the music in their heads will drive them crazy, but most get used to it. Scanning studies show that imagined music involves circuits activated by real music. Normal variation might include similar but milder brain changes, which could underlie normal religious experience, as in the research on faithful young Lutherans. But what if you study professionals?

Two scientists in Montreal put Carmelite nuns in a scanner and asked them to enter a state of communion with God. Although they had experienced such communion before, this was a very unspiritual environment. MRI scanners are big and make a lot of noise; you are slid headfirst into a big doughnut hole, then lie very still and follow instructions to the letter. Some patients need sedation. But the Carmelites were fine.

Fifteen nuns without psychiatric or neurological problems were scanned in three conditions: Baseline (restful, eyes closed), Mystical, and Control. The nuns told the scientists that God can't be summoned at will, but they played along. In the Mystical condition they were asked to close their eyes, remember, and relive "the most intense mystical experience ever felt in their lives as a member of the Carmelite order." In the Control condition they were to do the same for the most intense state of union with another human being. They rated the intensity of their experiences. Although they said that this MRI memory differed from the spontaneous episodes, many reported moderately intense subjective thoughts and feelings in both the Mystical and the Control conditions. Several said that during the relived mystical experience they felt God's presence—his infinite, unconditional love, and a sense of plenitude and peace.

What was going on in their brains? First, both the Mystical and the Control conditions showed quite different brain activity from Baseline; the nuns actually went through something as they relived these experiences. Second, the brain networks activated were surprisingly different in the two conditions—surprisingly, because so much thinking about the psychology of religion has centered on the ways these experiences *should* be similar. The caudate, involved in happiness, romantic love, and maternal love, was activated in both conditions, but differently—*only* the left caudate in recalling union with a person, the right *and* left in recalling communion with God—consistent with the right brain's less analytic role. The God challenge also activated the right temporal lobe (reminiscent of some epilepsy patients), while the person challenge did not. Finally, reliving communion with God, but not union with a person, engaged different parts of the prefrontal cortex.

God, we might say, is in the details. For now, it's reassuring if the same networks come up in different studies. In addition, some circuits that are active during spiritual experience in this and other studies mainly serve emotion, its embodiment, and its conscious interpretation. That alone should put to rest the notion that religion is purely cognitive. Finally, the differences between human and godly communion undermine another "nothing but" theory—namely, that faith is just social experience writ large.

We have considered the basis in the brain of a sensed presence or higher power; inspiring visions, music, and voices; belief in religious ideas; communion with God; prayer; and the subjective sense of being healed when prayed for. There is no reason that the same circuits should be activated in all of them, yet these are only a few of the many kinds of religious experience. Another experience common to hundreds of millions of believers worldwide is meditation, and brain scientists have studied that as well.

Eugene d'Aquili and Andrew Newberg, who founded "neuro-theology," say there are two main paths to altered states: meditation and ritual. The physiological states have technical names, but let's call them "quiescence" and "flow." Quiescence can be reached by meditation, but also by rest, reading, and other means. Flow is energetic; my San trance-dance experience is an example, as is my Jewish experience of *davening*—chanting prayers half-aloud while swaying rhythmically. The ultimate case might be Sufi whirling dervishes, but Tibetan Buddhist prostrations could also serve. Like quiescence, flow does not have to be spiritual; long-distance running, social dancing into the night, chopping wood, or the work of a master hibachi chef whose hands never stop moving could be examples. But when the goal is spiritual, the end point is different.

There is no hard boundary. Both meditation and ritual recruit brain circuits that regulate the autonomic nervous system, which governs internal states—breathing, heart rate, blood pressure, gastrointestinal and other functions. How *much* we can do this is arguable, but it *is* possible, and it is through the limbic system, or emotional brain, that we can change our bodily states. According to Newberg and d'Aquili, fast, energetic rituals exert a bottom-up effect from the rhythmic sounds and actions to the religious circuits in the brain, while meditation has a top-down impact. The end result is similar: an increased sense of oneness with natural and supernatural worlds.

What is the brain doing? Highly experienced Tibetan Buddhist meditators show increased prefrontal activity and decreased activity in the posterior superior parietal lobule, consistent with a decreased sense of the boundary of the self. Monks corrected me when I said that they were trying to suppress the self; for devout Buddhists the self does not exist, and one goal of meditation is to fully realize that. It's not easy.

David Silbersweig collaborated with David Vago to analyze brain studies of meditation. They distinguish between the autobiographical self and the integrative control network, each corresponding to widespread brain circuits. In meditation, the autobiographical self areas—"I" and "me"—are muted, while the integrative control network, which suppresses greed, desire, and anger, becomes more active. Tibetan Buddhist monks don't meditate on nothing or on a focused point in space. They meditate on an idea and a feeling central to their religious life: compassion for all sentient beings.

In an elegant brain-imaging experiment, Jenny Mascaro and her colleagues, including Geshe Lobsang Tenzin Negi, an advanced meditator and Tibetan Buddhist philosopher, trained naïve American subjects in compassion meditation. Their protocol derived from the religious model, but it removed specific Buddhist references. The control group took a health course for eight weeks. Meditation changed perception and the brain. On the "Reading the Mind from the Eyes" test (you have to guess the emotion a person is feeling from a photo of their eyes), which autistic people find difficult, the compassion meditators improved but the control group did not. The improvement correlated with increased activity in three brain areas—parts of the frontal and temporal lobes.

Finally, studies on how the brain produces belief have come from Sam Harris, the author of *The End of Faith*. He and his colleagues compared 15 committed Christians to 15 otherwise matched nonbelievers. Subjects were asked in an MRI scanner to answer yes or no to a series of statements. When someone in either group said yes to "Eagles really exist," the ventromedial prefrontal cortex region was active, and the same was true when the Christians said yes to "Angels really exist." Religious questions caused more activity in the insula (which monitors internal feelings), the ventral striatum (activated in reward or pleasure), and a part of the parietal lobe involved with the self. Nonreligious stimuli provoked more activity in left-brain memory networks. But as for the decision itself, about whether or not eagles or angels are real, belief is belief and yes is yes.

What of the trance state that I tried so hard to experience in Africa? In one study, trance was induced in experienced shamanic practitioners by exposing them to repetitive drumming that was part of their own tradition. Scientists identified hubs of brain-circuit activity that were strengthened during the trance state—notably the cingulate cortex and the insula; overall, results suggested that "an internally oriented neural stream was amplified by the modulatory control network" along with "perceptual decoupling." In other words, inward-looking brain activity was strengthened at the expense of external awareness.

To the extent that trance is a kind of self-hypnosis, hypnotizability may be relevant. Psychologists have long known that people differ in how susceptible they are to hypnosis, and imagers have begun studying what in the brain makes the different types of people tick. It turns out that high compared to low hypnotizability does imply activity in brain circuits that overlap with those of drumming-induced trance, including "greater functional connectivity between the left dorsolateral prefrontal cortex, an executive-control region of the brain, and the salience network composed of the dorsal anterior cingulate cortex, anterior insula, amygdala, and ventral striatum, involved in detecting, integrating, and filtering relevant somatic, autonomic, and emotional information." This finding is consistent with an inward-facing tendency in a brain more able to become detached from perceptual functions and pure reason.

If you're getting the idea that the neural correlates of religious experience are complex, that is certainly true, and this field is in its infancy. But if you're getting the idea that we're talking about the whole brain, we're not. We *are* talking about widely distributed networks, but ones that can potentially be specified. They are circuits known from many other studies to be involved in social cognition; in the boundaries of the self; in the control of desires and feelings; in emotions including joy, love, fear, and compassion; and in visions and voices. Other studies have identified brain regions active in forgiveness, justice, and other aspects of some religions. Some have identified circuits or connectivity patterns that might be specific to religious belief or activity.

Consider this respectfully offered analogy: Suppose some brain scientists set out to discover the neural basis of sex. Now, sex is much simpler than religion, but it isn't simple. Arousal would not activate the same circuits as orgasm, intercourse the same as masturbation, male experience the same as female. Pornography might well produce different brain dynamics in different people, and whether it is delivered through video, audio, or reading should matter. Different circuits could be activated in experienced people than are activated in novices, in casual sex than in sex with someone you love—and paid sex might be something else again. Yet it isn't a fool's errand to study how the human brain generates and responds to sex *or* religion. We now turn to a different window on religious experience: the aphrodisiacs of spiritual life.

5

Harvesting Faith

When Karl Marx called religion the opium of the people, he meant that it offers illusions of future happiness that lull us into accepting dreadful life conditions. But if religion is like opium, then opium and other mind-altering drugs could be like religion. People the world over have long known about natural mind-altering substances and used them in spiritual and religious activity. They come from plants believed sacred, and traditional uses lead to a sense of oneness, departure from the body, serenity, awe, or closeness to God. They are called "entheogens" because they evoke "the god within."

It is no news that these plants change the mind, but we are starting to know how the plants themselves change in the brain. This sort of stimulation is very different from the magnetic kind, and it reveals much that is not apparent from studies of epilepsy, brain damage, or brain scans. The insights are anatomical *and* chemical, and they show how the brain generates the range of religious experiences. And more: we can reverse-engineer the drug effects to probe the brain for the essence of the experiences. Take Marx's opium, or its long list of newer offspring: heroin, morphine, codeine, Oxycontin, hydrocodone, fentanyl, and many more. All treat physical pain, which was one of opium's first uses. They also help with the general pain of life; in the first US opiate epidemic, they were taken to help with grief.

But they also get you high. They are "euphorics"—euphoria being extreme happiness, elation, ecstasy, jubilation, rapture, exuberance, exhilaration, bliss. Opium itself, from the pretty poppy, has been in use in Europe and Egypt for at least four thousand years; the Minoan culture expected ecstatic states in shamans, who made predictions as a god "spoke" through them. The Greek earth-mother goddess, Cybele, is depicted holding poppies in her hands; some say the first poppies grew from tears that Aphrodite shed as she mourned Adonis. Germanic tribes also used opium to tell fortunes, and surgeons used it in fourth-century China. But in the last few centuries it became recreational everywhere.

Until the 1960s, scientists thought morphine (opium's essence) acted on all brain cells, but then the molecule was radioactively tagged and found to combine with specific receptors in certain places. If there were receptors, probably some *natural* brain molecules could activate them; these were found and named "endorphins," the brain's own morphine. Endorphins help produce the runner's high, and perhaps the high I experienced in the San trance dance. In fact, they could easily enter into any method of inducing an altered state without drugs. Among the different opioid receptors, the one written with the Greek letter mu (μ)—the μ-opioid receptor—binds morphine most strongly and is the most euphoric.

Mu (pronounced like a cat's "mew") is found in deep brain structures, including the emotion-related amygdala, hypothalamus, and nucleus accumbens (a center of reward and pleasure). Euphoria and ecstasy figure in many religions, and they are not centered in the cortex, although thought may induce them. (The cortex deserves the adjective "cerebral.") Dosage matters; the euphoria dose is usually higher than the pain-control dose, and if you go still higher you nod off—the narcotic, or sleep-inducing effect; higher still, you become comatose and die. What the ancients wanted from the poppy, however, was not sleep but truth—predicting the future. The states they sought were fundamentally emotional, although all human emotion also involves thought. The opioid receptors deep in the brain, provoked by poppy or natural endorphins, interact with cultural ideas.

So, religion is indeed (partly) the opium of the people, but it is also the cannabis, peyote, ayahuasca, amanita, coca, tobacco, alcohol, and chocolate of the people; each overlaps with some *non*-drug-induced religious experience, and each has been used in somebody's religion. Tobacco delivers nicotine, a stimulant that tweaks receptors for the brain chemical acetylcholine—or actually a subclass of them known as "nicotinic" receptors. They stimulate the sympathetic fight-or-flight system and have many brain destinations, including the cortex and the dopamine reward areas, which explain nicotine addiction. But nicotine has desired effects, including energy release (partly through adrenaline), concentration, a sense of calm, and reduced hunger.

All this can be euphoric. In one set of experiments, smokers were asked to press a button when they experienced "pleasurable sensations. . . . a rush, a buzz, or a high" while smoking their first cigarette of the day in the lab. They came on three different days, getting either a low-nicotine or a high-nicotine cigarette in random order on the first two days, and their usual brand on the third day. Forty percent pressed the button when they got the low-nicotine cigarette, 80 percent pressed it for a high-nicotine one, with their usual brand (having a nicotine level in between the two) getting an intermediate percentage of button presses. Nicotine can trigger hallucinations, and it is correlated with psychosis. North and South American natives knew the psychoactive properties of nicotine plants, valued them, and used them in varied religious ceremonies. Although it is difficult to say how far back such uses of tobacco go, nicotine has been found in mummies' hair and pipe residues many centuries old. People have ingested nicotine by chewing, licking, rectal insertion, snuffing, and of course smoking, which delivers nicotine to the brain in 7 seconds flat.

Among the Algonquins "smoking was indulged in on all solemn occasions, such as councils, and was a necessary part of most religious ceremonies. . . . Methods of picking up, filling, and lighting the pipe were usually rigidly prescribed, and the first smoke was offered to the spirits." Contracts and treaties were solemnized by the smoking of a pipe decorated with symbols of the gods. Smoking together, the parties invoked "the sun and the other gods as witnesses of the mutual obligations assumed. . . . blowing the smoke toward the sky, the four world quarters, and the earth."

Today, tobacco is used in traditional sweat lodge ceremonies— for purification, spiritual rebirth, and oneness. Pipes are smoked and tobacco put into the fire in the tight space of the lodge, making inhalation certain. In a Lakota Sioux rite, the power of the sun is captured in the pipe. In others, ritual smoking welcomes a girl into womanhood or purifies the souls of the dead. Tobacco, the pipe, and its rituals were first brought by a beautiful, sacred woman in white buckskin: "All these peoples, and all the things of the universe, are joined to you who smoke the pipe—all send their voices to *Wakan-Tanka*, the Great Spirit. . . . with this pipe, you pray for and with everything."

In Mayan art, the gods smoke cigars or cigarettes. In South America, shamans used tobacco much more intensely than does the average man or woman. Intoxication helped the shaman leave his body. Shaman healers among the Warao of Venezuela "incessantly" smoke a 2-foot-long cigar, leave their bodies in tobacco-induced trances, and fly to a mountaintop where a dead shaman's ancestor causes illness. After talking with the spirit, the healer—who has three pairs of pains in his breast—follows prescribed spirit roads and performs rites at stations along the way. The parallels with Bushman trance healers are clear, except that the Warao use tobacco.

In other South American groups, nicotine-drunk shamans change into jaguars. Tobacco makes the shaman like the big, sleek cat, with "acuteness of vision, night vision, wakefulness, a . . . raspy voice, a furred or rough tongue, and a pungent body odor." Nicotine stimulates "norepinephrine, epinephrine, and serotonin, among other compounds . . . implicated in the alteration of mood and affective states." Jaguar-men "experience real or imagined dangers . . . which they have been enculturated to . . . fight." Shamans are aroused, even enraged to protect those who believe in them and "confront their supernatural adversaries. . . . Shamans view pathogenic agents or . . . thunder and lightning as real natural and supernatural threats with no 'as ifs' about them." Their bodily changes parallel the stress-response, an adrenaline storm. "The jaguar-man takes . . . nicotine . . . until his 'battle' is fought and his body collapses in exhaustion," returning to human form. Among the Mapuche of Chile and Argentina, the pipe was open at both ends, so the shaman inhaled as his assistant blew from the other end, causing hyperventilation and quick, deep intoxication.

The Mapuche also smoked tobacco as a pastime, as did people throughout South America. Columbus brought gifts of tobacco home. The Taino, who gave those gifts, smoked recreationally, but their shamans *snuffed* tobacco to induce trances and visions, talk to their spirit helpers, treat disease, and tell the future. Our word "tobacco" comes from theirs for the forked snuffing tube. The plant enthralled Europe as Columbus's men on repeat voyages raped, tortured, and enslaved the Taino. Hundreds of thousands in five Caribbean chiefdoms were, in half a century, almost wiped out by European infections. Centuries later, tobacco smoke enslaves a billion people throughout the world, killing more than 6 million people each year—tragic, but perhaps the Tainos' revenge.

Many mild to moderate stimulants have been used around the world to give us a lift and improve concentration. Coca leaves are chewed or brewed widely in South America; their active ingredient is a small amount of cocaine, just enough to release some dopamine and give pleasure. Khat has been chewed similarly for thousands of years in the Horn of Africa and Arabia; its agent is amphetamine-like cathinone, which also releases dopamine. Betel leaves and nuts are the chew of choice in South and Southeast Asia; the acetylcholine receptors that their arecoline binds are different from those that nicotine uses. Kava root broth, drunk for centuries in the South Sea islands, has kavalactones that slow dopamine's breakdown while stimulating cannabis receptors.

Chocolate, in a bitter brew, was prized by Aztec and Maya elites and offered to their gods; it improves concentration and lifts mood with its mildly speed-like phenylethylamine (plus a bit of caffeine and theobromine) and at the same time calms with cannabis-like anandamide. Black tea, which goes back 4,000 years in China and has long been used in Zen Buddhist ceremonies, contains caffeine but also theanine, a relaxant; caffeine blocks the drowsy effects of brain adenosine, while theanine increases the alpha waves of alert relaxation. Ethiopian rituals used coffee.

All these plants were valued, used in rites, and offered to the gods. All promote alertness and energy and some relaxation without dulling the senses. Each is part of some culture's spiritual life; people find the well-being that these plants bring otherworldly. Some, like intensively smoked tobacco, alter the mind profoundly with delirium and the visions and voices crucial to many religions. Alcohol, cannabis, and the main hallucinogens—peyote, magic mushrooms, ayahuasca, and so on—have helped sustain many faiths. As with epilepsy, brain injury, and imaging, they also teach us how we are set up neurologically for certain experiences.

Take alcohol. More than a billion people reject it for religious reasons, yet a billion others use it in religious ritual. In the wedding at Cana, Jesus turns water into wine. At the Last Supper, he tells his disciples that when they break bread they are breaking and eating his body; drinking wine, they drink his blood. Today, many Christians take Communion, fulfilling Jesus's charge to his disciples.

Communion involves only a bit of wine, yet the symbolism carries forward an older tradition. The Last Supper was a Passover seder; ritually drinking four glasses of wine celebrates the Hebrews' release from slavery. Jews bless and drink wine every Friday night, marking the onset of the Sabbath. It is part of the marriage ceremony, and it or stronger brandies ceremonially close the Sabbath. In a biblical story, the vine refuses the trees' request to become their king: "Should I leave my wine, which causes God and men to rejoice, and go to wave over the trees?" (Judges 9:13). The traditional Jewish toast *l'chaim* ("to life") is made over wine or spirits on any occasion. On Passover you don't get drunk, but just relax, showing you are no longer a slave. You are free to drink like a Greek or Roman, joining in a symposium where ideas and words flow—with a little help from your local vineyard. Another seder was created by the mystical rabbis of the kabbalah for Tu B'shvat, celebrating trees and fruit. Four glasses of wine mark the seasons of the year—first white, then white mixed with a little red, then mainly red, and finally all red. The idea was that wine could bring you closer to God.

And twice a year Jews consider it a *mitzvah* (both "command-ment" and "good deed") to get drunk. One is Purim, a month before Passover, at a full moon, a day of costumes and revels for kids of all ages. It marks the triumph of the Jews of ancient Persia over their enemies, led by the king's viceroy Haman. In the book of Esther, the lovely protagonist and her Uncle Mordechai save the day. Yet you are supposed to get so drunk you can't tell the difference between "Blessed is Mordechai" and "Cursed is Haman." According to kab-balah, not being able to recognize the difference means you have (temporarily) entered the highest spiritual world, *Atzilut*, in which opposites unite.

More surprisingly, observant Jews also get drunk on Simchat Torah ("rejoicing in the law"), an evening of increasingly exuberant dancing and singing while carrying weighty sacred scrolls around the synagogue. If one scroll is dropped, the entire congregation has to fast, yet this rarely happens, despite the tipsy bearers. Hasidic Jews drink on other occasions too. Some say that drinking aids Torah study, and the *farbrengens* of Brooklyn's Lubavitcher Rebbe—hours-long Yiddish lectures to packed crowds on Friday nights—were punctuated by whiskey breaks. When Hasidism was born in the 1700s, Hasidic rabbis were condemned because they communed with God through song, dance, mysticism, and the pleasures of food and drink—not only solemn prayer, debate, and study. Their huge success and influence over other Jews suggests wisdom in their way, which is rather Dionysian—full of passion and liberation, as opposed to the Apollonian way of sober concentration on texts and prayer, abetted at times by fasting and self-denial.

The Bible does caution against drunkenness. A drunk Noah exposes his nakedness to his sons, and Lot actually has sex with his daughters—lasting abominations. "Wine is a mocker, strong drink a brawler" (Proverbs 20:1); "Who has woe? Who has sorrow? Who has strife? . . . Who has wounds without cause? Who has redness of eyes? Those who tarry long over wine. . . . Do not look at wine when it is red, when it sparkles in the cup and goes down smoothly. In the end it bites like a serpent and stings like an adder. Your eyes will see strange things, and your heart utter perverse things" (Proverbs 23:29–35). But yet, "Give strong drink to the one who is perishing, and wine to those in bitter distress" (Proverbs 31:6); and Psalm 104 honors "wine to gladden the heart of man."

If Hasidic Jews are Dionysian, what of the worshippers of the Greek god himself? Dionysus, also called Bacchus, was the god of winemaking, as well as of ritual ecstasy, even frenzy—first as worship, later as theater. In Greek as in Jewish lore, there are cautionary tales. In Euripides's play *The Bacchae*, women in a drunken, delusional mob tear the young prince Pentheus limb from limb because he disrespects their god and rites; tragically, one of these women is his mother. Plato warned explicitly against drunkenness and defended laws restricting alcohol. Yet Dionysus is the Liberator, because he frees people from care and restraint, while Pentheus is an uptight spoilsport who tries to prevent the new god from taking hold. He hears of women straying from home

in mock ecstasies among the thickets on the mountain,
dancing in honor of the latest divinity,
a certain Dionysus, whoever he may be!
In their midst stand bowls brimming with wine.
And then, one by one, the women wander off
to hidden nooks where they serve the lusts of men.
Priestesses of Bacchus they claim they are.

Pentheus jails them and anyone practicing Dionysian rites. His elders warn him to respect the god's power, but Pentheus learns the hard way. The chorus—the voice of reason—rejects his blasphemy, praising the god for his blessings, including

the loosing of cares
when the shining wine is spilled
at the feast of the gods,
and the wine-bowl casts its sleep
on feasters crowned with ivy.

Later they chant, "To rich and poor he gives / the simple gift of wine, / the gladness of the grape"; decry the young scoffer's arrogance; and say, "What the common people do, the things that simple men believe, I too believe and do." And in the last passage of the play, the chorus says, "The gods have many shapes. / The gods bring many things." By the time the play told of his triumph, Dionysus was widely worshipped, and his festivals fostered theater.

Fermenting fruit or grain naturally yields ethanol, and even wild animals grow giddy after imbibing. Wherever grains or grapes were sown, beer- and winemaking spread or were invented. The oldest archeological evidence of routine alcohol use is from China, where drinking and drunkenness have been celebrated in poetry for millennia. Funerals included alcohol in much of the ancient world. But in Egypt 6,000 years ago, we have the first clear evidence of alcohol sacrifices and intoxication in worship. Beer was made wherever grain was grown. Large stores graced the pharaohs' tombs, as did wine later. Egyptian art depicts extensive drinking of both, and beer was stored in temples 5,000 years ago. In myth, the lion-goddess Sekhmet savagely eats people, threatening to wipe out humanity. But the clever prey create a lake of pomegranate-crimsoned beer, which the goddess mistakes for blood. The humans escape while she is drunk, and she later morphs into the goddess Basmet—literally a pussycat.

Women reenacted this event in rituals, drinking to excess on a special "porch of drunkenness." Commenting on digs that turned up wall paintings and inscriptions from 3,500 years ago, Johns Hopkins University archeologist Betsy Bryan said, "We are talking about a festival in which people come together in a community to get drunk. Not high, not socially fun, but drunk—knee-walking, absolutely passed-out drunk." The festival followed the first flooding of the Nile, and beer was the drink of choice. A few months later the annual "festival of the beautiful valley" had ritual celebrants getting drunk on wine. Some inscriptions linked to the porch of drunkenness describe the celebrants "traveling through the marshes," ancient Egyptian slang for having sex. These rites are echoed by what Greek historian Herodotus saw in Egypt a thousand years later:

> They sail men and women together, and a great multitude . . . in every boat; and some of the women have rattles . . . while some of the men play the flute . . . and the rest, both women and men, sing and clap their hands . . . they bring the boat to land, and some of the women . . . cry aloud and jeer at the women in that city, some dance, and some stand up and pull up

their garments. This they do by every city along the river-bank; [at] Bubastis they hold festival celebrating great sacrifices, and more wine of grapes is consumed . . . than during the whole of the rest of the year. To this place . . . they come together year by year even to the number of seventy myriads of men and women, besides children.

That's about 700,000 drunken, frolicking worshippers. During the thousand years between Bryan's porch of drunkenness and Herodotus's Nile tour, the Greeks carried wine, the winemaking craft, and the cult of Dionysus around the Mediterranean. But Euripides dramatized a confrontation that was real in many places that the Greeks colonized. Dionysus was a god of the common people, linked with the great Earth Mother goddess, who was loved by farmers and vintners; the Greeks absorbed her and Dionysus into their inclusive religion.

Polytheism can do this, rather than suppress local beliefs. But with Dionysus and the Earth Mother a clash was inevitable, because the people's worship of the pair was in many places an "activist and explosive fervor." About 3,200 years ago, a dark age began in Greek-dominated lands, as large landowners bent on commercial agriculture, especially growing grapes for wine, pushed small farmers off their soil. These folk embraced the ecstatic, wine-empowered Dionysian religion:

The ancient cults of fertility, of the earth, of plenty, gained strength again as dispossessed migrants spread. . . . Cults were more apt to be dedicated to the divine child, Dionysus, than to the Great Earth Goddess, [with] a greater phallic emphasis as well as a greater violence. . . . The sexually potent bull, or the goat and the donkey of similar repute . . . had become important. And what a polymorphous group of rioters they were: maenads, satyrs, nymphs, and others. The ecstatic, even orgiastic . . . cult of fertility was transformed into a wild and bloody form of sacramental communion. Feverish dances, disordered acts, shouts and other noises were typical of the ceremonies.

But Greek *elites* embraced another imported god, Apollo, about as different as he could be from Dionysus. Nietzsche saw the Dionysian and Apollonian as two approaches to life: the first a kind of wildness, the realm of the poet and the dreamer; the second all about order— and hierarchy. Here *The Bacchae* becomes real. Dionysus (and wine) inspired dispossessed masses to rebel, and when their Apollonian masters tried to crush their religion, widespread violence resulted. Athens's rulers compromised, shaping Dionysus worship into festivals and drama. Less flexible rulers paid with their lives.

All this turns Marx's dictum on its head. The Dionysian religion of wine and ecstatic dance fomented mass rebellion and led to political change. Alcohol-fueled anger, channeled in myth, made the masses *less* docile. Under the wandering god's eye, fermented grapes led Greek commerce far and wide. Wine grew on inhospitable, unirrigated slopes; it was delicious, addicting, clean in a time of dirty water, and blessed by gods. William James understood this: "The sway of alcohol over mankind is unquestionably due to its power to stimulate the mystical faculties of human nature, usually crushed to earth. Sobriety diminishes, discriminates, and says no; drunkenness expands, unites, and says yes. It is in fact the great exciter of the *Yes* function in man. It brings its votary from the chill periphery of things to the radiant core. It makes him for the moment one with truth." Or, in the words of Greek poet Anacreon, translated by Irish poet Thomas Moore,

If all the goblet's bliss were o'er,
When fate had once our doom decreed,
Then dying would be death indeed!
Nor could I think, unblest by wine,
Divinity itself divine!

We don't fully know what ethanol does to the brain, but here are some basics. It's a simple molecule that blocks a chemical called GABA (short for gamma-aminobutyric acid). GABA brakes dopamine in the brain's reward center, so easing off the brakes makes drinking very rewarding. By blocking GABA, ethanol provides indirectly what cocaine and many other drugs do directly: dopamine reward. Addiction may result. But the small molecule with the big impact has many targets. Ethanol blocks the neurotransmitter NMDA (*N*-methyl-D-aspartate), which is involved in thought. It affects the frontal lobes, lifting inhibitions and yielding strange imaginings. It mimics some cannabis, opiate, and nicotine effects. Recently, ethanol was found to have its own special pocket—seen down to the level of atoms—where it fits snugly in the protein of a channel in the cell wall; this binding of ethanol to the channel protein allows ions to flow out of the cell, potentially affecting millions of neurons.

Religions have used many other substances. Hashish and marijuana have long been a part of life even in many Islamic countries where alcohol is forbidden. Assyrians called cannabis "the drug that takes away the mind." Ancient Chinese physicians prescribed it, warning that seeing devils was a side effect. Hashish was popular in mid-nineteenth-century France, where the poet Charles Baudelaire described "groundless gaiety" and "distortions of sounds and colors," and a psychiatrist's experiments caused "happiness, excitement and dissociation of ideas, errors of time and space . . . delusions, fluctuations of emotions, irresistible impulses, and illusions and hallucinations." Baudelaire, in *Les paradis artificiels*, hailed "this delightful and singular state . . . an intermittent haunting from which we must draw, if we are wise, the certainty of a better existence."

Cannabis has been part of India's religious life for millennia. Some believe Shiva, a major Hindu god, created it; today, holy men consecrated to his worship smoke, eat, and drink it to heal and bring on godly visions. Tibetan Buddhism gives cannabis a key place; Buddha himself was said to have lived for a time on one hemp seed a day. Most Buddhists favor natural meditation, but Tantric yogis use the plant to deepen it, and some art shows the Buddha with cannabis leaves in his begging bowl.

The "divine nectar" acts on receptors that were found in the brain in the 1960s. The brain's natural equivalent—"endocannabinoids"—were discovered around 1980. The brain's own cannabis was named "anandamide," from the Sanskrit *ananda* ("bliss"). But trips are not always mellow; phantasms can be unpleasant, even psychotic, in those susceptible. Yet there is no hashish-club equivalent of a bar brawl; aggression is rare. THC, the active ingredient, lasts hours, unlike the brain's own transient version. But our natural cannabinoids may limit anxiety and stress. Cannabis indirectly stimulates two different dopamine receptors in the basal ganglia, critical for emotion, thought, and action. The entire cerebral cortex sends them continuous messages, and they return the favor, in a shifting but never-ending circle. Cannabis synchronizes streams that don't normally converge—a likely basis of delusions. Dopamine serves double duty: overstimulating D_2 dopamine receptors causes delusions; but reward occurs in both D_1 and D_2 connections. A "bad trip" might result from higher doses, individuality, or past experience.

In moving from the mellowing to the visionary—or, on the downside, psychosis-like—effects of cannabis, we come to the core of humanity's entheogen arsenal: the legendary "plants of the gods." Most of the drugs we've considered—euphorics like opiates and ethanol, stimulants like nicotine, coca, khat, betel, and kava, and even marijuana—will produce visions in high doses. But others have this result as their main effect. Plants containing such drugs have been used in spiritual traditions from time immemorial.

One classic is the mushroom *Amanita muscaria*, the "fly agaric" of shamans throughout Siberia and the New World. It and other hallucinogens are neither necessary nor sufficient for ecstatic religious experience, yet they have often been at its core. Consider a passage from Mircea Eliade's classic, *Shamanism*:

> The Tremyugan shaman begins beating his drum and playing the guitar until he falls into ecstasy. Abandoning his body, his soul enters the underworld and goes in search of the patient's soul. He persuades the dead to let him bring it back to earth by promising them the gift of a shirt or other things; some-times . . . he is obliged to use more forcible means. When he wakes [he] has the patient's soul in his closed right hand and replaces it in the body through the right ear.

The parallels with the San trance healer are striking; he enters trance, travels to the world of the spirits, talks them out of killing the person who is ill, and brings that person back to life. The Tremyugan sha-man does all this without drugs, through music—the San add stodgy, repetitive dancing—or even without physical or musical exertion if he is adept enough. But among the Ostyak,

> the technique is markedly different. . . . The shaman performs fumigations and dedicates a piece of cloth to Sänke, the celes-tial Supreme Being. After fasting all day, at nightfall he takes a bath, eats three or seven mushrooms, and goes to sleep. Some hours later he suddenly wakes and, trembling all over, commu-nicates what the spirits . . . have revealed to him: the spirit to which sacrifice must be made, the man who made the hunt fail, and so on. The shaman then relapses into deep sleep and on the following day the specified sacrifices are offered.

Women shamans also make mushroom voyages, but they speak to Sänke directly. "Ecstasy through intoxication by mushrooms is known throughout Siberia. In other parts of the world it has its counterpart in ecstasy produced by narcotics or tobacco."

The same mushroom entranced a novice among native Athabascans in Northwest Canada, who said of the shaman helping him, "He had snatched me. . . . I had no power of my own. I didn't eat, didn't sleep, I didn't think—I wasn't in my body any longer." Another episode was described like this: "Cleansed and ripe for vision, I rise, a bursting ball of seeds in space. . . . I have sung the note that shatters structure. And the note that shatters chaos, and been bloody. . . . I have been with the dead and attempted the labyrinth." On his first try he was dismembered, on his second he met the spirit. For the fruit of a fungus, the fly agaric is a pretty thing, with a pure-white stem and a reddish-orange flattop or cap speckled with raised, white spots and flecks. The active ingredients are ibotenic acid and muscimol, which resemble the brain chemicals glutamate (exciting) and GABA (inhibiting), respectively, but no one knows how exactly they produce visions.

Peyote, though, used for millennia in Texas and Mexico, we do understand. It's a small cactus that grows within inches of the ground, with a richly green or blue-green crown 2 to 5 inches wide and studded with whitish shoots. People collect the crowns not just carefully but ritually—sometimes "hunting" them with bows and arrows—and separate them into buttons you can chew or boil in water as a tea. Just a tablespoon of the dried buttons is mind-altering. The agent is mescaline, which neurophysiologist John Smythies studied. This natural molecule, like lab-made LSD, works mainly by stimulating serotonin 2A receptors. Two other New World ritual plants have similar effects: the "magic mushrooms" of many Mexican cultures and "ayahuasca," a drink made from *Banisteriopsis*, used by South American shamans. Magic mushrooms contain psilocybin; ayahuasca contains dimethyltryptamine, or DMT.

Both psilocybin and DMT work on the brain in the same way

that mescaline and LSD do. And they do work. In studies by Roland Griffiths and his colleagues, 14 men and 22 women without hallucinogen experience were well prepared and given (in separate sessions) different doses of psilocybin or methylphenidate (Ritalin), a stimulant prescribed for attention deficit disorder. They were in a safe living-room environment, lying on a couch, wearing eye masks, listening to classical music, with two supportive, knowledgeable monitors at hand, for 7 hours; they took before and after questionnaires; and they were followed up on. They had prompt responses, proportional to psilocybin dose: a sense of unity, transcendence of time and space, ineffability (they couldn't express it in words), sacredness, noetic quality (knowledge that seems true but not logical), and positive mood.

Those who scored higher than 6 out of 10 on all these were judged to have had a complete mystical experience. Some felt "oceanic boundlessness," "dread of ego dissolution," "visionary restructuralization," euphoria, dysphoria, and other mental states. During the session (compared with Ritalin), psilocybin produced less talking but more arousal, tearing or crying, anxiety or fear, joy or intense happiness, and peace or harmony. Subjects went through volatile emotional changes, positive and negative—much like the shamans who used magic mushrooms.

All was not sweetness and light. Eight of the participants reported anxiety or sadness, and six of these had mild, transient problems like paranoid thinking. While reassurance calmed them and these feelings did not continue after the session, "Two of the eight volunteers compared the experience to being in a war and three indicated that they would never wish to repeat an experience like that again." Yet most of those who had bad trips still "rated the overall experience as having personal meaning and spiritual significance and no volunteer rated the experience as having decreased their sense of well being or life satisfaction." But the really remarkable findings came later.

At the two-month follow-up, those who had been given psilocybin were more than twice as likely to describe positive changes in attitude, mood, and altruism. Two-thirds of the psilocybin group rated the session as among the five most meaningful experiences of their lives, and a substantial minority called it their single most meaningful experience. In addition, each volunteer named three family members or coworkers to be interviewed about them before the sessions and two months after. Friends and relatives of those who took psilocybin rated them as positively changed, but no change was reported for the stimulant group. The positive changes persisted at least a year.

In another study, 18 volunteers took psilocybin in five different doses, increasing or decreasing from session to session. They had predictable dose-response reactions, and the findings at two-month and fourteen-month follow-ups echoed those in prior research. Hallucinogens are being tested for use in depression, addictions, and the distress of physical illness. But these studies also show how shamans worldwide could have the stunning experiences they describe over long careers—facing danger with vision, conviction, altruism, and well-being. Their traditional plants contain drugs used in research, but instead of a living room, classical music, and monitors, they have age-old cultural frameworks for support, guidance, interpretation, and meaning.

The small, yellow-orange psilocybin mushrooms *look* magical, like gold coins strewn in the grass, and the ancient Aztec name for them was *teonanácatl* ("flesh of the gods"), but the native peoples who use them today call them "little flowers" and "holy children." Among the Mazatec of Oaxaca in Mexico, a famous *curandera* (healer), María Sabina, told hallucinogen experts, "There is a world beyond ours, a world that is far away, nearby, and invisible. And there is where God lives, where the dead live, the spirits and the saints. A world where everything has already happened and everything is known. It is they, the sacred mushrooms, that speak in a way I can understand. I ask them and they answer me. When I return from the trip that I have taken with them, I tell what they have told me and what they have shown me." Her chants were confident:

Woman who thunders am I, woman who sounds am I.
Spiderwoman am I, hummingbird woman am I . . .
Eagle woman am I, important eagle woman am I.
Whirling woman of the whirlwind am I, woman of a sacred,
    enchanted place am I,
Woman of the shooting stars am I.

She also said, "I take the 'little one who springs up out of the earth' and I see God. I see him springing up out of the earth."

Ayahuasca—Quechua for "vine of the ancestors or souls"—is actually a drink made from a combination of two plants: a hardy common vine and the leaves of a shrub. The shrub's leaves contain the hallucinogen DMT, which is in the monoamine family, while the vine supplies a monoamine oxidase inhibitor, preventing the removal of the DMT. This tandem action has for centuries aided shamans throughout the Amazon basin. The mix is central to many cultures. In Glenn Shepard's description of the Matsigenka of Peru,

Few sensory experiences can match the furor and exaltation . . . the existentially bitter taste of the brew; the giddy alternating waves of nausea and euphoria; the showers of rainbow-colored fractals; the ethereal resonance of the shaman's chanting; a speechless sense of mystery and wonder; and the unshakeable sensation of being transported to a place beyond time, ordinary reason, and the laws of physics. [There is a] mixing of the senses . . . healing sessions take place in absolute darkness, since the faintest spark or illumination could burn the vulnerable, free-roaming souls of participants. By banishing ordinary sight, Matsigenka shamans open their perceptions to "true vision."

A shaman of the Secoya of Ecuador and Peru described his own ayahuasca journey:

> You're sitting in the hammock, but at the same time, you're in
> another world, seeing the truth of everything that exists. . . .
> The angels come and give you a flute. You play it. It is not the
> healer who teaches you, but the angels themselves who make us
> sing when we are inebriated. It's so beautiful to see the animals
> in their entirety, even those living underwater! . . . I managed
> to see the sun, the rainbow . . . everything. The vision ended
> and I noticed that my heart was hot, like a pot that's just been
> burned. I felt the burning heat inside me. Even without work-
> ing, I was sweating all day. Continuous visions assaulted me.
> Every so often I would be bathed in sweat. I felt capable of
> doing witchcraft and killing others, even though I never did it
> since my father's advice held me back.

And Yaminahua shamans in an ayahuasca trance relate visions in
continuous songs: "Songs are a shaman's most highly prized posses-
sions, the vehicles of his powers and the repositories of his knowledge. . . . Learning to be a shaman is learning to sing, to intone
the powerful chant rhythms, to carefully thread together verbal
images. . . . 'A song is a path—you make it straight and clean then
you walk along it.'"

Singing helps maintain the trance, and its metaphors—"language-
twisting-twisting"—cure the sick. A shaman came to a woman who
bled for two days after childbirth. Beside her hammock, he began to
sing to the moon for her, retelling a widespread Amazonian story that
explains the moon's origins from the head of an incestuous brother.
The moon is linked to menstrual blood and fertility. But the song
evoked the sun's path from dawn to dusk, and the red sunset sky, her
bleeding:

Painted cliff people . . .
It is real human blood
Falling on this earth
Their big blood
Has touched the woman's womb
It has touched your womb . . .
Right there it is stopping
Real human blood
There I am cutting it off

Shamans have a shared consciousness of how things came to be; a trance can show what has gone wrong and how nature and our lives can be set right again.

A peyote pilgrimage among the Huichol of Mexico's Sierra Madre was seen in the 1500s by Bernardino de Sahagún, a Franciscan friar. The Huichol put peyote "above wine or mushrooms. . . . In the desert, they sang all night, all day . . . they wept exceedingly. They said their eyes were washed." Recently, anthropologist Peter Furst found the Huichol blending only a little Christianity with the "powers of creation." The rising Sun is a strong father, water the Springs of Our Mothers, Fire the first shaman. The people hunt Deer-Peyote far into the mountains and, finding the cactus they call Elder Brother, beg him to forgive them for cutting and eating him. His death is not death, yet they weep.

The night was passed in singing and dancing around the ceremonial fire, chewing peyote in astounding quantities, and listening to the ancient stories. . . . [Some people were] subdued and quiet. Some . . . had entered trances. Veradera had been sitting motionless for hours, hands clasped around her knees, eyes closed. When night fell, Lupe placed candles around her to protect her against attacks by sorcerers while her soul was traveling outside her body. . . . The singing, dancing, and speechmaking, punctuated by laughter and trumpet-blowing, went on with few interruptions until well past midnight, when Ramón laid aside his fiddle and allowed the peyote to take hold of him completely, so that he might speak directly with [the supernaturals] and listen to their counsel.

In this state the shaman finds new names for the pilgrims (Offering of the Blue Maize, Votive Gourd of the Sun, Arrows of Fire Shaman). "These names are said to emerge from the center of the fire like brilliantly colored, luminous ribbons. Ordinary Huichol, leaving this sacred place, beg the spirits *not* to leave it, pledging the 300-mile trek again next year, singing,

Nothing but flowers here . . .
The hills very pretty for walking,
For shouting and laughing . . .
And being together with all one's companions.
Do not weep, brothers, do not weep,
For we came to enjoy it,
We came on this trek
To find our life.
For we are all,
We are all,
We are all the children of,
We are all the sons of,
A brilliantly colored flower,
A flaming flower.
And there is no one,
There is no one,
Who regrets what we are.

6

Convergences

Only the most parochial logicians or religious fundamentalists would deny such devout people as the Huichol the dignity of their faith. But how do shamanistic rites, especially under the influence of dream stuff, shed light on major religions? First, we use psychoactive drugs—cannabis in some Hindu practices, alcohol in Jewish ones. Second, other mind-altering tools—fasting, sleep deprivation, social isolation, silence, meditation, prayer, pilgrimages, prostrations—figure in all major religions. Third, studies show similarities between substance-induced spirituality and the more conventional kind.

The classic Marsh Chapel Experiment—a.k.a. the Good Friday Experiment—was the focus of a 1963 thesis by Walter Pahnke, a Harvard-trained physician, psychiatrist, and minister. Supervised by Timothy Leary and Richard Alpert (Ram Dass)—psychologists studying psychedelic drugs—Pahnke published only a summary. But in a long-term follow-up, Rick Doblin had access to Pahnke's papers and most of his subjects.

On Good Friday 1962, Pahnke took 20 male graduate students in a liberal Protestant theology program to a private chapel in Boston. Of these 20 students, 10 took psilocybin, and the other 10 took nicotinic acid (vitamin B_3, or niacin), because its effects on heart rate might make the control subjects think they had consumed psilocybin. Under supervision 90 minutes later, they heard a live service over loudspeakers. The service ran two and a half hours, with organ music, solos, readings, prayers, and meditation. The men were observed and afterward assessed according to a mysticism scale measuring nine dimensions: Unity (internal and external), Transcendence of Time and Space, Deeply Felt Positive Mood (joy, blessedness, peace, love), Sense of Sacredness, (seeming) Objectivity and Reality, Paradoxicality, Alleged Ineffability (inability to find words), Transiency, and Persisting Positive Changes in Attitude and Behavior (toward self, others, life, and the experience). The results were impressive, as was the six-month follow-up. Group differences were highly significant for all nine dimensions; psilocybin subjects scored two to fourteen *times* higher than the controls, who were in the same small chapel on one of the holiest days of the Christian year.

But Doblin's long-term follow-up—a quarter century later, when studies like this were illegal—was equally remarkable. He interviewed 16 of the original 20 volunteers—7 from the psilocybin group and 9 controls. Five in each group were currently working as ministers. Doblin criticized the original report for minimizing the dark side; one psilocybin subject needed a tranquilizer. Unfortunately, the one with the worst "trip" refused the twenty-five-year follow-up. In addition, because all the subjects were together during the trial, the controls realized who had received psilocybin.

Doblin used the same questionnaires that Pahnke had used. After twenty-five years, in eight of nine categories the psilocybin subjects scored even higher than they had at six months, the differences significant for every dimension. In open-ended comments, "experimental subjects wrote that the experience helped them to resolve career decisions, recognize the arbitrariness of ego boundaries, increase their depth of faith [and] appreciation of eternal life, deepen their sense of the meaning of Christ, and heighten their sense of joy and beauty." Nothing like this was reported by the vitamin group.

Most of the psilocybin subjects described other feelings in dreams, prayer, or nature that they likened to their Good Friday experiences, but with a narrower emotional range. Participant "T.B." could not think of any spiritual experience of that magnitude, but it "was the last of the great four in my life." The first was when he had scarlet fever at age nine and was expected to die. "I saw a light coming out of the sky . . . and it came toward me and it was like the figure of Christ and I said, 'No, let me live and I'll serve you.' And I'm alive and I've served." In seventh grade, T.B. was in a prayer state and "intentionally went for an experience with God. . . . I also went for an experience with God at the Good Friday experience." Later, at West Point, he had another prayer experience in which he saw the face of Christ and felt saved.

Although the man with the worst experience declined follow-up, everyone who could be interviewed looked back favorably on that day and felt it had changed his life. "K.B." said, "It left me with a completely unquestioned certainty that there is an environment bigger than the one I'm conscious of. . . . I expect things from meditation and prayer . . . that I might have been a bit more skeptical about before." Several said it made them more active in the civil rights and antiwar movements; one was surprised because "drugs are an escape from social obligations."

All remembered their long-ago drug experience. "Reverend S.J." recalled feeling "drawn out into infinity" and "caught up in the vastness of creation. . . . You would look up and see the light on the altar and it would just be a blinding sort of light and radiation. . . . The main thing . . . was a sense of timelessness."

"L.J." said, "I was on the floor underneath the chapel pew. . . . I was hearing my uncle who had died, the one who was a minister, saying, 'I want you to die, I want you to die, I want you to die.' . . . The more that I let go and sort of died, the more I felt this eternal life, saying to myself . . . 'it has always been this way. . . . O, isn't it wonderful, there's nothing to fear, this is what it means to die, or to taste of eternal life. . . .' Just in that one session I think I gained experience I . . . could never have gotten from a hundred hours of reading, a thousand hours."

"Reverend L.R.," despite having had "a very strong paranoid experience," said, "The inner awareness and feelings I had during the drug experience were the dropping away of the external world . . . and then the sudden sense of singleness, oneness. And the rest of normal waking consciousness is really . . . illusion."

"Reverend Y.M.," whose journey was also partly negative, said, "I closed my eyes and . . . it was as if I was in an ocean of bands, streams of color, streaming past me. . . . Then that swirl dissolved itself into a radial pattern. . . . I was at the center and I could swim out any one of those colors and it would be a whole different life's experience." At the time of the study, Y.M. had been making hard career choices, "and when I couldn't decide, I died. . . . My insides were literally being scooped out, and it was very painful." He made the big decision while on the drug, and remained confident about it 25 years later.

Reverend K.B. had a specifically Christian experience. "Words are a familiar environment for me . . . but I didn't find any for this. And I haven't yet. . . . I closed my eyes and it seemed to be darker than usual. And then there was a sudden bolt of light which I think was entirely internal . . . like a shock. . . . It wasn't violent but it was . . . like taking hold of a wire." It was "a fine time" to meditate on the Passion and "the procession to the cross."

> I had an unusually vivid scene of the procession going by . . . apart from me but very vivid. I had a definite sense of being an infant or being born . . . a sense of death, too. . . . I had my hands on my legs and there wasn't any flesh, there were bare bones. . . . That part wasn't frightening, I was just kind of amazed. . . . I must have gone along through the life of Christ identifying in a very total sort of way—reliving the life in some way until finally dying and going into the tomb.

Others' experience was not particularly Christian. Two volunteers who randomly got the vitamin pill later tried a psychedelic drug— akin to the kind of experiment that uses the subjects themselves as their own controls. One had a psilocybin subject from the original Good Friday study as his guide. "It seemed like an eternity of being in heaven and everything," he said. "One of the most beautiful experiences in my entire life." He would like his kids to take it. The other got psilocybin in a hospital during a later experiment. Anxious at one point, he felt as if he were finding out what it was like to be crazy, but that didn't last:

> I just had this incredible sense of joy and humor, too. I was laughing, real ecstasy. . . . The thing that struck me was how anybody could worry or not trust, that just struck me as an absurdity. It was very exciting. There was an energy, it was almost a sexual thing, an intensity and a joy. . . . We were all part of the same thing. You didn't sense a difference between the music or the physical objects . . . you can certainly have a religious experience without the religious symbols. Certainly the religious symbols can lead you to a mystical experience. Unfortunately, they can also be divisive. . . . The mystic experience as I understand it comes down more on the commons.

We will return to this divisiveness, but consider this: in divinity students, psilocybin causes mystical experiences resembling those of shamans. Some likened it to other mystical events in their lives. Almost all looked back positively twenty-five years later, and the majority who were clergy felt it had shed light on their calling.

A recent study used the shamans' potion ayahuasca to compare two modern groups who use ayahuasca for spiritual purposes—as many now do. A surge of drug tourism to South America, and several churches originating in Brazil—Santo Daime, for example—combine

Christianity with ayahuasca ceremonies; the movement has centers in Japan, Australia, the US, and Europe. The researchers recruited 131 ayahuasca users; they interviewed 50 in person and gave questionnaires to the rest, comparing them with 46 religious Catholics attending a weekend contemplation retreat.

The ayahuasca group had varied religious affiliations, including Buddhist, pagan, agnostic, and Christian. They had at least some prior experience with ayahuasca and/or other psychedelics. Large majorities of both groups engaged in a spiritual practice four to five times a week. The ayahuasca ceremonies took place at night in a private retreat with "natural beauty. A shaman or leader was present for 80% of the people who took ayahuasca, and almost all reported feeling safe. . . . Most groups had live singing of *icaros* (traditional songs) and music consisting of rhythmic drums and rattles with some flutes and guitars." Users scored modestly higher on a Spiritual Experience Questionnaire. But the 50 interviewed got "messages" while on ayahuasca: "love yourself more, open your heart to yourself and others, empower yourself, another's pain is your pain, normal waking consciousness is just one of many realities, love what is."

Many said that the experience had changed their lives and that they had reduced or stopped alcohol and other drug use, had lost weight, had started eating healthier food, and had become less anxious. One reported losing his "emotional triggers"; others noted an increased sense of community or improved relations with parents. One said, "I'm becoming my own best friend"; another, "I'm part of the Cosmos"; another, "I better understand the strength I draw from past trauma." Many described renewed or deepened faith and love of God, increased awareness of nature, and shared consciousness. Some had gained wisdom in dreams. Others said they now believed in the sentience of plants and could ask ayahuasca for help. One spoke of "regular contact with spirit guides—something I never believed in before."

Asked if they had a personal relationship with the spirit of ayahuasca, three-fourths said yes, describing it as "a wise teacher, grandmother, or healer from a higher spiritual dimension and intelligence who provides guidance and loving, comforting, protective support." They felt loved, "connected to the Great Mystery," and forgiving of themselves, grateful, or humbled. One said, "I glow light." Probing for negative experiences revealed very few, qualified by comments about how much the participants had learned. This research blurs the distinction between sacred-plant shamanism and modern spiritual life. The use of ayahuasca, peyote, and mind-altering substances from other traditional plants is growing among seekers of transcendence, who find commonalities, even communion, with a distant and exotic cultural past.

———

WE HAVE TOUCHED on wine's role in the Gospels and in Christian ritual. Alcohol may produce religious insights in Judaism as cannabis does for Hindu holy men. At pivotal points in history, spiritual discoveries have been made in altered states of consciousness achieved by sensory deprivation, isolation, sleeplessness, and fasting, without drugs. But in one religion practiced today by about a billion people, a hallucinogenic substance was central in the beginning.

Scholars have searched for and argued over *soma*, the sacred drink made from a plant of ancient India; none doubt its importance. The Rig-Veda (the oldest Hindu scripture, at 3,500 years) includes 1,000 hymns, 120 *about* soma—a strong and holy drink, a nectar of gods like Indra and Agni that can make humans godlike—a worthy offering to the gods, even a god itself, addressed in prayer. Some experts say that soma was *Amanita* or other mushrooms; some, a mixture of plants containing ephedrine and harmaline; some, cannabis. But none question its key religious role. Consider one hymn:

> *I have tasted the sweet drink of life . . .*
> *We have drunk the Soma; we have become immortal; we have gone*
> *to the light; we have found the gods. . . .*

The glorious drops that I have drunk set me free in wide space.... Inflame me like a fire kindled by friction; make us see far; make us richer, better. For when I am intoxicated with you, Soma, I think myself rich....
Weakness and diseases have gone; the forces of darkness have fled ...
Soma, you give us the force of life on every side.

Whatever its exact identity, soma was a drink, not a metaphor, and hymns like this played a foundational role in the Hindu faith, revealing the nature of the gods and the limits of human aspirations. But methods other than drugs can also change body and brain.

Moses on Mount Sinai is said to have received the Law from God, over a period of forty days and nights when he did not have much to eat. Matthew 4:1–4 says, "Jesus was led up by the Spirit into the wilderness to be tempted by the devil. And after fasting forty days and forty nights, he was hungry. And the tempter came and said to him, 'If you are the Son of God, command these stones to become loaves of bread.' But he answered ... 'Man shall not live by bread alone, but by every word that comes from the mouth of God.'" Mohammed went on isolated mountain retreats, receiving the Qur'an from the angel Gabriel over twenty-three years. Buddha, it is said, lived six years eating one hemp seed a day.

Taoism has roots in ancient Chinese shamanism, and Confucianism and Buddhism retain shamanic rituals. Many millions in supposedly Communist China continue them in some form. Archeologists associate them with alcohol, cannabis, and other psychoactive drugs used in ancient China—perhaps hemp's original home. The popular Shinto religion of Japan, which, like Taoism in China, persists combined with Buddhism, had shamanic roots too. Some neurologists claim that Joan of Arc had temporal lobe seizures and that Hildegard of Bingen's visions were due to migraine. These ideas direct us to brain circuits, even while some see those circuits as God's antennas.

The fact that hallucinogens use serotonin neurons should help us with the brain's spiritual pathways—the God map. But *where* are the key serotonin neurons? In a high-tech extension of the Good Friday Experiment, Robin Carhart-Harris's group scanned the brains of people taking psilocybin. They found that certain "hubs" in the brain— the thalamus, the anterior and posterior cingulate cortex, and the medial prefrontal cortex—were less active; a kind of current running between the center of the brain and the part between the eyes becomes quieter, enabling "unrestrained cognition." There were adverse effects, including vivid memories of prior trauma, but reports were mostly positive. The "unrestrained cognition" included ten items showing huge psilocybin effects, such as "Things looked strange," "My imagination was extremely vivid," "My sense of size or space was altered," "My thoughts wandered away," "My sense of time was altered," and "The experience had a dreamlike quality."

Crucially, the score on these statements correlated with the decreased activity of the medial prefrontal cortex and the adjacent anterior cingulate cortex, both of which interact with the limbic system—the emotional brain. The deactivations fit with what we have seen: hallucinogens prod serotonin 2A receptors, causing GABA release, which in turn inhibits the pivotal pyramidal cells in the cortex. Many 2A receptors are found in the very regions damped down by psilocybin—regions normally "noisier" than the rest of the cortex. Depression is related to *increased* activity in the medial prefrontal cortex (deactivated here), and pessimism is related to decreased serotonin 2A responsiveness. Psilocybin improves depression and increases openness, consistent with the mood alteration and mind expansion described by traditional entheogen users. The psilocybin effects may resemble rather than counteract a different disorder: psychosis. This doesn't mean that depression and psychosis are opposites. But depression includes rigidity of pessimistic thinking, while psychosis can seem like *too much* openness.

In a second study, scanning for functional connectivity was taken to another level through different methods. Two circuits are normally *not* coordinated: an internal network active when we're thinking about ourselves, and an external one for focused attention. It's easy to see why keeping the two circuits separate would be adaptive. But under psilocybin, the two blend together; as one volunteer said, "*It was quite difficult at times to know where I ended and where I melted into everything around me*" (italics added).

How does this relate to spirituality *without* hallucinogens? Recall that, drugs aside, more religious people had fewer serotonin 1A receptors, which normally inhibit serotonin. Jacqueline Borg and her colleagues gave 15 "normal" men a personality test, using PET scans to reveal their 1A receptors. Only one of seven personality traits related to the 1A receptors: "self-transcendence," which was both the most stable dimension and one of the key things distinguishing us from each other. The aspect of self-transcendence that was most correlated with the brain measure was "spiritual acceptance"; high scorers "endorse extrasensory perception and ideation, whether named deities or a common unifying force. Low scorers ... favor a reductionistic and empirical worldview." So, spiritual people are less likely to inhibit the same neurons that hallucinogens stimulate.

It's complicated, I know, but let's take stock of what we tentatively know now about what I have called "the God map."

1. Some psychotic thoughts have religious content. Dopamine-blocking drugs can suppress psychotic thoughts.
2. Temporal lobe epilepsy involves unusual activity in that lobe. Some patients feel religious during seizures. It isn't a "God spot," but it's on the God map.
3. Some limbic—emotional brain—circuits are hyperactive in schizophrenic hallucinations; the frontal lobes, which inhibit the limbic system, are less active.

4. Prayer by devout Christians activates the tip of the temporal lobe, the temporal-parietal junction (involved in social cognition and relationships), the caudate nucleus (trust and reward), and the medial prefrontal cortex (relationships).

5. Patients who had parts of their parietal lobes removed had an immediate, long-lasting increase in self-transcendence, but those with frontal damage did not.

6. The left frontal lobe is involved more in ritual; the right, more in spirituality. One split-brain patient's right hemisphere believed in God, while his left did not.

7. Patients with damaged ventromedial prefrontal cortex (vmPFC) became more authoritarian and fundamentalist.

8. Nuns in an MRI study activated only the left caudate for communion with a person, but both left and right, and the right temporal lobe, for communion with God.

9. Meditation activates prefrontal areas (integrative control) but deactivates parietal areas that mark the boundary of the self (the "I" and "me" circuits).

10. Hallucinogens (including peyote, magic mushrooms, the ayahuasca ingredients, and other sacred plants) activate serotonin 2A receptors. Religious people have fewer 1A receptors, which inhibit serotonin cells. Hubs in the midline of the brain become quieter with hallucinogens, and externally and internally oriented brain networks conflate.

11. Effects of substances used in religions range from stimulation (low-dose nicotine) to hallucination (higher doses of nicotine, or the substances noted in number 10 above) to euphoria and ecstasy (opium, high-dose alcohol). Common pathways cause pleasure, suppress pain, and release inhibitions.

These bits of knowledge don't add up to a full grasp of how religion and spirituality live in our brains. Correlations depend on which aspect of religion we mean—ritual, belief, self-transcendence, experience of a presence, meditation, prayer, communion, group identity, affiliation with institutions, attendance at religious services, life-cycle rites, and others. Why should a domain of life that varies so much have one circuit, however complex—much less one spot? Brain research on religion confirms the following:

- Religion is not just cognitive, but emotional, social, bodily, and mystical.
- The wide varieties of religious experience involve overlapping but different brain circuits.
- Religion can in principle be explained, but not explained away.

7

Good to Think?

Neuroscientists seek and sometimes find religion and spirituality in brain circuits and chemicals; meanwhile, research by psychologists, anthropologists, and philosophers shows how religion is formed not only in the brain but in the mind.

Cognitive anthropologist Scott Atran published his wide-ranging book *In Gods We Trust* just a century after William James's *Varieties*, and I think it remains the best secular book about religion since James. Although Atran says, "There is no such entity as 'religion,'" he clearly means that in the sense we have established: religion is too many different things to be *an* entity. But he also says that the following are found in every known society:

1. Widespread counterfactual belief in supernatural agents
2. Hard-to-fake public expressions of costly material commitments to supernatural agents—personal sacrifice
3. A central focus of supernatural agents on people's existential anxieties
4. Ritualized and often rhythmic coordination of 1, 2, and 3—or, communion

In every society, convergence of these common elements leads to *"passionate communal displays of costly commitments to counterintuitive worlds governed by supernatural agents.*" The words I have italicized almost define religion, but we don't want to exclude noncommunal experiences, nor would we find in Buddhist societies that supernatural agents (which many Buddhists believe in) *govern* the counterintuitive world. Some would object to the words "counterfactual" and "counterintuitive," but let's just say that what we mean by them is *outside the evidence-based explanations of ordinary experience.* So, we can, perhaps, with these friendly amendments, define religion as *passionate, often communal, commitments to and experiences of supernatural agents and forces that do not require evidence-based explanations.*

The trend toward cognitive-psychology explanations began with a book by an anthropologist: Stewart Guthrie's *Faces in the Clouds.* Guthrie proposed that religion is, in essence, animistic and anthropomorphic. That is, we tend to see the inanimate world as alive with unseen creatures that cause seemingly random events, and we project our own abilities and foibles, writ large enough to be superpowers, onto those creatures. Guthrie knew the standard social explanations. But he was doing *psychological* anthropology: what is it about the human mind that wants or creates religious explanations of so many experiences? His animism and anthropomorphism resemble today's cognitive explanations.

An explicitly cognitive anthropologist, Pascal Boyer, refined part of Guthrie's theory: one of the cognitive modules (functional components of the mind) that arose in evolution is a mental device for seeing agency (conscious, motivated action) where there may be none. This was similar to Guthrie's animism. Because, like Guthrie and Atran, Boyer used many ethnographic examples, he escaped the narrowness of some psychological theories. His "framework for a cognitive neuroscience of religion" includes the following:

1. Gods and spirits are seen as agents with goals, because of human capacities to detect such agency from infancy, and

eventually development of the superior temporal sulcus
and the parietal cortex.

2. Because of what psychologists call "mind reading," partly
done by the medial frontal cortex, gods and spirits are said
to have thoughts, perceptions, and beliefs.

3. Likewise, the dead are believed to have minds and to be
agents we can relate to because of our shared ability to read
minds and our social capacities generally.

4. Ideas about purity, pollution, taboo, and the sacred are
adaptations to fear of real contagion; such fear is based in
limbic system structures, and rituals ease it.

5. Because of limbic and cortical structures that link morality with emotional states, we think that gods make moral
judgments and are interested in what we do.

6. Because of the brain's capacity for delusions, imaginary
companions, and blurring of the self/nonself distinction,
gods and spirits seem real.

7. Social exchanges can be made with gods; people make sacrifices to get gifts or avoid punishments from them, using
brain circuits evolved for human exchanges.

8. Altered states of consciousness result in "fusion" with the
supernatural world.

Boyer accepts the variety of things we call religious and sees a role
for emotions, unusual mental states, and compulsive behavior, but he
views religion as a "by-product of the normal operation of human cognition," with an emphasis on social cognition.

Psychologist Justin L. Barrett and his colleagues conducted a series
of relevant experiments that led them to postulate not just agent detection but a "hypersensitive agency detection device" (HADD) common to all humans, and evolved for such things as predator detection.
As Guthrie had said about animism and anthropomorphism, better

mistake a boulder for a bear, or a tree for an enemy, than vice versa. Anthropology and cognitive psychology were converging. Reviewing a book by Boyer, *The Naturalness of Religious Ideas*, Barrett summarized his message like this: "People are universally equipped with cognitive intuitions [that] provide the inferential core of religious ideas; thus only counterintuitive or novel properties need to be culturally transmitted." He concluded, "Whether or not this text foreshadows a 'cognitive revolution' in religion, it certainly qualifies as a well-armed uprising."

The uprising became a revolution as more experiments tested these ideas. For example, Barrett and Frank Keil showed that people's concept of God or gods is more anthropomorphic than they claim it is. In questionnaires, university students of several religions agreed with the modern theology of an abstract God not limited like a person. Then the students read stories and had to recall what God did in the story. In one story, God saves a boy from drowning. "Though God was answering another prayer in another part of the world . . . before long God responded by pushing one of the rocks so the boy could get his leg out." The students tended to think God had to *finish* answering the first prayer before he could help the boy, rather than doing both at once. So they gave God limitations that they had denied in the abstract questionnaire. They humanized God.

Barrett's group did parallel work with Hindus in northern India, translating the questionnaires and stories to study people's ideas about four gods: Brahma, who in Hindu theology is abstract and important; Krishna, who is explicitly a god in human form; and Shiva and Vishnu, who are manifestations of Brahma that are often depicted anthropomorphically and so occupy an intermediate position. There were four different versions of the questionnaires and the stories. Once again, the contrast was sharp. Subjects were clearly more likely to anthropomorphize in misremembering the story elements, while in answering the questionnaires, they depicted all four gods with fewer humanlike limitations. And, like the subjects in the American experiment, they made far fewer mistakes in recalling secular stories.

Todd Tremlin's *Minds and Gods* focused on two universal cognitive features: an agency detection device (ADD) and a theory-of-mind module (ToMM) prompt us not only to look for an agent—an actor—behind every event, but also to expect that that actor will have a mind. Again, we err on the side of attributing agency in situations where there isn't any—a tendency that served our ancestors well. We also endow the imagined agent with mental properties that, despite superpowers, parallel our own much weaker ones.

The ToMM is something more than Guthrie's faces in the clouds; "theory of mind" has to do with how we represent the intentions, beliefs, and other mental processes of fellow creatures. But in reducing religious experience to these two (quite useful) elements, much is left behind. As Tremlin says, "ADD and ToMM are not the only mental mechanisms that underpin religious thought . . . gods evoke intense feelings and emotional experiences," and he wisely goes on to say that "belief in gods indeed is largely an activity of the heart."

Philosopher and cognitive scientist Robert McCauley extended the approach in *Why Religion Is Natural and Science Is Not.* Together with comparative religion scholar E. Thomas Lawson, he developed arguments in favor of explaining religion without rejecting it or its cultural interpretation, and then focused on the explanation of ritual with respect to its impact on human memory and emotions. McCauley's claims are relatively modest, and he wisely says, "The sciences do not provide full or comprehensive accounts of anything. Only religions propose those. This is why faulting scientific proposals for their incompleteness . . . is always an empty complaint."

Like Atran, Boyer, and Tremlin, McCauley seeks basically inborn perceptual and cognitive functions (which he calls "maturationally natural cognition") that predispose us toward religious thinking and ritual. Yet these functions may (like language) be deeply *culturally infiltrated* despite some of their main circuits being prewired. They are *maturationally* natural because they tend to arise early in life and don't have to be deliberately taught or practiced. McCauley argues that "maturationally natural cognitive systems influence religion far more than they influence science."

Atran uses more conventional terms, like "innate releasing mechanism" and "instinct" to refer to core processes: "From an evolutionary standpoint, these structures are . . . no different in origin and kind from the genetic instincts and mechanical processes that govern the life of other animals." This broad concept includes the "infant-mother paradigm," the "agent-detection module," "a near universal association of mountains with sacred places," the "primary emotions" identified by Darwin ("surprise, fear, anger, disgust, sadness, happiness"), and others. I have no problem with biologically prepared mental and behavioral capacities.

Like the cognitive theorists, however, Atran insists that there is no special adaptation for religion itself—that it is not in itself important but is a by-product of something that is. Others of comparable sophistication (for example, E. O. Wilson) have seen religion as having been in some sense specifically selected for as an adaptation in its own right. We'll return to this debate, but for now I will simply say that I find it difficult to rule out the latter view. Even more difficult to rule out is the idea that religion was an "exaptation"—a feature of an organism that starts out as a by-product and subsequently becomes adaptive. I'll also say in passing that it is pretty difficult to believe both that religion is adaptive and that it should be abolished, which helps explain the heated nature of this debate. I see religion as an *emergent* property of human brain function, arising from a complex interplay of human cognitive, emotional, and social capacities to become a whole that is more than the sum of its parts—adaptive, and therefore selected for in its own right, for most of the human past.

Psychological approaches to religion apart from the cognitive one confirm McCauley's insistence that cognitive science "does not provide a comprehensive theory" of religion because "we are not only cognitive systems." James—partly because he was trained as a physician—emphasized meditative states, trances, and conversion experiences with huge emotional power, as well as fasting, other types of abstinence, and a life of service to others. Freud emphasized the feeling of oneness with the world or others, a desired dissolution of the self. Trying to pin all this on a few cognitive principles leaves us feeling that they help explain the thoughts, but that the experiences themselves are more fundamental functions of brain and body. They are more intense in some people, who inspire others. We saw that

- Certain forms of epilepsy and psychosis involve religious thinking and may lead to new commitments or abandonments of faith.
- Traditional plant products that stimulate or inhibit certain circuits—long a part of many religions—produce visions, voices, and feelings of a dissolving self.
- Brain damage can enhance or interfere with religiosity.
- Prayer and meditation modify brain circuits and states of body and mind.

Prayer involves beliefs that can be explained in part by animism, anthropomorphism, agency detection, and other cognitive processes that lead to ideas about supernatural beings, but meditation often does not. Much meditation *strives for no ideas at all*, and that experience, too, can be profoundly religious. Personality psychology has explored individual differences in faith, whether due to genes or to learning.

Yet these explorations hardly exhaust the potential of scientific psychology. Consider what are called dissociations and dissociative disorders. Examples include often feeling that you are not who you are (depersonalization), that the world around you is unreal (derealization), that you can't remember basic facts about your life, or that you have multiple personalities (dissociative identity disorder). Such disorders are often said to result from childhood trauma, but this conclusion is controversial, and very unlikely to apply to all cases. Dissociative identity disorder was a diagnostic fad in the 1980s (as multiple personality disorder); it is now once again considered rare.

Other, more common dissociative disorders are like experiences we all have had. We daydream, fantasize, and let our attention wander. We fall asleep or wake up with dreamlike visions. We can be so lost in thought or so involved in a task that we ignore our environments. We feel alienated from ourselves or exclaim, "This can't be real!" And we sometimes briefly feel we are outside ourselves, watching our own actions. We differ in these tendencies; as with many diagnoses, dissociative disorders are one end of a continuum of human behavior.

Lisa Butler refers to "normative dissociations" and "the dissociations of everyday life." She argues that complete absorption in a mental state or a task allows for "healthy temporary escape into alternate universes or a level of engagement that promotes optimal performance. . . . In daydreaming, absorption engages persistent concerns or unaddressed challenges, with . . . testing and rehearsal of alternatives in fantasy. . . . In dreaming, we may identify dissociation in its involuntariness and memory deficits and in the discontinuity . . . with the waking state." Terms for these things during waking life include "spacing out," being "in the zone," and "highway hypnosis." Many tasks we deliberately choose, from gardening and woodwork to reading and watching television, lead to normative dissociation. The state we are in when a task is completely absorbing and going well is called "flow," a dimension of well-being.

Solitude is a deliberate dissociation from the social world; it is not the same as loneliness, and for many of us it contributes to well-being. It figured in the faith of Moses, Jesus, Muhammad, Buddha, and other religious founders, as well as in the practices of followers. Yet, one result of solitude is to highlight the importance of relationships—whether with supernatural agents, a sacred community, or all sentient beings. The human needs for attachment and meaning underlie faith. Uniquely among animals, we foresee our physical nonexistence. We ask why we are here and whether life has a purpose, but day to day, we worry about being alone. Faith recruits cognitive mechanisms, but they are fueled by fear, loneliness, and longing. Parents, friends, mentors, and leaders abandon us, but gods and spirits do not. They may be malevolent, but they are not indifferent. They take an interest in our actions and our destiny, and they know what we do for good and ill; even without them, in Buddhism, the karmic cycle infuses every moment with meaning. Any claim to explain belief must take into account not just thinking but the strong needs that energize thinking. This means we must listen to children, who have perhaps the strongest needs.

The Voice of the Child

O ne of Richard Dawkins's rhetorical gambits is to show a picture from the British paper the *Independent*: a Nativity play with the three wise men played by, according to the caption, "Shadbreet (a Sikh), Musharaff (a Muslim), and Adele (a Christian), all aged four." The message, clearly, was meant to be ecumenical. Dawkins asks us to imagine this change: "Shadbreet (a monetarist), Musharaff (a Keynesian), and Adele (a Marxist), all aged four." He goes on:

> It is child abuse to label a child of four with the religion of their parents. The child is too young to know what its religious views are. There is no such thing as a Catholic child. If you hear the words "Catholic child," and the child is young, it should sound like fingernails scraping on a blackboard. There's no such thing as a Protestant child. There's no such thing as a Muslim child.

In case we missed the point, he has another version with the caption "Shadbreet (an Atheist), Musharaff (an Agnostic), and Adele (a Secular Humanist), all aged four." He begs us to "please all raise our consciousness to the child abuse that is involved whenever anybody talks about a Catholic child, a Protestant child, a Christian child."

This debater's trick asks us to ignore that the substitutions are of different kinds. A monetarist thinks regulating the money supply is the way to stabilize economies, a Keynesian thinks it should be done with government spending, and so on. A child can't have these ideas. But when we call a child Catholic, we do not mean that she understands Catholic theology; we mean she is growing up in a Catholic family with Catholic parents who are raising her in that faith. I dare say that by age 4 she would be more comfortable in a Catholic church than in a mosque or a synagogue, not to mention at a San trance dance or a Huichol peyote ceremony.

Saying that a child is Catholic or Muslim is much more like saying she is English or Japanese or Nigerian than it is like calling her a monetarist or a Marxist. The economic theory comparison is easily dismissed. But there is more in Dawkins's remarks: the label "child abuse." He is serious about this, and so are other aggressive atheists. The claim comes from an influential speech by English psychologist Nicholas Humphrey—"What Shall We Tell the Children?"—the 1997 Amnesty International Lecture at Oxford:

> Children, I'll argue, have a human right not to have their minds crippled by exposure to other people's bad ideas—no matter *who* these other people are. Parents . . . have no god-given license to enculturate their children in whatever ways they personally choose: no right to limit the horizons of their children's knowledge, to bring them up in an atmosphere of dogma and superstition, or to insist they follow the straight and narrow paths of their own faith. In short, children have a right not to have their minds addled by nonsense. And we as a society have a duty to protect them from it. So we should no more allow parents to teach their children to believe, for example, in the literal truth of the Bible, or that the planets rule their lives, than we should allow parents to knock their children's teeth out or lock them in a dungeon.

I sometimes ask educated audiences, especially scientists, whose kids they think would most likely be the first to be taken away if it became okay for the state to decree what parents may teach their children. Then I point around the room.

This is not a philosophical argument, but it is an argument: Parents will draw a line in the sand when it comes to what they may teach their children. And often in history, not just for religious reasons, the sand along that line has been soaked with blood. Humphrey compares teaching children any faith to female genital mutilation and ritual child sacrifice. These and other forms of physical, sexual, and emotional abuse have been considered just cause for state control. So, Humphrey is calling for the systematic interruption and destruction by the state of all religious tradition, starting in childhood.

State control over religious expression has been tried historically with, let's say, mixed results. After generations of state suppression, religions thrive in "Red" China and the former Soviet Union, although nonbelievers thrive too, in large numbers. These two states substituted, for the faiths they tried to destroy, quasi-religious ideologies with intense indoctrination and at least equal destructiveness. Soviet indoctrination lasted seventy years, yet in today's Russia, autocratic secular rule must compromise with the Orthodox church and its 100 million followers. Even the small Jewish minority, whose religion was banned for all that time, revived its traditions; in 1993, about two years after the Soviet fall, the Congress of the Jewish Religious Organizations and Associations in Russia formed; within a decade it represented 160 organizations. In China, after sixty-five years of communism, the great majority of the people, affiliated or not, practice some form of religion, including Confucianism, Taoism, Buddhism, polytheistic folk traditions, ancestor worship, or a blend.

As Dawkins has remarked, religion is oddly persistent. Freud, in *The Future of an Illusion*, said that he wanted to see what would happen if children were raised without religious indoctrination. We now know the answer: most of those children grow up normally without religious beliefs, although many say they are spiritual. Yet it is simplistic to view the development of faith as pure indoctrination. Religiosity, variously defined, is etched in the brain, and the brain develops.

Cognitive capacities for belief grow in infancy and childhood. So does our sense of self, our feeling of unity with the world and people, and our capacities for attachment, identification, imitation, emulation, and communion. But the fact that religiousness often intensifies in adolescence belies the claim that faith is infantile. Faith trajectories in adulthood point to both maturing thought about the future and a search for meaning as life goes on. These need not end in religious commitment, but often they do. Ideally, they involve some kind of commitment—generativity, integration—that not all achieve without faith. We vary for biological reasons in how much we lean toward faith, and these differences prove that culture—indoctrination—cannot explain it all.

Research on twins—identical and nonidentical, raised together or apart—as well as adoption and other family studies, consistently shows that religion has a moderate genetic component. Identical twins, even raised apart, resemble each other more in religiosity than do nonidentical twins, and children adopted at birth resemble their biological parents. It is surprising that something as subject to personal influences—family, friends, upbringing, affiliation, marriage—as religion or spirituality could be shaped at all by genes. Many see genes as constraints on freedom, and to some extent they are, but they are also part of the essence of individuality.

How could genes do something like this? We envision a child growing up with "Now I lay me down to sleep" as a nightly ritual, mom or dad kneeling beside her, or a child on the other side of the planet in her mother's lap while the drama of the trance dance unfolds—and we are not surprised that children grow up believing in this religious form or that. But different children have different susceptibilities. Although the "Now I lay me" child who becomes very religious will have different ideas from the devout trance-dance child, both will have the essence of faith: the belief in things unseen, and the emotions that go with it. But some children with those same experiences become skeptics as adults in either culture. Some incline toward a private religious life, some toward a public one, some toward the conventional, some with only a vague sense of the spiritual, and some with nothing at all.

By adulthood, these different children will have had different experiences, but they also will have started life with different brains. We have seen how the brain gives us—some of us—the experiences we call spiritual or religious. Some people have religious experiences because of brain activity that doctors call abnormal. Often, structural differences underlie this activity. Genes guide the initial building of circuits. But many human genes are expressed only in the brain and only in infancy. Some are shared by all normal people; they give us attachment, relationships, agency detection, mind reading, normal dissociation, and more. Other genes make us individuals.

Some genes are expressed in the brain throughout life, coding enzymes that manufacture or remove dopamine, opioids, cannabinoids, and serotonin, as well as the receptors for those chemicals. Religious people have fewer serotonin 1A receptors, which could mean that they have more *natural* day-to-day stimulation of the 2A receptors involved in the brain's own hallucinogenic effects. This is speculation, but it shows how genes *could* matter in religious experience. The role of genes is moderate. From studies of 72 pairs of same-sex twins (35 identical) raised apart, Thomas J. Bouchard and colleagues estimated the heritability of two kinds of religiosity—intrinsic (spirituality, belief, private experience) and extrinsic (affiliation, churchgoing, and the like)—to be 0.43 and 0.39, respectively. This would mean that being religious is about half as heritable as height, yet twice as heritable as giving or risk taking.

These are ballpark estimates, affected by gender, environment, and research methods. But it is fair to say that height is about 80 percent heritable and religiousness about half that, meaning that genes explain most of the variation in height, but less than half—even so, a substantial influence—of religiousness. Still, we can't just think of religion as genes or environment; it involves many more specific things, and how we define and measure it is a lot more complicated than for height.

As with height, personality, and much else, the heritability of certain aspects of religion increases with age, because differences in the pace of development obscure the end point and the environment is more influential early in life. Either factor can hide heritability. In addition, the way the environment works on religiousness is not typical of most behavioral traits. For most, the shared family environment explains very little of the variation; that doesn't mean the environment is unimportant, just that the important influences come from things that siblings experience separately—peers, schools, illnesses, accidents, and different siblings—namely, each other. But for religion, the *shared* environment matters more, especially in childhood and adolescence. This is the part that parents are trying to transmit to all their kids alike, and research shows that it works—for a time.

While you are in the family fold, your religious inclinations and habits (or lack of them) reflect those of the family, but when you grow up you can become your own version of yourself, in your self-tailored environment. For example, ultra-Orthodox Jewish teens may be cut off from their families when they reveal that they are gay. After this rejection they can stop pretending to be like those around them; their genes and their new chosen environment will matter more. A teenage San boy may dream of trance dancing, but if he finds out he can't easily enter an altered state of consciousness—or is reprimanded for flirting while trying—he may become more aloof from the ritual. A girl who is at 15 a devout Christian may find at 20 that her scientific bent leads her to Darwin and Einstein, and a teacher may encourage her to doubt. Someone raised in a secular family may feel moved by the words of a TV megachurch pastor.

There are revealing specifics. Matt Bradshaw and Christopher Ellison in a 2008 twin study broke down religiousness into four parts: organizational involvement, personal religiosity and spirituality, conservative ideologies, and transformations and commitments; these were further broken down into eight. The lowest heritability was 19 percent, for *childhood* religiosity. "Genetic influences are sizable for several commonly employed measures of religion, including religious or spiritual service attendance (32 percent), religious salience (27 percent), spirituality (29 percent), daily guidance and coping (42 percent), biblical literalism (44 percent), exclusivist beliefs (41 percent), and being born-again or making a religious or spiritual commitment (65 percent)." These are significant effects of genes.

Tanya Button and her colleagues added a developmental dimension, studying well over a thousand twin pairs ranging from ages 12 to 18, and some of the younger pairs were studied again from the time they were 17 years old until they reached the age of 29. For an assessment of religious values, they were asked,

How important is it to you . . .

1. To be able to rely on religious counsel or teaching when you have a problem?
2. To believe in God?
3. To rely on your religious beliefs as a guide for day-to-day living?
4. To be able to turn to prayer when you're facing a personal problem?
5. To attend religious services regularly?

Answers were scored from 1 (not at all important) to 4 (very important). Religious attendance was measured by the number of times the twins had been to religious services in the past year. Heritability of values increased from 29 to 41 percent between adolescence and young adulthood, while heritability of attendance changed from 9 to 34 percent. The freedom of young adulthood affected habits more than values, but genes asserted themselves in both.

Other developmental studies of religiousness add personality—the idea being that if genes (or environments), influence religious feelings, attitudes, and behavior, they might work through personality types. A standard method is the "Big Five" model: if you ask people hundreds of questions about their likes, dislikes, habits, and tendencies, you can order the answers best with statistics that sort them along five dimensions: Neuroticism, Extraversion, Openness, Agreeableness, and Conscientiousness. If you think of the common meaning of these labels, you won't be far from how scientists see them. They are designed statistically to be independent; none of them predicts much about the others. The Big Five model is a time-tested method, with decades of refinement and thousands of studies. In many different countries, personality tests yield the same factors.

One impressive application was a meta-analysis of 71 samples— over 20,000 people in 19 countries. Three main faith dimensions appeared: religiosity, spirituality, and fundamentalism. "Agreeableness and Conscientiousness were reliable correlates of religion across most samples." This finding "generalized across adolescents, young adults, and adults. However, the relation between religiousness and the two personality factors was stronger among adults." We can guess cause and effect from follow-up studies: personality predicts future religiousness, not the other way around. Other correlates emerge in some cultures. But Agreeableness and Conscientiousness predicted religiosity without regard to nationality, religion, sex, or age, and more strongly for adults than for teens. Earlier studies relating *values* to the Big Five showed that Christians, Muslims, and Jews share a hierarchy of values that embraces tradition, conformity, and benevolence but tends to reject hedonism and stimulation. These values are predicted by Agreeableness and Conscientiousness—not by how neurotic or introverted you are.

Separate twins research confirmed: these two dimensions predict religiosity. Yet there is more to *genetic* religiousness than any Big Five factors can explain. "Religiousness itself may reflect a basic individual attribute rather than an outcome" of a personality type. Ralph Piedmont pioneered a scale for spiritual transcendence, defined as "the capacity of individuals to stand outside of their immediate sense of time and place to view life from a larger, cooler perspective. In this transcendent view, a person sees a fundamental unity underlying the diverse strivings of nature and finds a bonding with others that cannot be severed, even by death." Piedmont asked people how strongly they agree or disagree with statements like "I have had at least one 'peak' experience" and "I feel that on a higher level all of us share a common bond." He proposed that spirituality should be a sixth factor *separate from* the Big Five.

Piedmont and Mark Leach tested this idea among hundreds of Hindus, Christians, and Muslims in India. Among Muslims and Christians, women had higher scores on the three components—universality, prayer fulfillment, and connectedness—but the three religious groups had remarkably similar average scores. In India as in the US, personality explained little: "Spirituality represents the raw psychological material from which religious behaviors arise," although "the form of one's religiousness is determined by specific historical, social, and cultural imperatives" that don't "affect the relevance of transcendence. . . . The human drive to create a unified cosmological picture, although diverse in its expression, does represent a singular, pancultural motivational construct. . . . Spirituality needs to be recognized as a universal aspect of human experience."

However, the Piedmont spirituality questionnaire contained many conventional religious ideas. Pavel Rican and Pavlina Janosova developed the Prague Spirituality Questionnaire, specifically to assess spiritual leanings in "the extremely secularized Czech youth who largely reject organized religion." None of their questions referred to God or prayer, but instead tapped into feelings about the sacredness of nature and human relationships and a sense of purpose, meaning, and moral standards. Having validated the questionnaire (and finding substantial individual differences even among these secular young people), Rican and Janosova combined their scales with those for the Big Five, and found they needed a sixth—a nonconventional spiritual dimension.

Now, you could say this is no surprise, since the usual Big Five questionnaires don't ask about spirituality. But why don't they? Probably because scientific psychologists haven't paid much attention to religion until recently. But if you add questions on spirituality, you find a sixth factor, even among Nones. They may all be secular, but some are more spiritual than others. Rican and Janosova see spirituality as "a universal human phenomenon, largely independent of concrete confessions of religious organizations or movements" and assume "that a person may be highly spiritual whether he is a Christian, a Jew, a Muslim or an atheist."

To recap, we have evidence of a spiritual dimension with a heritability of 30 to 40 percent, linked with known brain circuits and neurotransmitters, relevant to those with little conventional belief, perhaps its own dimension of personality. Twin studies show that genes matter, but not which genes; a complex trait like religiousness, or even one component like spirituality or church attendance, will be affected by many genes. Yet the era of single genes is here—as in the study of the serotonin 1A receptor. Some individual differences correlate with a gene for that receptor.

Another study, looking at variants of the dopamine receptor, used a word game to prime subjects. Religion-primed subjects were given a word string like "felt she eradicate spirit the" and were asked to remove one word and rearrange the others grammatically—in this case, to yield "she felt the spirit." Controls played the same game with no religious content. They completed a test of religiosity and then got a questionnaire on volunteerism in environmental causes. Religion priming in the word game did predict volunteerism overall, but dopamine receptors mattered; those with one variant showed a slight decrease in volunteering after religion priming, while those with the other variant showed a marked *increase* after the same priming. These are baby steps toward specifying genes that play a role in religion. But if genes consistently contribute to religiousness, and religious people consistently have more children, the future of religion will be secure—all else being equal. All else, however, is very rarely equal.

Many atheists believe that we have evolved to be moral, and that since the moral sense develops in childhood without training or religion (it does in most children), deliberate inculcation of ethics is unnecessary (this doesn't necessarily follow). We'll return to this idea, but let's first focus on faith itself. Religious ideas arise naturally in most children growing up in any cultural environment that includes relevant influences. Ideas about gods and spirits exist in every culture, and many children have spiritual inner lives.

Classic interview studies by psychiatrist Robert Coles addressed children's thinking about poverty, race, and other aspects of their lives. For a book on faith, he talked to children between ages 8 and 12 from varied religions, asking them how they make use of what they are taught—about God, heaven, the devil, spirits, and life after death. Many felt that God was always with them and described how this belief helped them deal with challenges, pain, and loss. One girl had recently been one of the first African American children to enter a newly integrated elementary school in 1962. She had walked through a raging mob of bigoted white adults and children. "I was all alone," she said, "and those people were screaming, and suddenly I saw God smiling, and I smiled." A woman standing by the school door yelled at her, " 'Hey, you little nigger, what you smiling at?' I looked right at her face, and I said, 'At God.' Then she looked up at the sky, and then she looked at me, and she didn't call me any more names."

Religious differences also exacerbate hatreds; religion and ethnicity make a toxic blend. Yet children's grasp of the differences between their own and others' beliefs can be positive. Natalie, a Hopi 10-year-old in the southwestern US, was described by her teachers as a rather dull child who would not give a good interview, but she had a deep spiritual life. Coles noticed her gazing at a thundercloud. She pointed and said, "The home of the noise," and then contrasted her beliefs with Anglo ones:

> The sky watches us and listens to us. It talks to us, and it hopes we are ready to talk back. The sky is where the God of the Anglos lives, a teacher told us. She asked where our God lives. I said, "I don't know." I was telling the truth! Our God is the sky, and lives wherever the sky is. Our God is the sun and the moon, too; and our God is our people, if we remember to stay here. This is where we're supposed to be, and if we leave, we lose God.

She prayed for the Anglos, and she also talked about the bitter Hopi-Navajo land dispute: "They want the land, and we believe it has been here for us, and it would miss us . . . the land can feel the difference." Yet she felt sorry for both of the other ethnic groups, because they "don't feel at home near their mesa, so they want all the mesas in the world! . . . Their ancestors must go from one mesa to the next, and they must cry, because they don't know where they can stay and be together, and they don't know if they'll ever be seen by the people." She loved to watch hawks in flight because they were the souls of the Hopi ancestors, gliding above one place in the landscape, watching over her.

But Hopi religious indoctrination had a harsh side, in kachina initiation rituals. Children were set apart in a sanctuary called the *kiva*, where they were frightened by adults dressed up as supernatural spirits with yucca whips—as described by anthropologist Esther Goldfrank, "a We'e'e Kachina in a blue mask and carrying a long black and white ringed pole . . . [and] two Natackas with fierce bulging eyes and huge black bills fashioned from large gourds, each with a bow in the left hand and a saw or a large knife in the right hand." The goal was to scare children into being good. Goldfrank continues,

> The children tremble and some begin to cry and to scream. The Ho Kachinas keep up their grunting, howling, rattling, trampling and brandishing of their yucca whips. . . . Someone places a candidate on the sand mosaic, holds his (or her) hands upward and one of the Ho Kachinas whips the little victim quite severely. . . . Some of the children go through the process with set teeth and without flinching, others squirm, try to jump away and scream. . . . Some of the boys, probably as a result of fear and pain, involuntarily [urinated] and . . . even defecated.

This is not the spiritual support that young Natalie described to Coles—indeed, it is consistent with Professor Humphrey's worst fears linking religion to child abuse—but it was traditionally part of Hopi children's religious experience. As all religions claim, it is for the children's benefit—"to save their lives," the Hopis say—and to exact a needed obedience. When children learn that the drama was not real, they feel angry and disappointed, but as one woman put it, "I now know it was best and the only way to teach the children."

Remarkably, the Puritan Christian tradition also considered punishments essential for moral development. The Puritans were wrong, but fear has been an aspect of religions major and minor. So on the one hand, God—or a god or spirit—is the imaginary friend your parents want you to believe in, who can protect you; yet the same or another supernatural being is the punitive parent unseen but all-seeing, the

Santa Claus who knows if you've been bad or good, delivering a toy or a lump of coal accordingly.

Which brings us to how religious susceptibility grows. We start with near-universal features of the developing mind that help us understand why religion is so widespread. These features depend on brain development. They allow for individual variation, inborn and learned, but in some ways they happen to almost all children in a religious environment. In James Fowler's pioneering model, the proposed stages were (1) primal, (2) intuitive-projective, (3) mythic-literal, (4) synthetic-conventional, (5) individuative-reflective, (6) conjunctive, and (7) universalizing faith—some of which are not reached until adulthood, if at all. This model has been applied in varied religious communities, but it has been in some ways superseded by subtler approaches.

One focus has been the emergence of faith in early childhood, which some have tried to integrate with psychodynamic models of attachment and the self. These models develop the claims of Freud and others that religious faith comes initially out of the process of individuation within our intense dependency on and love for our parents. These older approaches offered more than stage models of cognitive development to explore emotion and relationships, but remained oversimplifications. Current models are better.

Patricia Ebstyne King and Chris Boyatzis, two leaders in a current explosion of research on religion in childhood, put stage and attachment theories in perspective. Stage theories adapted Jean Piaget's approach to cognitive development. Some held that the animistic ideas of "primitive" cultures were like an early-childhood phase of mental development. Anthropologist Margaret Mead, *in 1928*, published her research on 41 children among the Manus of New Guinea. Like Piaget and others, she interviewed them about cause and effect for various happenings—a canoe drifting away, or the sounding of wind chimes. By age 5, Manus boys have a guardian ancestral spirit, whose skull may hang in their home. Adults are highly animistic in their thinking. But children, even 5-year-olds, gave pragmatic answers: the canoe "wasn't fastened right" and "The wind winds. The glass hits. It sounds." Mead wrote, "The Manus child is less . . . animistic than is the Manus adult." Simpler societies were not like children frozen in mental development; children had to *learn* animistic beliefs.

New research has confirmed this conclusion, highlighting both cross-cultural and individual differences in children's religious thinking. Cristine Legare, in a study of Sesotho-speaking children and adults in South Africa, found that at all ages, biological explanations coexist in the same person with ideas about bewitchment, but bewitchment explanations are offered more by adults. "Contrary to traditional accounts . . . supernatural explanations often increase rather than decrease with age," which "supports the proposal that reasoning about supernatural phenomena is an integral and enduring aspect of human cognition." A 2017 study in Vanuatu, an island in Melanesia, confirmed that explanations coexist at all ages, but in *this* culture, supernatural explanations were more likely in children. "Coexistence reasoning . . . is pervasive across cultures . . . reflecting the nuanced differences in local ecologies and cultural beliefs."

We'll return to *coexistence reasoning*, important in explaining religion in children and adults. Nevertheless, children are different. King and Boyatzis credit Fowler's mythic-literal stage, corresponding to middle childhood (and Piaget's stage of concrete operations) as a time when "religious principles are taken at face value, . . . symbols are one-dimensional [and] faith is built around concrete story-like narratives." Young teens—the synthetic-conventional stage—are conformists, accepting the "tyranny of the they." Older teens, in the individuative-reflective phase, approach "an examined explicit faith orientation that is more truly one's own."

Attachment models cut across the stages. No one takes too seriously the idea that the young infant feels at one with the universe—pain and pleasure give it a pretty clear idea of the boundary—but it's reasonable to think of Fowler's primal stage as one in which trust or lack of it begins. Twenty-first-century psychodynamic approaches to religion are of two main kinds: *correspondence models*, in which our attachment to our parents—secure, insecure, angry, and so on—is reproduced in our relationship to God or the supernatural; and *compensation models*, in which weak or unstable attachment makes us want from God what we didn't get from our parents. There is evidence for both.

Recall from the genetic studies that *shared* family environment determines more what the child does than what the older teen or adult does; both genes and individual experience show up more strongly in adulthood. So it is not surprising that attachment models find more support in adults. One study compared 30 "priests and religious" (5 nuns, 10 novices, 5 priests, and 10 seminarians) in a small Italian town to a matched sample of lay townspeople. A standard Adult Attachment Interview showed that those in the religious group were more attached to their own parents. Interpersonal attachment styles also corresponded to attachment to God among Israeli Jews.

Research on 181 university students found support for both models. Secure attachment was found in "once-born" religious people (those who continued in the religion of their parents), while "twice-born" people who had conversions or born-again experiences were more likely to be compensating for *insecure* attachment. And in 119 Christian recent college graduates, those "with low parental security . . . articulated reciprocal experiences of secure, intimate attachment with God." Other studies suggest that relationships to God and people can each compensate for rejection in the other. Special categories of people are also instructive. People with autism spectrum disorders have more anxiety-provoking perceptions of God as ruling and punitive than others do. People with disorganized attachment experiences are more inclined to mysticism because they have greater access to normal altered states of consciousness.

IN *UNWEAVING THE RAINBOW*, Richard Dawkins recalls "trying gently to amuse a six-year-old child at Christmas time by reckoning up with her how long it would take Father Christmas to go down all the chimneys in the world." He proceeded with the calculation—100 million houses with children, each chimney 20 feet long, the time taken to tiptoe. "She saw the point and realized that there was a problem, but it didn't worry her in the least. . . . The obvious possibility that her parents had been telling falsehoods never seemed to cross her mind." Yet, says Dawkins, "the years of childhood innocence may pass too soon. I love my parents for taking me for a ride, high as a kite, through the treetops; for telling me about the Tooth Fairy and Father Christmas, about Merlin and his spells, about baby Jesus and the Three Wise Men," making childhood "a time of enchantment." Dawkins has no use, though, for any beliefs about the supernatural *after* childhood.

A normal 6-year-old, such as the one he reckoned chimneys with, is entering Piaget's stage of concrete operations, so it is not surprising that she sees the implications of the reckoning; she just doesn't care. It's not because she is bamboozled by her parents' falsehoods; it's because she wants the enchantment. As Cristine Legare found, many children never outgrow the supernatural, maintaining scientific and supernatural beliefs in one and the same mind. But they do outgrow Santa Claus and the tooth fairy. How? And why, for so many, is it different from the story of baby Jesus?

One thing of note is that Dawkins's young friend was probably about to lose her belief in Father Christmas. A classic study of 4-, 6-, and 8-year-olds found that 85, 65, and 25 percent, respectively, believed in Santa. For the Easter bunny the percentages were similar, while for the tooth fairy more 6- and 8-year-olds (60 percent) than 4-year-olds (20 percent) believed, probably because of the age of tooth loss. Firm *dis*belief rose with age for all three groups: most for the Easter bunny (15, 20, and 60 percent at 4, 6, and 8), next for the tooth fairy (5, 20, and 35 percent), and least for Santa (5, 10, and 20 percent).

But, really intriguingly, fully 55 percent of 8-year-olds were rated as transitional for Santa, as opposed to 5 percent for the Easter bunny and none for the tooth fairy. Why? Well, Santa Claus is a far more high-stakes cultural item for parents, communities, even economies. Parents "organize" their kids' belief in Santa much more actively, colluding with them. Some parents say that they believe in Santa Claus, and many express sadness when their children stop believing. The history of Santa Claus suggests a growing commitment to him even as religion has declined.

My wife, developmental psychologist Ann Cale Kruger, has said,

I can still feel the excitement and the intimacy and the wonder of there being someone who knows my wishes, who works all year not just for me but for all children. Another part of my brain reflects on that and on what happens if you lose that feeling of wonder and of generosity and of being cared for. I think there's something about the intimacy—that he only comes to children, and he only comes if you believe in him. If you stop, you've denied that there is such a being who cares for children in such a giving way. If you're a child with a rich imagination, you have a private relationship with Santa Claus that is meaningful and special and intimate. If you stop believing, you create a rupture; you end a sweet intimacy.

I remember the moment that I realized that the whole thing with the reindeer going around the world couldn't be true. I'd been pushing it out of my mind for years. It's embarrassing. I was in sixth grade, and I was still hanging on to Santa Claus. I mean my relationship with him. The idea of him. But right then and there, I decided I would not stop believing in him, even though I knew the details couldn't be possible. I don't think there's a man on the North Pole sorting presents. I retain a love for the story. I don't believe in the supernatural Santa, but I believe in the feelings associated with the story. I loved making that story true for my daughter. I got to keep him alive by helping her believe in him.

Her description of how she went forward from age 12 or so is a clear instance of Legare's coexistence reasoning.

A study of 140 Jewish American children showed that belief in both Santa Claus and the tooth fairy, while less prevalent than in Christian children, was common; it declined from ages 3 to 10 and was unrelated to parents' encouragement or even experience with the rituals. A 2015 study of 47 children ages 3 to 9 showed that their conceptual understanding of physical law helped determine what they thought about Santa, just as Dawkins suspected. However, the children also came up with provisional explanations about how the Santa myth might be true despite its physical impossibility—yet another case of coexistence reasoning.

But what does all this say about gods? In "Why Santa Claus Is Not a God," Justin Barrett argues that "God concepts must be (1) counter-intuitive, (2) an intentional agent, (3) possessing strategic information, (4) able to act in the human world in detectable ways and (5) capable of motivating behaviors that reinforce belief." Santa is all those things, but despite being more important than Mickey Mouse or even the tooth fairy, he is not a god because he does not meet those criteria for adults, but only for children—with adult support. Gods are less concrete than Santa, and expectations about what they will do are not as well defined, or as limited to a particular time of year.

Kruger mentions being a child with a rich imagination, and a growing number of studies focus on that quality in children, with regard to pretend play and imaginary friends. Contrary to some assumptions, these studies consistently show that pretend play reflects intellectual capacity, including executive functions and a capacity for emotion regulation. Such children are less shy. The flexibility of fantasy relates to some very practical mental abilities; apparently, it's healthy. But some kids take fantasy play a step farther, creating imaginary companions. Is that also a plus?

You might think of Santa as an imaginary companion that you share with other children and become especially aware of one season a year. But between 15 and 25 percent of preschool-age children have imaginary companions (ICs) that they have *invented*—without parental encouragement, or even with the opposite—and that belong to them alone. ICs are associated with theory of mind and predict emotion understanding later in childhood. They are not a substitute for friends; children with ICs are *more* likely than others to describe mental characteristics of their real friends. For some children, ICs and their benefits extend into middle childhood.

It's said that God is the imaginary companion your parents don't want you to outgrow. Tanya Luhrmann studied evangelicals who feel that Christ is often with them and who cultivate situations and mental states that make that more likely—such as coffee dates. The African American child whom Robert Coles interviewed said that God's presence had helped her find the courage to walk through a crowd of screaming bigots into a segregated school. Companionship (not a substitute for human companionship, but another kind of alliance) is a key function of many religions—one often missed by critical atheists, who tend to focus on fear of death. But how *does* death awareness function in children's lives?

The Puritans instilled fear of God in the context of death rates that made the end seem only a breath away. Not all cultures where death is common drive children to guilt and fear, but given the Puritans' extravagant beliefs about the afterlife, they felt they had to ensure salvation; even their harshest punishments would be kind next to hellfire.

Yet children have to deal with death even where it is timely, and they start during the transition to middle childhood. Before age 5 they tend to think death is reversible, like travel, sleep, or sickness, although it has occurred to them that their parents might die. But by around age 7, they begin to see it as inevitable and irreversible.

Death remains remote for most children until the age of 10 or 11, when they know its universality means *me too*. But children vary, and cross-cultural studies reveal additional differences. In a 2017 study comparing children, adolescents, and adults in Vanuatu with those in Austin, Texas, both cultures showed beliefs in the persistence of some aspects of individual life after death, although details of exactly what persists differed between the cultures. In rural Madagascar, adolescents and adults see an enduring mental life for their ancestors, who are central to their faith.

In a touching and sensitive study, Bonnie Hewlett interviewed children in two neighboring cultures—Ngandu farmers and Aka hunter-gatherers—in the Central African Republic, each with high mortality rates. All adolescents in both cultures understood the finality of death, yet many believed that good people had spirits that would soar to a place resembling heaven, while the spirits of bad people might be cast into the forest to cry. Emotional and physical support for bereaved children was strong in both groups, despite different burial customs and longer formal grieving in the Ngandu. Children and adolescents expressed deep feelings of love and loss.

Until the recent development of None subcultures, everywhere in the world most people believed that something important persists after death. Examples include cultures with ancestor worship, those in which the dead are punished or rewarded, those in which spirits go to or coexist with gods, and those in which you are reborn in another living form. This belief in rebirth after death almost always involves forgetting past lives, but it is very, very important spiritually and morally. Children in many cultures increase the complexity of their thinking about, and their commitment to, such ideas, temporarily or permanently, in adolescence. If religious belief were solely the result of childhood indoctrination, why would it increase as childhood recedes and independence is established?

Some psychological and behavioral change is due to programmed hormonal dynamics. Genes play a role, but cultural factors, including peer influences, are at least as important: teens exposed to sex, violence, and substance abuse are much more likely to have a developmental crisis. Many traditions guide adolescent development more than Western ones do. We say, if only tacitly, "Soon you will have to take care of yourself," and oppositional behavior is partly due to this message. In traditional cultures, expected adult roles are clearer and options fewer, but you know you have an assured place in the world you grew up in and always will. Yet such cultures make demands, often through ritual. They mark life's transitions—birth, marriage, parenthood, death—with symbolic rites to show that these events are not just biological; there are right and wrong ways to go through them. Rites of passage, often around puberty, are found in many cultures: 79 percent of societies have initiation rituals for girls; 68 percent, for boys.

For Australian aborigines, ceremonies began with the preparation of sacred ground, often a circular space connected to a second circle. Men ritually separated themselves from women. Among the Kamilaroi, one circle has a tall pole decorated with emu feathers; the other, two trees fixed in the ground with their roots in the air, anointed with human blood. Two older men climb the trees and chant the traditions of the *bora*, which re-creates the very first such rite, with gods, ancestors, animals, and the first young men to go through it at the start of human time, reintegrated with the present in every performance. In various parts of Australia, pubescent boys were subjected to silence, deprivation of food and water, or painful interventions such as circumcision and subincision (cutting a long gash on the underside of the penis). "The neophyte is at once prepared for the responsibilities of adult life and progressively awakened to the life of the spirit . . . by instruction through myths, dances, pantomimes. The physical ordeals have a goal—to introduce the youth into the tribal culture, to make him 'open' to spiritual values. Ethnologists have been struck by the intense interest with which novices listen to mythical traditions and take part in ceremonial life."

Among the San, girls have their ritual at first menstruation. When the girl sees a trace of blood, wherever she is, day or night, she must sit on the ground, keep silent, and wait—though lions or hyenas could get wind of her. But the women in her family are ready, and they soon track her and carry her to a place near the village. They build a grass hut just for her. All the women begin a dance and, as day and night pass, they grow rowdy. Women strip to a small leather pubic apron, tossed around carelessly. Sometimes they pull it up to flash their genitals, provoking peals of laughter. They sing, dance, and clap continuously. No men dare approach. Through it all, the menstruating girl sits in the hut, expressionless, neither speaking nor laughing, but she gets the message: a celebration of San womanhood, to which she now belongs.

Among the Baka, hunter-gatherers of Cameroon, boys past age 11 or 12 will have their teeth painfully chipped and filed—a permanent sign of endurance and maturity, not to mention making them more handsome. The boy lies still, biting down on a piece of wood, while a relative chisels away at his front teeth. If he whimpers, another man may apply warm plantain skin to comfort him. Children watch and tease the boy as he leaves childhood behind. (If this seems cruel, consider orthodontics.)

The Native American vision quest was stressful in a different way. Among Great Plains bison hunters, boys purified themselves in the sweat lodge, their bodies painted with white clay. Each boy had to go out alone and naked to an isolated place, nearer to the spirits, for days, during which he fasted with one goal: an altered mental state that would bring him his vision. In essence, he had to become delirious from exposure, solitude, hunger, thirst, and the fear of mountain lions, bears, and enemy war parties. In his vision, a spirit came personally to him—an ancestor, animal, plant, even a storm; this was his guardian spirit, which gave him a new identity beyond boyhood.

In the Jewish *bar mitzvah* ("son of the commandment") at age 13, a boy becomes, in religious terms, a man. Traditionally, the boy said a blessing before and after a Torah passage was read, and he took on responsibility for his own sins. The rite is usually more elaborate today, and it can be stressful. The child must master the complex music for the week's Torah portion, chant long passages of it in Hebrew, often lead the congregation in a substantial part of the Hebrew service, and deliver a speech in English of his own composition. Beginning in the twentieth century, girls increasingly took on an analogous ritual, the *bat mitzvah*. For either sex it's a big effort, taking months to years of preparation. Like all initiation rites, it has strong symbolic power.

All of these coming-of-age rituals serve at least three purposes. First, they often involve stress, pain, or fear, intended to impart a strong adult identity: "I can take it as the grownups once did, so I must no longer be a child" (in the emotional logic of ritual, "Whatever doesn't kill me makes me stronger"). Second, like college fraternity hazing, pubertal rites make initiates feel a part of the community. They are *in*, and those who are too young or who belong to other cultures (or the other sex) are out—pitied or disdained. Third, the ritual is a teachable moment. Formal instruction is usually included, even in cultures lacking formal instruction in other contexts. At these times the child's eyes are wide with fear and stress, then finally exhilaration. Your elders say explicitly, *This is what it means to be a Sioux man, a San woman, a Jewish adult. These are our customs. Now they are your obligations and privileges.*

The ritual makes the lessons vividly memorable, and the stress ingrains them at a deep emotional level. In addition, the rites have a strong religious dimension. In most cultures, life is inseparable from

religion and spirituality, and becoming a woman or a man is inseparable from initiation into your ancestors' faith. These rites prepare you
to give rise to the next generation, which will in turn hand down the
beliefs of the past.

Adolescence is a paradox of divergence. Bad behaviors support the
concept that this is a problem phase of life. But it can also be a time of
high ideals—charity, patriotism, religiosity, music, Scouting, athlet-
ics, conservation, pacifism, racial integration, military discipline, mis-
sions to the poor, holy war, and martyrdom, along with more specific
goals that set teens on the path to becoming (in Western cultures), car-
penters, pilots, firefighters, doctors, ministers, dancers, or soldiers. We
diverge at puberty through unique biology, experience, and chance.

The quest for ideas and ideals is common to many cultures. Youth
have been key to revolutions throughout history: they are naïve, risk
prone, idealistic, and oppositional. They can imagine a better future,
and their fearless demands provoke change. Traditional initiation harnesses these forces, but the emotional dynamics are ongoing, beyond
rites, begging for a strong social context. Peers, romantic partners, siblings, parents, schools, teachers, clergy, other adults, and media transmit culture during this period.

Can initiation protect youth against the dark side? In the introduction to Eliade's *Rites and Symbols of Initiation*, Michael Meade warns,
"Instead of participating in a prepared rite for leaving childhood games
through ordeals of emotional struggle and spiritual alertness, gangs
of blindly-wounded youth hurl their woundedness at the darkness
and spit angry bullets at groups that are their mirror image, attacking
masks of themselves. . . . Denying that each individual must struggle
at the thresholds of spiritual and emotional self-discovery eventually
destroys any shared awareness of the sanctity of life."

It's an extreme view of what happens without initiation rites, but
growing evidence supports protective effects of religious frameworks.
Personal religiosity buffers teens against juvenile delinquency, as does

family. A longitudinal study of 3,000 youths ages 12 to 16 in a representative US sample used structural equation modeling to tease out causality. Familial religiosity predicted more effective parenting, closer bonds with parents, and more commitment to school, all reducing delinquency. In a 2017 study of 1,300 African American adolescents, both extrinsic (attending church) and intrinsic (prayer and rating faith as important) religiosity buffered against depression in response to stressful life events, including racism. Most teens in this study scored high on extrinsic *and* intrinsic religiosity, although both types of religiosity declined as the teens grew older.

Other studies find complex patterns. In one, looking at 220 youngsters, a "high-religious" group of teens (believing and participating communally) were less likely to show externalizing and/or internalizing psychopathology than either a "low-religious" group or a mixed group that was high on some measures but low on private religious practices. In addition, different types of religiosity can have positive or negative effects on teens' health-related behavior.

Clearly there is more to be learned. Adolescents often increase their religious exploration and commitment, sometimes subsequently rebelling or losing faith. (That was my path.) As we've seen, heritability for many psychological traits looks weaker in the teens because there is so much "noise"—hormonal, experiential, sexual, political, school, and peer influences—to interfere with the neat correlations. It has been well said that in childhood, connection always trumps authenticity. In young adulthood, people start to settle into who they feel they really are.

Clearly, simple indoctrination cannot explain the complexity of religious development. There *is* indoctrination—one might say the same about language, nationality, and sports—but there are also genes, positive and negative attachment, imagination, individuality, altered states of consciousness, identity crises, family values, peers, and searching, to name a few.

King and Boyatzis propose the term "reciprocating spirituality" to try to capture the two-way flow of internal changes and external influences that produce the adaptations that young people develop as they move to adult beliefs—or lack of them. I think it's a better approximation than "indoctrination." But if there are inborn aspects of spirituality, why are they there?

Awe Evolving

An observation of wild chimpanzees: Harold Bauer, then working with Jane Goodall at Tanzania's Gombe Stream, followed a well-known male through the forest until the chimp stopped near a waterfall. It was an awesome spot: a stream of water cascaded from a 25-foot height, crashing into the pool below and casting mist 70 feet back into the air. Stunning to come upon—for a person, anyway. Watching it, the chimp seemed lost in reverie. He moved closer and rocked rhythmically, showing excitement with pant-hoots. More aroused, he ran back and forth, jumped, made louder calls, and drummed on nearby trees with his fists. Roughly, the behavior resembled what Goodall saw in chimpanzee groups during storms: the "rain dance." But this chimp was alone.

He kept the "dance" up long enough to need explaining, and he repeated it at the waterfall on other days. Others did it too. None had any practical stake in the waterfall. They did not drink from the cascade or cross the stream. To the extent that it might be dangerous, it could have been easily avoided. But for some it was a spectacle, a sight they stared at and returned to, lingered on, grew excited about. Was it a thing of beauty, an object of curiosity, a challenge, a fetish, an imagined creature, a revelation, a god, or just inchoate fear and fascination that caught them and drew them back? We don't know.

But, for a similar creature 6 million years ago, when we split from chimpanzees, some things in nature must have evoked such a response. If not a waterfall, perhaps a view from a mountaintop, a sunset among storm clouds, a volcano, the edge of a roiling sea—something that stopped the creature in its tracks and made it watch, and move, and watch again; something that made it return to the spot, though nothing "biological" happened there—no feeding, drinking, reproducing, sleeping, fighting, fleeing, nothing animal. Such a moment, for such a creature, was the dawn of awe, of wonder. In a recent account, Jane Goodall stood at the waterfall and said,

When the chimpanzees approach, they hear this roaring sound, and you see the hair stand a little on end, and then they move a bit quickly. . . . They'll rhythmically sway, often upright, picking up big rocks and throwing them for maybe ten minutes. Sometimes climbing up the vines at the side and swinging out into the spray. . . . Afterwards, you'll see them sitting on a rock, actually in the stream, looking up, watching the water with their eyes as it falls down, and then, watching it going away. I can't help feeling that this wonderful display or dance is perhaps triggered by feelings of awe, wonder, that we feel. The chimpanzee's brain is so like ours; they have emotions that are clearly similar to or the same as those that we call happiness, sadness, fear, despair . . . so why wouldn't they also have feelings of some kind of spirituality, which is really being amazed at things.

She goes on to discuss the "rain dance":

It's the same at the start of heavy rain. I've seen it a couple of times, when a sudden wind came roaring through the valley. . . . Maybe it's defying the elements, defying the rain. Maybe it's the same kind of amazement [as] with the waterfall. I think chimpanzees are as spiritual as we are, but they can't . . . describe what they feel. . . . It's all locked up inside them, and the only way they can express it is through this fantastic rhythmic dance.

The rain dance has been seen in chimps elsewhere in Africa. And in 2010, Jill Pruetz and Thomas LaDuke observed similar behavior toward a wildfire in Senegal. Chimps are normally calm about wildfires, probably because they can collectively predict where and how fast a fire will go. (This ability may tap into a protohuman agency detection device.) But during one fire in a streambed, the chimps climbed a baobab, not to feed,

> although [fruiting] vines could be found there. . . . In ascending the tree, they moved closer, initially, to the fire and then to heights of greater than 10 m. The remaining dominant male exhibited a slow and exaggerated display "toward" the fire in a manner analogous to the "rain dance." . . . As the fire approached, individuals moved into the very top of the crown. Immediately before the fire reached the tree, however, the entire party filed out and moved ahead of the fire. The flames climbed more than halfway to the top of the tree.

Pruetz thinks they had to conceptualize fire to overcome fear. "Chimps everywhere have what is called a rain dance and it's just a big male display. . . . Males display . . . for different reasons, but when there's a big thunderstorm approaching they do this exaggerated display, it's almost like slow motion. . . . When I was with this one party of chimps at Fongoli, the dominant male did the same . . . towards the fire, so I called it the fire dance. It wasn't directed at other members of the group but at the fire itself."

Although evolution—change over time in animal species—was

embraced by some ancient Romans, clear ideas about the process came much later: "Animals engage in a struggle for existence; for resources, to avoid being eaten, and to breed. Environmental factors influence organisms to develop new characteristics to ensure survival . . . thus transforming into new species. Animals that survive to breed can pass on their characteristics to offspring." This is a good brief summary of how evolution works, and it might have come from Darwin. But actually it was written by the ninth-century Baghdad philosopher Al-Jahiz. The process was rediscovered by Darwin (and by Alfred Russel Wallace independently) at a luckier moment in history, when Darwin could assemble a large body of systematic evidence, including comparative anatomy, embryology, changes in animals and plants under domestication, and the fossil record.

But the key observation, first made during Darwin's voyage around the world, was that organisms are exquisitely adapted to their environments. This was one of the three pillars of his theory: (1) organisms are adapted, but—within a population—some are better adapted than others; (2) the different adaptations must be to *some* extent inherited; and (3) these partly inherited differences result in different numbers of offspring, or reproductive success. Darwin did not say much about religion, although he was troubled by the tension between his view of the history of life and Christian faith. One reason he delayed publication of *The Origin of Species* was that his much-loved, devout wife, Emma, feared for his immortal soul, doubting she would see him in heaven.

He understood. As early as 1838, he wrote in his notebook, "Origin of man now proved. . . . He who understands baboon would do more towards metaphysics than Locke." Near the end of *The Origin of Species* he wrote, "Psychology will be securely based on . . . the acquirement of each mental power and capacity by gradation. Much light will be thrown on the origin of man and his history." And he closed the book by saying that "from the war of nature, from famine and death, the most exalted object of which we are capable of conceiving, namely, the production of the higher animals, directly follows. There is grandeur in this view of life, with its several powers, having been breathed by the Creator into a few forms or into one; and that, whilst this cycling on according to the fixed law of gravity, endless forms most beautiful and most wonderful have been, and are being, evolved." His goal was not atheistic but a new view of "the Creator" and the process of creation.

Despite the seeming teleology, we know that Darwin did not (as some did and do) see humanity as the inexorable goal of evolution, the tippy top of the tree of life. He saw us as one twig on a vast, branchy bush. In fact, he left a sketch of it among his papers, below the hand-written "I think." And privately he could sound a darker tone, as in this note written to botanist Joseph Hooker a few years earlier, "What a book a Devil's chaplain might write on the clumsy, wasteful, blundering low and horribly cruel works of nature!"

A year after *Origin*, Darwin wrote in a calmer mood to Reverend Asa Gray, about religion: "I feel most strongly that the whole subject is too profound for the human intellect. A dog might as well speculate on the mind of Newton." Yet, many years later, in *The Descent of Man*, Darwin did muse a bit, describing religious faith as "consisting of love, complete submission to an exalted and mysterious superior, a strong sense of dependence, fear, reverence, gratitude, hope for the future, and perhaps other elements. No being could experience so complex an emotion until advanced in his intellectual and moral faculties to at least a moderately high level." He shows his usual respect for complexity, and the idea that such a big dimension of life must serve many functions.

Yet he lists things that not all religions share. The San have intense experiences in an intricate belief system that has dependence but not love, mystery but not exaltation, fear but not reverence, hope for the future but not much gratitude. They are polytheistic, with different gods having different traits. The "village of the spirits" includes the souls of the dead, who also influence the living. But their impact is not benign, so people's stance toward the spirit world is not one of thankfulness or praise.

The Eipo, gardeners, pig farmers, and (traditionally) warriors of mountainous western New Guinea, were similarly skeptical of the ancestral and nature spirits that surrounded them. These spirits' dangerous powers could be activated immediately by violation of social norms, and they needed to be placated by elaborate rituals. Other rituals ensured hunting success by propitiating the prey's spirits, or had the goal of facilitating childbirth.

Similar things may be said of the shamanistic faiths we encountered among the world's hunter-gatherers; of the religions incorporating witchcraft in many traditional cultures; of the hostile religious powers in ancient civilizations, from gods who are ravenous for beating human hearts to ones that rise with the sea to wipe out helpless villages; of the destructive power of Shiva and the dangers of Buddhist demons; of the devil and his satanic legion of imps and goblins—holdovers, perhaps, of a dualistic Zoroastrian split between good and evil gods. There is a lot to explain.

So it is not surprising that theorizing about religion's origins is now a cottage industry, including the ideas that: it is a specifically evolved adaptation to manage anxiety and depression; it improved group cohesion and was favored by group selection; it gave some individuals in a group control over others; it evolved as a costly display of commitment and altruism that increased reproductive success; or it was just a byproduct of new cognitive powers, which had adaptive value while faith itself did not.

All these theories may be partly true. Most focus on community, precisely the dimension of faith that William James set aside. He did recognize that some of his special people—saints and such—impress those who come after them with their commitment, founding new religions. But James was also fascinated by the little people, the born-again, the prayerful, the meditators, the ones who stumble privately on insight and ecstasy. I like to ask the modelers of faith as community whether Robinson Crusoe would have any use for religion on his desert island. I believe he would, perhaps more than the rest of us.

Some say Robinson Crusoe's experience is too rare to be relevant to evolution. I don't think so. In fact, I think it's our general experience. We are alone on our private islands, however much we love and are loved, however successful we are in communal life. Many Nones find things to do in solitude that bring comfort without religion: gardening, woodworking, flower arranging, painting, writing—it's part of mental health for many. The chimps show apparent awe at a waterfall alone *or* with others. But many people find, in solitude, a spiritual companion: the Hopi girl who found companions in the hawk and the thundercloud; Plains Indian boys with their personal spirit from a vision quest; the African American girl smiling "at God."

Stanford anthropologist Tanya Luhrmann's research on evangelicals shows them carefully cultivating relationships with Jesus—having dates with him, or setting out an extra cup of coffee for him when alone on an average morning. As she says in *When God Talks Back*, "they experience part of their mind as the presence of God." Luhrmann emphasizes learning, especially self-training—she calls it the "absorption hypothesis"—as a path toward this state of mind. You might say this is the opposite of the "brainwashing" hypothesis common among belligerent atheists.

For the San, the ancestral spirits may be malign, but they are always there, and they are interested in you; they give your every act and thought meaning. A friend of mine, a 90-year-old Orthodox rabbi with a mischievous sense of humor, says, "God is an observant Jew." God is always watching. God is interested in him, you, me—everyone, although he believes God expects more of Jews. That is why he repeats dozens of blessings every day between waking and sleeping, from "Blessed are you, O God, who brings forth bread from the earth" to thanking God—after leaving the bathroom—for making all the parts of his body work because "if even one were to fail," life would fail. Observant Jews believe God watches them, and they are mostly grateful.

Mystically inclined Jews see God's presence as the *Shekhina*— according to kabbalah, the feminine, compassionate aspect of God. Rabbi Levi Yitzhak, a leader of the revolutionary Jewish religious movement Hasidism, was known for criticizing God. He was also known for an ecstatic song, a melody in Yiddish based on Psalm 139, full of the haunting refrain *"Du, Du, Du"*:

> *Where I go, You,*
> *Where I stay, You,*
> *Only You, Only You . . .*
> *When I am happy, You,*
> *When I am sad, You,*
> *You, everywhere You,*
> *You, You, You . . .*

This may seem more deistic or pantheistic than Jewish, but it is personal, and it presages Martin Buber's much later *I and Thou*.

A Hindu family I know well through three former students, all now physicians like their parents, has prospered. The father, a surgeon originally trained in India, looked around at his home one night and said, "Lakshmi has been good to us." His wife, a family physician, agreed. Lakshmi is the goddess of prosperity, and these highly educated, highly effective doctors believe in some sense that she is with their family. They would say, I think, that they believe in one God (the God of the Vedas perhaps), but for them God's care is manifest in Lakshmi's generosity, just as for many Jews God is in the *Shekhina*, and for Christians, in Jesus.

Skeptics say that these people are deluding themselves, replacing real human bonds with imagined supernatural ones. But most are also in close relationships with other people—who have their own supernatural bonds. If faith evolved as a communal adaptation, how can it also keep people apart? Supernatural companionship matters. Atheists who think religion is all about fear of death miss key human functions, one of which is a companionship that makes every moment of life *seen*, and meaningful. The "Watch me, Mommy!" need that every human child has (and no chimpanzee does), identified by psychologist Ann Kruger as communion, is also played out when a part of your mind is God. A religious Robinson Crusoe does not feel alone.

Consider some formal evolutionary explanations. The minimalist claim is that religion is a by-product of human mental, emotional, and social abilities evolved for other reasons—other adaptive purposes—and serves no additional function. It's just the price we pay to be smart, attuned, and sociable. I will explain why I find this idea implausible. Other, more persuasive evolutionary arguments include enhanced group solidarity in the face of external threats; anxiety reduction in the face of disease and natural disaster; preservation of order when at least some people behave immorally and exploit others; and encouragement of reproduction by valuing children and helping families flourish.

We will come back to the evidence for these explanations, but first let's look at what has happened in religion's long history. We've considered Edward Tylor and Émile Durkheim's "elementary forms" in the simplest societies—confirmed, rejected, or developed over two centuries of anthropology. We've delved into the trance-dance religion of the Kalahari San (Bushmen) and found these brave, spirited people practicing an ancient tradition using complex music, dance, and profoundly altered states of consciousness to gain access to the ancestors and gods and try to influence them—not beg, but cajole or even berate—to back off on the harm they do to the human world. Their culture is built around this ritual and the awe it inspires.

We've looked at ritual initiations, centered on the time in life when the adolescent mind is open to inspiration and instruction, changing vague children into adults who know what it means to be a participant and a believer in a particular faith, culture, and social world; a time when the young are deliberately taught, not just encouraged to observe and imitate, when parents and grandparents reaffirm through their children their own faith and commitment to tradition. But there is more to any "primitive" religion. In the Mbuti of the Congo's Ituri Forest, young men—older than the boys who have their teeth filed at puberty—learn how to kill elephants; a successful hunt is followed by a day of ritual and narrative that promotes solidarity. When the Sirionó of eastern Bolivia kill a valued harpy eagle, they ritually rub their bodies with its feathers, to absorb its power.

Megan Biesele's book on !Kung myths was called *Women Like Meat*. In two other hunter-gatherer groups—the Hadza and the Ache—admiration for successful big-game hunters leads women to choose them as mates, although the meat is widely shared. Even many non-hunter-gatherer cultures—such as the Maasai of Kenya—made hunting central to rituals of manhood, and a visit to any major art museum shows how the hunt has been celebrated. Literary traditions from ancient Greece and China to Tolstoy and Faulkner describe the rituals of the hunt.

Most cultures make marriage a sacred moment, and have rites for the dead. Even a primitive species like *Homo naledi* disposed of its dead in a deep cave for generations. Neanderthals probably had systematic rituals and deliberate burials. At La Ferrassie in France, a rock shelter dated to 60,000 years ago was apparently a family burial plot, with remains including a man, a woman, two children, and two infants. The woman and man were laid head to head, the children were set at the man's feet, and one of the infants, a newborn, was buried with three well-designed flint tools. At a site in the Middle East, a boy's grave was ringed by pairs of goat horns, and at Shanidar Cave, an old man was buried with evergreen branches and flowers.

Biological and cultural evolution had continued in Africa, and some modern humans left Africa and began to populate the world. Their spread across Asia was relatively rapid, some along coastlines; their coastal subsistence ecology—fishing, shellfish collecting, and hunting the land animals feeding on the fish—did not need to change dramatically during the time it took to reach Australia.

Modern humans entering Europe had new tools and weapons of stone, bone, antler, and ivory, iron pyrite for making fire, and fine bone and ivory flutes that made good music, and they created cave art. In our modern love of wildlife we have nothing over our ancestors. The Cave of Altamira in northern Spain has a herd of brightly colored bison on the ceiling, along with a horse, two deer, and some wild boar; at Font-de-Gaume in France, a reindeer male sniffs the head of a kneeling female; at Trois-Frères an engraved chaotic group of big game, along with a pair of snowy owls guarding their chick, appears beside an odd figure with antlers, staglike ears and body, human hands and feet, a prominent human phallus, a horse's tail, and striking eyes in a mouthless, bearded face. Chauvet in southern France shows realistic lionesses, bison, and rhinoceroses dating back 33,000 years, plus stereotyped sketches of woolly mammoths and parts of humans (pubic triangles with vulvas) as well as stripes and circles. Lascaux has a yellow-and-black horse in a rain of arrows; a herd of small, ornately antlered stags; a horse with a fluffy mane; two bison tail to tail; a large, red, dappled cow; and a 5-yard-long, big-eyed, black bull.

Were rites involved? Holley Moyes's book about the ritual use of caves, *Sacred Darkness*, begins, "Caves are special places. They are mysterious. They captivate us. They draw us in. They can protect or entrap. Whether they fascinate or frighten, we recognize caves as otherworldly." The Paleolithic caves could be accessed only with great effort, often requiring crawling through cramped spaces, so some think there may have been a kind of ritual theater—perhaps a pubertal initiation rite—a torch-lit, obstacle-filled approach being the prelude. Or, inaccessibility may have had more to do with secrecy—hunting magic, totemism, shamanism. We can't know for sure. But this art, considered to be among the greatest in history, was probably part of a religious adaptation.

———

MUCH CURRENT THINKING about the origins of religion is grounded in the societies found in the anthropological record. Starting with the oldest and most basic type of fully human culture, a group at the University of Cambridge in 2016 analyzed 33 hunting-gathering societies. Mathematically reconstructing the *cultural* evolution of those groups, they confirmed Edward Tylor's intuition that animism—the belief that objects like waterfalls and wildfires are inhabited by willful spirits—was the first human religious form. Every one of the 33 cultures had that kind of faith, consistent with the "faces in the clouds" idea: we humans attribute agency and minds nearly instinctually. Twenty-six (79 percent) had two other features we've encountered: shamanism and belief in an afterlife. Ancestor worship was a distant fourth, at 45 percent; next, the belief in high gods, at 39 percent. The belief that high gods are *actively involved* in human life was last, at 15 percent. So we can say provisionally that our fully human ancestors—say, 100,000 years ago—were animists, most believed in an afterlife and had shamans, about half worshipped their ancestors in some sense, and few believed in high gods involved in human affairs.

This synopsis is consistent with the relatively egalitarian nature of hunting-gathering societies. We have long known that high gods are most common in cultures with high humans—kings and queens. In all major religions, these high gods became objects of fear and worship, and sooner or later monumental architecture of some type was erected throughout the world in their honor. Awe was transferred from the waterfall and the fire to buildings, towers, sanctuaries, and altars—and to hereditary monarchs worshipped as gods. The ancient empires had hierarchies of gods who were very involved in human affairs, punishing people, demanding sacrifices, taking sides in wars. Monotheism came late to these empires but was logical: one king, one God.

Yet for hundreds of thousands of years, we lived in *relatively* egalitarian communities, although, in lush times and places, high population density made hierarchy possible. The culmination came about 12,000 years ago, 2,000 years before agriculture, when hunter-gatherer populations were growing and settling down. By the time of the transition to agriculture, major architectural *religious* forms had emerged—like Göbekli Tepe in Turkey, "one of the most important archeological discoveries of modern times." It includes a ring of pillars resembling the much later Stonehenge, not as large but much more richly carved with apparent symbols, a religious sanctuary not close to settlements—a gathering point and place of pilgrimage. While there was some agriculture, including evidence of beer in rituals, people depended on hunting and gathering, amassing bones of gazelles, aurochs, wild asses, and other game.

Unlike at Stonehenge, gorgeous carvings of wild animals adorn the pillars, some anthropomorphized, an "explosion of images" that requires no stretch of the imagination to see as having ritual significance, "part of a system of symbolic communication that preceded writing [for] storing cultural knowledge. These people must have had a highly complicated mythology, including a capacity for abstraction." There is evidence of feasting, probably part of ritual observance at the sacred site. The placement of the stones and carvings may have astronomical significance. It is the forerunner of organized, hierarchical religions marked by monumental architecture from the Parthenon and the biblical Hebrews' temple to the Egyptian and Aztec pyramids—awe-inspiring symbols of high gods. Because such gods have been central for so long, many have speculated on why they emerged—and how, if at all, they are adaptive.

One widely discussed model is that of social psychologist Ara

Norenzayan. His 2013 book, *Big Gods*, and a 2016 paper with several colleagues have provoked extensive commentary from experts on religion. The debates give a good sense of current thinking about how and why *major* religions arose. The book opens with "The Eight Principles of Big Gods":

1. *Watched people are nice people.*
2. *Religion is more in the situation than in the person.*
3. *Hell is stronger than heaven.*
4. *Trust people who trust in God.*
5. *Religious actions speak louder than words.*
6. *Unworshipped Gods are impotent Gods.*
7. *Big Gods for Big Groups.*
8. *Religious groups cooperate in order to compete.*

These are all statements about human behavior: (1) People behave better when they think they are watched. (2) Religion is not intrinsic but contextual. (3) Fear of punishment motivates people more than hope of reward does. (4) Religious people trust other religious people. (5) To gain such trust you have to do costly things. (6) Gods and religions don't get big unless a lot of people do such things. (7) Big punitive gods rise with and sustain big groups. (8) Cooperation within big groups enables them to defeat and engulf other groups. In a nutshell, what anthropologists call "moralizing high gods" promoted cooperation within groups, which enlarged those groups until they took over the world.

These sweeping claims have critics. Scholars of religion often find the model superficial. Social scientists and evolutionary theorists also have issues. The Abrahamic religions play a large role in the theory, and their influence in the world could be a historical accident. Others object to the emphasis on extrinsic factors, which ignores or belittles religious impulses and passions. Still others point out that demographic, economic, and political forces produced the large-scale cooperative societies of the ancient world, some of which had "big gods" while others didn't, and even for those that did, it's difficult to separate the effect of the big gods from the other factors. Buddhism (almost ignored by the theory) spread widely with massive cooperation but without big gods. And ritual promoted cooperation long before big gods.

Anthropologist Augustin Fuentes points out that extensive cooperation with non-kin precedes by hundreds of thousands of years the emergence of big gods, and that the huge scaling up that began about 12,000 years ago has been well explained by generations of anthropologists as a dynamic involving increased population density, intensifying social hierarchy, emerging religious elites, concentration of wealth, and wars of conquest. Fuentes points to "the lived experience of religion" as a needed focus before we get to "overarching structural and adaptationist explanations." Hillary Lenfesty and Jeffrey Schloss note that "the gods of cosmopolitan Greek, Roman, Mayan, Aztec, Chinese, and Hindu religions" are "generally uninterested in human morality, and "that the sequence from small foraging bands, to chiefdoms, to large kingdoms was not driven by but rather informed the notion of Big Gods."

Richard Sosis and his colleagues apply the principles of behavioral ecology to religion's evolution. This means actually calculating the costs and benefits of religious commitment. Sosis compared the longevity of scores of American commune experiments during the eighteenth and nineteenth centuries; religious ones lasted longer. The Israeli kibbutz showed a similar trend; despite being socialist, those with religious commitments outlasted secular communes, and the degree of devotion also predicted success, even among religious ones. Costly signaling of commitment is key, and here personal passions and sacrifices converge with public displays of faith to increase group solidarity and reciprocal cooperation.

Snake-handling religions are a classic example. Making pilgrimages to Mecca, taking your mother to the Ganges to be cremated, waking up every day before dawn to go to synagogue, tithing in an evangelical church, or dancing intensely into the night to enter a trance "like death" are all "hard to fake" displays of commitment. Eleanor Power, in a 2017 study of Hindus and Christians in two villages in southern India, used a new mathematical model to show that individuals who attend temple or church more regularly—or, for Hindus, perform public religious acts, from sacrificing a goat to firewalking—are perceived by others as more trustworthy and more likely to reciprocate if you help them.

Religion is a complex adaptive system with many functions—including social cohesion, valued in peace, vital in war. When one group replaces or absorbs another, the consequences may be genetic—through killing, raping, and seizing wives and concubines—but they are also always cultural. Those who survive in the subject population accommodate as best they can to the dominant culture's rules, including religious ones. This is the basic story of the spread of Christianity, Islam, Buddhism (with no high god), and other major religions. Some, like historian of religion Karen Armstrong, think the tie between religion and war is incidental; faith is a sort of flag carried by armies. I see it as part of a system of predatory expansion, along with economic motives and domination. Wars and genocide have been motivated by nonreligious causes (Hitler, Stalin, Mao, Pol Pot). But many wars were explicitly religious, and many conquerors had convert-or-die mandates, ultimately essential to the dominance of the largest religions.

Here is my sketch of religious history: For the first few hundred thousand years, our species lived in small, nomadic groups with animistic, shamanistic, and ancestral-spirit beliefs, although larger populations waxed and waned in times and places. Rituals, including dance and music, bound communities together. They involved costs, risks, and pain—public displays of commitment. Reciprocal aid was its own reward, and lack of it led to ostracism. Better-functioning groups attracted members from groups that did not function as well—part of a process of cultural group selection. One recent theory gives raiding and war a central role throughout our evolution. Some fossil evidence supports this, but recent hunter-gatherers do not; these small-scale societies had violence within groups, including homicide, but little between groups. We know intergroup violence grew with increased population density at the end of the hunting-gathering era, more so with the rise of agriculture.

From at least that time until ours, conflicts between groups have been the rule, and preparations for them continuous—at the levels of tribes, villages, cities, empires, nation-states, and alliances among them. The good news is that, since the ancient "civilizations" emerged from the mud of irrigated soil with the blood of conquest oozing from every pore, the actual death rate from violent conflict has declined fairly steadily, because of the consolidation of power in larger entities and later the rise of democracy, education, women's equality, and the increase in life expectancy, giving us more to lose.

Big gods came late to this gruesome game, and their moralizing probably began no earlier than 3,000 years ago. That's one-third of the time since ancient empires began to clash. Smaller gods got "involved" in wars, as vividly described in *The Iliad*—but as champions of certain favored human warriors, who were then used as levers in the gods' battles with each other. The soap opera of the gods was not about morals, but about human foibles writ large and playing favorites with human leaders.

Compare the flood story in the Bible with one of its predecessors, the Babylonian Gilgamesh epic. Both are dramas of human weakness and godly power. But the Gilgamesh flood and its heroic human survivor are pawns in a conflict among the gods. In Genesis, God is alone in the heavens. Noah, the best man on Earth, uniquely obeys God's will and so is chosen to be saved. The flood is no power struggle, because God's power is unique and unopposed, able to end the world. The Hebrew story is about right, not power, and it became part of the narrative of all three Abrahamic religions, now adhered to by about half the world. Their success could be due partly to Norenzayan's effect of a moralizing high god enforcing cooperation in far-flung populations.

Aggressive atheists say that religion is the main cause of intergroup violence. Karen Armstrong says no, wars are caused by economic and political interests that use religion as a label on the way to other goals. Group differences—far from always practical—begin wars, but they often spiral out of control, imposing greater costs and grief than intended by either side. But "civilizations" were always organizations for predatory expansion. Bias against out-groups is intrinsic and universal, as is the tendency of human males toward physical aggression. The Crusades and the Thirty Years' War were mainly about religion, with true believers and moralizing high gods on both sides. In the Nazi expansion, religion was in the deep background of anti-Semitism, but the *Gott mit uns* military belt buckle was more a wish than a cause. For Stalin and Mao, religion was a target. Buddhism conquered without a big god.

We know that in all intergroup violent conflict, the reproductive success of winners is augmented through rape and the seizure of wives and concubines. Thus, not only cultural group selection but conventional genetic adaptation through enhanced reproductive success has rewarded generation after generation of warriors, and especially their leaders. Culture and genes evolve partly independently, but they also interact. Culture can (as conventionally assumed) buffer against selection on genes and substitute for genetic evolution, or it can amplify genetic evolution by creating new, intense selection pressures.

But since cultural change is fairly obvious—all major religions spread by proselytizing, often at sword- or gunpoint, but also with economic and political domination—let's look at how religion shapes genetic evolution. Religious people have children. Call it part of their prosocial program, or their unreasonable optimism about the future, or the way they think about the key to evolution—sex.

Any way you look at it, if you think that religion is on the way out (as some intellectuals have thought for two centuries), you have to deal with the simple fact that in every major religion, the devout (celibates excepted) outbreed the lukewarm, and they certainly outbreed atheists. True, cultural evolution is faster than genetic evolution, but so far, one of its main effects has been to (relatively speaking) sterilize people lacking faith. Someone much more religious than I might say it's God's plan to create a slowly swelling tide of believers—people whose faith is stronger than your logic.

One of the functions of religion consistently overlooked by belligerent atheists, and even by some faith leaders, is to nurture family. The Dalai Lama describes himself asking a rabbi the secret of Jewish survival in the diaspora—something he is very concerned about for his own exiled Tibetan people. The rabbi pointed to the Friday-night dinner, and the Dalai Lama said he did not understand why a ritual would be so important. I fear His Holiness missed the point, which is the home, not the ritual. The most observed Jewish ritual is the Passover seder, around a set table in the home, not the synagogue. This revered celibate leader among celibate monks may have overlooked the way faith sustains families.

This family factor is evident in Bradd Shore's eloquent account of Salem camp meetings, a Methodist summer tradition for two centuries. Hundreds of families from far and wide meet at a Georgia camp for a week apart from the "time famine" hustle of modern life. They escape the heat by converging on breezier porches for direct, face-to-face talk during 8 unscheduled hours daily. There are prayer services with famous preachers, dual pianos, and emblematic hymns. Shared faith brings these families together. But the down time—"gossiping, catching up, and reminiscing . . . provides a basis for meaning making . . . uniting spiritual revival and family reunion." As at Jewish

Friday-night dinners and Passover seders, the family takes on a spiritual dimension.

Equally important, "camp meeting is both a storehouse and a theater of family memory." Photos, slide shows, and stories effect a "constant shifting between distant past, recent past, and present . . . a blurring of time and a continuity of place." The Jewish Sabbath is a sacred time, not a sacred place; camp meeting is both. Old objects matter, and even sawdust lingers for months in Bibles and clothing—a welcome reminder of the sacred week; one woman said she would like it mixed with her ashes.

Meals, prayer, and music bind people beyond families, but the event functions crucially within them. Parents spend time just watching their children, more in nostalgia than in concern, reliving their own memories that match the ones their parents had and their children are having. Raising a family is hard, but traditions make it easier— and sacred. For elders, "identity updating" is shaped by the reactions and sympathy of peers. All in all, these traditions "inform narrative expression and create a powerful sense of identification in 'family' over the generations. . . . what Mircea Eliade has called 'eternal return,'" and "something both precious and fragile: the distinct sense of a life." There is a Jewish expression, "l'dor vador"—"from generation to generation"—that is used in formal speech and casual observations, especially at events involving children. It expresses history, nostalgia, costly commitment, family, love, and hope.

Goodness!

I attended a conference once that was supposed to include Daniel Dennett, author of *Breaking the Spell* and other books. He couldn't come, because he was recovering from one of life's most serious anatomical mishaps. A little over a week before, he had had a dissecting aortic aneurysm—a sudden coming apart of a large part of the inner wall of this greatest of all arteries, preventing blood from circulating and backing it up to the heart. It is a surgical emergency, frequently fatal. Fortunately, he was successfully treated, and he sent an essay to be read at the meeting. As a longtime fan of Dennett's, I liked it a lot. I have already said how much I admired the way Christopher Hitchens faced his death from cancer—a model of courage, disproving the adage that there are no atheists in foxholes. Dennett seemed to me similarly courageous.

His essay was called "Thank Goodness!" It began with an account of analytic philosopher A. J. Ayer's near-death experience, which Ayer reported on not long before his actual death, saying that it had weakened his "inflexible attitude" toward the belief in life after death. Did Daniel Dennett also have an epiphany? He wrote,

> Yes, I did have an epiphany. I saw with greater clarity than ever before in my life that when I say, "Thank goodness!" this is not merely a euphemism for "Thank God!" (We atheists don't believe that there is any God to thank.) I really do mean

thank goodness! There is a lot of goodness in this world, and more goodness every day, and this fantastic human-made fabric of excellence is genuinely responsible for the fact that I am alive today.

Continuing, Dennett extended his thanks to the doctor who had noticed his aortic dissection in a routine exam (his symptoms were unusually mild), to the surgeons, neurologist, anesthesiologist, and perfusionist who had kept him alive during the operation, as well as to "the dozen or so physician assistants, and to nurses and physical therapists and x-ray technicians and a small army of phlebotomists so deft that you hardly know they are drawing your blood, and the people who brought the meals, kept my room clean, did the mountains of laundry generated by such a messy case, wheel-chaired me to x-ray, and so forth." They came from all over the world but worked together to save his life. He thanked an old friend who had shared the Nobel Prize for inventing the CT scan, and all the other discoverers of the diagnostic and therapeutic triumphs that had saved him. He even thanked the editors and reviewers of the medical and other scientific journals for the research that had led to his treatment.

He saw no point in thanking or praying to God, and to those friends and relatives who told him they had done that on his behalf, he had to resist "the temptation to respond 'Thanks . . . but did you also sacrifice a goat?'" In the end he wrote, "I excuse those who pray for me," and compared them to scientists who hold on to an outmoded theory. I thought the essay expressed something important: whether or not we thank God, we can't ignore the fact that we have people to thank as well, for their kindness, will, energy, knowledge, and skill in helping strangers. Having been to medical school and had serious illnesses in my family, I know that income alone would not motivate medical teams to do all they do, so we *should* thank them for their goodness.

When I returned home, I pulled Dennett's essay out of my briefcase to share with my wife. It's not long or difficult, and in a few minutes she turned the last page. And threw it across the room—a first in our happy marriage.

"What was that?" I asked, rather stunned.

"Doesn't he realize that all those people believe in God?" She understood that this was an exaggeration and not something she could exactly know. But I immediately thought of a study showing that over 60 percent of American physicians believe in God. That could mean a majority, although not a large one, of the doctors who took such good care of Dennett. As I thought about it, it seemed likely that the percentage of nurses would be higher, the technicians higher than that, and so on, widening out to the people in the kitchen and the laundry, where Nones would likely be pretty hard to find.

I am not saying that goodness depends on religious faith. I am just saying that my wife's statement had a piece of the truth: most of those who care for us in hospitals believe in God. The question of whether such belief has any bearing on their goodness (positive or negative) is an empirical one—a scientific one. It's not something we should take on faith, whether a theologian says it matters or a philosopher says it doesn't. Does belief in God make a phlebotomist try harder to puncture the vein with minimum pain? Does it make a surgeon less likely to get drunk the night before she has to operate at 6:00 a.m.? Does it help the woman who brings patients lunches to be kind when her toddler kept her up all night after her roommate robbed her? I don't know, but I will not take anyone's word for it, one way or the other. This question is open to scientific study.

Let's look first at the findings relevant to the folks who took care of Dr. Dennett. Start with a study by physicians and scientists at the University of Chicago of religious beliefs in a stratified national sample of almost 1,500 physicians in the US, compared with a general sample of Americans. (The US is still by far the most religious industrial country, an important point to consider.) Some highlights:

- 76 percent of 1,144 practicing physicians said they believe in God, compared with 83 percent of Americans generally.

- 58 percent (versus 73 percent) said they *Agree* or *Strongly agree* with the statement "I try hard to carry my religious beliefs over into all my other dealings in life."

- 48 percent (versus 64 percent) said, "I look to God for strength, support, and guidance *A great deal* or *Quite a bit.*

- Minority religions in the US were overrepresented among physicians.

These data were collected in 1998, so it's important to bring them up to date, since religiosity is now declining in the US. A 2017 study, based on 2,097 practicing physicians surveyed in 2014, found that 65.2 percent believe in God, and that 76 percent consider themselves either religious (51.2 percent) or spiritual (24.8 percent); 29 percent said that religion influenced their decision to become a doctor, and 44.7 percent said they pray frequently.

The findings were similar across specialties except psychiatry, which was less religious. These numbers may underestimate religion's impact, since they reflect only current religiousness, and many doctors will have been raised religious and possibly influenced by that upbringing, despite being religious no longer. I have taught thousands of pre-med students over more than four decades, both before and after going to medical school myself. They have to take rigorous science courses and do well in them. This requirement ensures that they are smart and adept at scientific thinking, having been selected from among those who couldn't do this as well as they could.

They are not asked to study religion or to attend religious services. In college, they are more likely to be exposed to arguments against than for God. Not a single one of these students was influenced by me to become religious, although I have helped some in their search in one way or another. I teach the facts and theory of evolution. Yet my students became part of the US physician cohorts of 1998 and 2014 who were sampled by the two studies cited here, a majority of whom were found to be believers. Generally, nurses are found to be more religiously inclined than physicians. A study of 339 oncology nurses and physicians at four Boston area hospitals found that 79 percent of nurses and 51 percent of doctors wanted more training so that they could deliver spiritual care to cancer patients (not the same as believing, but relevant). As for the other people Dennett thanked, such as the orderlies wheeling him around the hospital and the laundry workers cleaning his sheets, if they are like the general US population, they are more religious than the doctors.

What about other countries? A 2012 study of 324 Polish physicians found that religiosity (independent of denomination) was significantly correlated with altruism, holistic approaches, and empathy toward patients. An ambitious 2014 study looked at 1,255 physicians from (in order of self-reported religiosity) India, Thailand, Ireland, Canada, Japan, and China. Overall, religiosity was positively correlated with idealism and negatively correlated with relativism (situational ethics). A very large international collaborative study of religiosity and practice among health professionals on six continents is under way and will teach us a lot more soon.

It would be good to have similar research on firefighters, emergency medical technicians, and other first responders and rescue workers, but few such studies have been done. One study points to the possibility of negative as well as positive religious coping. We know that religion promotes prosocial behavior in many ways, both within and beyond religious in-groups. There is a large body of research on this now, and there is no way we can do justice to it here, but consider a few examples.

A 2016 meta-analysis combined data from many studies of the effect of religious priming—reminding people about God and religion—on cooperation and generosity in economic games and other experimental settings. "Results across 93 studies and 11,653 participants show . . . robust effects across a variety of outcome measures—prosocial measures included. Religious priming does not, however, reliably affect non-religious participants—suggesting that priming depends on the cognitive activation of culturally transmitted religious beliefs." Another 2016 meta-analysis looked at 48 case studies of communities "in which religion played some role in community-based resource management (CBRM)." The "findings suggest that beliefs in supernatural enforcement are common features of CBRM and that these duties are ascribed to entities ranging from ancestral spirits to gods."

A series of six cross-cultural studies published in 2017 on 2,137 subjects used verbal and pictorial measures to evaluate the impact of awe on what is called "the small self"—a sense of humility. Real-life and laboratory "experiences of awe, but not other positive emotions, diminish the sense of the self. These findings were observed across collectivist and individualistic cultures. . . . The influence of awe upon the small self accounted for increases in collective engagement, fitting with claims that awe promotes integration into social groups."

Other studies look at the impact of religious holidays and rituals on cooperation and altruism. Two field experiments with 405 people in Portugal showed that "women, on a religious day, were more inclined to agree to a prosocial behavior than on a non-religious day," although men were not affected. Another experiment, with shopkeepers in the souks (markets) of Marrakesh, presented them with a variant of the dictator game, in which you are given a sum of money and can choose to give any amount, including zero, to an anonymous second person. Shopkeepers who played the game while the Muslim call to prayer was audible were more generous than those who played when it was not.

Another approach involves self-reported game or test results; the experimenter knows whether the subject is cheating when reporting. Observers of extreme rituals such as undergoing multiple body piercings or walking on swords for hours during a Hindu festival cheated less than nonobservers. In a milder challenge, culturally appropriate religious instrumental music that was played during a test reduced cheating among religious Hindus in the same community (compared to Bollywood film music), and the same was true of religious test takers at a university in Czechoslovakia or at Duke University in North Carolina. All this evidence and much more suggests that religious priming makes people, especially religious people, give or cooperate more and cheat less.

I can pretty much guarantee that in the coming months you will see headlines about religiously inspired terrorist violence. Some headlines you won't see?

CHURCHGOING BAPTIST LADY VOLUNTEERS AT SOUP KITCHEN
DESPITE BAD BACKACHE

DEVOUT MUSLIM PHLEBOTOMIST IS ESPECIALLY KIND, CAREFUL,
AND FUNNY WITH CHILDREN WHO HAVE SMALL VEINS

CATHOLIC SOCIAL WORKER STAYS LATE WITHOUT PAY TO CLOSE THE
FILES ON A FEW MORE ABUSED GIRLS

BUDDHIST MAN FINDS TWENTY DOLLARS ON STREET, LOOKS AT SKY,
DONATES MONEY

RABBI AND MINISTER LEAD INTERFAITH GROUP, ALL WHITE, TO
JOIN "BLACK LIVES MATTER" MARCH

HINDU ORTHOPEDIST THANKS LAKSHMI FOR HIS SUCCESS, PRAYS TO
GANESH FOR SKILL DURING SURGERY

Do I think atheists do good things too? Of course. I know they do. But the question begged by the scientists and philosophers who want to eliminate religion is, Would the amount of good done in the world by humanity stay the same or increase? There is little evidence at present to support a yes answer to that question, and there is considerable reason—in empirical research—to think the answer is no.

———

ANOTHER EMPIRICAL QUESTION is whether religion has direct positive effects on illness and health, aside from inspiring those who take care of us. More and more research suggests that it does. Here are a few examples.

- A 2017 study found that among 5,449 US adults 40 to 65 years old, people who went to church at least once a year had better physiological stress measures and lower mortality on follow-up than people who did not. Those going more than once a week had a *55 percent lower death rate* from all causes than non-churchgoers had.
- The Black Women's Health Study followed 36,613 women from 1996 to 2010. After controlling for demographic and pre-existing health variables, women who attended church several times a week had 36 percent fewer deaths.
- The Nurses Health Study followed 74,534 women from 1992 to 2012. There were 13,537 deaths during this period, including 2,721 from cardiovascular causes and 4,479 from cancer. Those who attended a religious service more than once a week had 33 percent fewer deaths compared to women who never attended; both heart disease and cancer deaths were markedly reduced.
- A 2015 meta-analysis that focused on cancer included more than 32,000 adult patients in 101 samples, measuring religiosity and spirituality. Physical health was better in those with greater religion/spirituality, *especially* the emotional dimensions called "spiritual well-being" and "spiritual distress."

These effects are not limited to the US, a very religious country.

- Almost 37,000 patients in Tokyo were followed from 2005 to 2010. Nearly 14,000 of them said they were at least somewhat religious—mostly Shinto or Buddhist. The more religious were less likely to smoke or abuse alcohol, more likely to exercise, and less likely to develop diabetes.
- On Crete, in a rural town, about 200 older Orthodox Christians were followed from 1988 to 2012. Religiosity, spirituality, and "a sense of coherence" were measured by standard questionnaires. Those high in religiosity/spirituality had one-third less thickening of the carotid arteries in their necks (meaning much less stroke risk), showed one-third lower levels of the stress hormone cortisol, and were less likely to develop diabetes than were their nonreligious peers.
- In Thailand, 48 women with established diabetes—19 Buddhist and 29 Muslim—were assessed in 2008 and 2009. Religion, spiritual practice, and family support all contributed to the women's management of their blood sugar.
- In Saudi Arabia, 310 kidney dialysis patients (99.4 percent Muslim) were studied to see how well they were faring under this stressful treatment regime. "Psychological functioning was better and social support higher among those who were more religious. The religious also had better physical functioning, better cognitive functioning, and were less likely to smoke, despite having more severe overall illness and being on dialysis for longer than less religious patients."
- 5,442 Canadians were followed in a community health survey. People who attended religious services more than once a week had 40 percent lower diabetes rates and were 18 percent less likely to have high blood pressure than those who went less than once a year.

Aside from prevention and management of illness, coping with severe stresses has also been studied to see whether religion and spirituality have a buffering effect.

- After a recent catastrophic earthquake in Italy, 901 people (almost all Christian) were evaluated on trauma and loss scales, along with a measure of religiousness/spirituality. The earthquake tended to weaken the faith of those having difficulty coping, yet at the same time it served as a buffer for those who coped well.
- 792 Hindus in rural northern India were studied with respect to the ordinary stresses of life. All identified as Hindu, but those who identified more strongly had a greater sense of efficacy in coping and greater *overall* subjective well-being. However, they scored lower on some measures of well-being.
- 81 young African American women were tested on routine cardiovascular measures. They were asked about their use of prayer in coping, evaluated on a Perceived Racism Scale, and given a racism recall task. Those who reported more prayer coping had lower stress levels and lower blood pressure during the racism recall task.

Even the most secular countries show such effects. In Denmark, one of the least conventionally religious societies, a 2013 study of severely ill lung patients found that almost two-thirds had some belief in God and/ or a spiritual power. Those who said they believed in both had a better quality of life by standard measures than did those who only believed in a spiritual power. However, negative religious coping (self-blame or fear of punishment) was associated with a lower quality of life.

And in Hungary, in 2002—thirteen years after Communist rule ended—religion and its protective effects persisted. Among 12,643 people (mean age 47), those practicing religion had better mental and physical health, with the healthiest being those practicing regularly in a religious community rather than those who were religious in their own personal way. "We can conclude that even after an anti-religious totalitarian political system practicing religion still remained a health protecting factor."

Obviously, such effects transcend borders and religions, persisting in places where religion has declined or was long suppressed. Skeptics argue that it has nothing to do with faith really; it's just about affiliation, and regular attendance at a church or a mosque could be substituted with, say, a bowling league. "You don't look well," one of the regulars says, "you should see a doctor," and pretty soon you are getting better care than you would if you didn't bowl. Or, any sort of fellowship is psychologically good for you. Some of these studies suggest that this looking out for one another works and that (as many evolutionary models propose) much of the adaptive value of religion is in community. Jesse Graham and Jonathan Haidt, for example, find that religious people are happier, more charitable, and make up the majority of the world, and their explanation is that religion binds people together in moral communities. But others suggest this isn't all, that spirituality and faith work in more mysterious ways too—nothing supernatural, just psychological fostering of health habits and perhaps the immune system.

A 2017 study by Becky Read-Wahidi and Jason DeCaro explored immigration stress in rural Scott County, Mississippi. They interviewed 60 Mexican immigrants sharing devotions to the Virgin of Guadalupe. They used a standard immigration stressor scale, asked subjects to rate their well-being physically and psychosocially, and developed a scale for "cultural consonance" with Guadalupan devotion. Those with high cultural consonance—many beliefs and practices, such as keeping a statue of the virgin in their homes or cars, bringing her flowers, or saying that her festival is important to them—showed no decrease in physical or psychosocial adaptation with increasing immigration stress. But those low in cultural consonance declined in well-being as stress increased. Those who scored high did so for different reasons. Praying to the virgin even when you are not in trouble is different from attending a communal event in her honor. So there were varied paths to high consonance. Anthropologists would call the Virgin of Guadalupe a "master symbol"—one with many meanings and functions.

Her following is strong in Mexico; there, it is said, a poor peasant named Juan Diego was climbing a mountain five centuries ago when she appeared to him. He reported this appearance to his bishop, who was dismissive. But on another climb, she appeared to Juan in winter and filled his cloak with flowers. The bishop, seeing the flowers, as well as the virgin's image on Juan's cloak, became a believer, and customs honoring the virgin grew in the church. As has often happened with Catholicism's spread, the virgin's shrine was at the site of a pagan goddess's demolished temple.

Scott County immigrants identify with Juan Diego, reframing poverty as humility. He was native, yet, under colonialism, a stranger in a strange land. Scott County immigrants are also disempowered. Many do hard, dangerous work in the poultry industry, and families include documented and undocumented people. Most lack health insurance. Many are afraid. But those who are high in devotion are buffered against stress.

Critics of religion might argue that religion simply helps these immigrants to accept what they should resist, but for them, fighting back is highly impractical. Just going forward day to day is resistance. Spiritually or psychologically, the Virgin of Guadalupe is helping her Scott County followers come through. And theirs is the story of generation after generation of immigrants, legal and otherwise, willing and enslaved. They come through for themselves, their families, their unborn American grandchildren. If faith helps them, it is not just opium for the people; it is also sustenance for the people's future.

If Not Religion, What?

As we have seen, one eminent figure of scientific atheism is the Nobel-laureate theoretical physicist Steven Weinberg. Like Dawkins, Dennett, and Harris, he is an implacable enemy of religion; he says unequivocally that "the world needs to wake up from its long nightmare of religious belief," and that helping the world to do that might in the end be science's greatest contribution. But while he is in the inner circle—"one of the staunchest atheists on the planet," according to Dawkins—he parts company with them when he takes very seriously the question "If not religion, what?"

There is a difference between an atheist wise enough to see a worldwide end of faith as a potentially serious loss, and one who says, in effect, *no problem*. I've called Dawkins, Harris, Dennett, and the late Christopher Hitchens the Quartet, but they are a brass quartet, while Weinberg, the tragic humanist, is to the side, playing a slightly mournful solo violin, and the music and its meaning are different. Tragic humanism is different from "no problem" atheism, because it admits the dark side of life. It does not claim that the scientific worldview can take the place of religion, even if it succeeds in eliminating religion. It shares with religion a sense of loss during our brief, often painful lives, our inevitable separation from the people we love, our aching search for beauty and meaning in lives that are often anguishing and sometimes seem pointless.

Of course, there is the surpassing beauty of improved human lives: the impact of vaccines, the eradication of smallpox, the treatment of HIV/AIDS, the prevention of heart disease, advances in agriculture, the industrial technology that has liberated billions, the information technology that may yet unify the world, lifesaving mathematical models of hurricane movements, the preservation of diversity and beauty in the plant and animal world, and the science of global climate change that can help avert catastrophe.

But science does not just make life safer and more comfortable; it creates great beauty—neuronal connections under a microscope, the vast worlds-upon-worlds view of the Eagle Nebula photographed on the Saturn flyby, the first views of Earth from space—but also in the elegance of the explanations themselves: Euclid's geometry, the system of planetary ellipses reduced to the law of gravity, the periodic table of elements, Maxwell's laws of electromagnetism, evolution by natural selection, the germ theory, Einstein's relativity, the majesty of continental plates inching colossally under our feet, and the structure of DNA, a lockstep spiral molecular galaxy that explains life. But to suppose that all these products of science, together with many more, can take the place of faith reveals an impoverished view of religion.

It also risks ignoring or disdaining the role of art and its relationship, for much of the human past at least, with religion. In the context of responding to Steven Weinberg, who called religion a "crazy old aunt" who might be missed when she's gone, Richard Dawkins declared he wouldn't miss her a bit. But he then qualified the dismissal: "We would miss the music. The B Minor Mass, the Matthew Passion, these happen to be on a religious theme, but they might as well not be. They're beautiful music on a great poetic theme, but we could still go on enjoying them without believing in any of that supernatural rubbish." When asked once what music he would take to a desert island, he recalled that he "chose 'Mache dich mein Herz herein' from the St. Matthew Passion as the most gorgeous piece of music."

"These happen to be on a religious theme, but they might as well not be." But how would we know that the composer's religiosity didn't matter? In fact, in Bach's case the opposite is much more likely. Scholars find that he was a man of faith and that his long career of writing church music drew on that faith. Among other similar notations, Bach wrote in the margins of his study Bible, "Where there is devotional music, God with his grace is always present." This is not to say that atheists don't write great music; they do and probably always have. It is just to say that some great art is intertwined with faith, and in those cases it is a fool's errand to try to disentangle them or to say that "they might as well not be."

Dawkins has also addressed the question of art and science in his book *Unweaving the Rainbow*. The title, he says, "is from Keats, who believed that Newton had destroyed all the poetry of the rainbow by reducing it to the prismatic colors. Keats could hardly have been more wrong." Here are the offending lines of the great young English poet (who was, incidentally, a surgeon):

> *There was an awful rainbow once in heaven;*
> *We know her texture; she is given*
> *In the dull catalog of common things,*
> *Philosophy will clip an angel's wings,*
> *Conquer all mysteries by rule and line,*
> *Empty the haunted air, and gnomed mine*
> *Unweave a rainbow . . .*

Dawkins proceeds to unweave the rainbow very deftly, satisfying my curiosity at least, but in no sense addressing Keats's fears:

> Light from the sun enters a raindrop through the upper quadrant of the surface facing the sun, and leaves through the lower quadrant. But of course there is nothing to stop sunlight enter-

ing the lower quadrant. Under the right conditions, it can then be reflected *twice* round the inside of the sphere, leaving the lower quadrant of the drop in such a way as to enter the observer's eye, also refracted, to produce a second rainbow, 8 degrees higher than the first and half as bright.

Citing a great contemporary of Keats, he concludes, "I think that if Wordsworth had realized all this, he might have improved upon 'My heart leaps up when I behold / a rainbow in the sky . . . '" Dawkins also quotes an eighteenth-century English poet, Mark Akenside, whose lines extolling Newton's prismatics have the misfortune to appear only a page away from Keats. Why is Keats so widely read and loved, while Akenside is not? A nineteenth-century critic, even in praising his verse, said, "At his very best Akenside is sometimes like a sort of frozen Keats."

To demand that poems have Newtonian precision is a bit like reading the Psalms and pointing out that hills don't skip like rams, or seeing in Mercutio's magnificent riff on Queen Mab a throwback to a benighted age of imps and demons. In fact, Keats *cannot* have been wrong, because it was not his aim to be right in any way that Dawkins means. He was right in the only way that mattered to him: having expressed the fear he felt toward Newton's prismatics in what I might call (metaphorically, despite my knowledge of the brain) his heart and soul.

Walt Whitman wrote, a century and a half after Newton, "There shall be love between the poet and the man of demonstrable science. In the beauty of poems are the tuft and final applause of science." Yet an astronomy lecture inspired him to write,

When I heard the learn'd astronomer,
When the proofs, the figures, were ranged in columns before me,
When I was shown the charts and diagrams, to add, divide, and
    measure them,

When I sitting heard the astronomer where he lectured with much
   applause ...
How soon unaccountable I became tired and sick,
Till rising and gliding out I wander'd off by myself,
In the mystical moist night-air, and from time to time,
Look'd up in perfect silence at the stars.

Now I, for one, don't get sick and tired in lectures like that, unless
they're bad. I get energized and see the beauty in the measurements
and models. I see the beauty, too, in Newton's prismatics. But at a certain point I want to see the rainbow and have my heart leap up—an
anatomical impossibility but an expression of delight. After the stimulating lecture, in the mystical moist night air, I want to put the analysis out
of my mind for a while and, like Whitman, gaze in silence at the stars.

   That is awe—perhaps an evolved form of the chimp's response at
the waterfall; perhaps not so different. Einstein said, "The most beautiful thing we can experience is the mysterious. It is the source of all
true art and science." He continued,

> He to whom the emotion is a stranger, who can no longer pause
> to wonder and stand wrapped in awe, is as good as dead—his
> eyes are closed. The insight into the mystery of life, coupled
> though it be with fear, has also given rise to religion. To know
> what is impenetrable to us really exists, manifesting itself as the
> highest wisdom and the most radiant beauty, which our dull
> faculties can comprehend only in their most primitive forms—
> this knowledge, this feeling is at the center of true religiousness.

The key phrase here is "which our dull faculties can comprehend only
in their most primitive forms." Science and art take this experience of
awe in different directions. Religion is like art, and for many of us art
is a partial substitute for faith.

Science is analytic and largely practical. Awe must be set aside for a time while we slog through the experiments, make the measurements, derive the equations. Then we go back and reexperience awe with greater understanding. I daresay I experience as great an awe at the starlit sky, *with* my knowledge of what the Milky Way is, the fact that there are billions more like it, and that they are racing away from each other at unimaginable speed and have done so since Lumina (the Big Bang), as the ancient Greeks did when they saw their gods in constellations or the Bushmen do when they see their ancestors' eyes. But the moment of my awe at the stars cannot include pages of discourse about science. If it is awe, it floods the mind. I can feel awe in contemplating $E = mc^2$, but I have to leave that state in order to derive, test, or improve on the equation.

Art, like religion, evokes awe not by analyzing but by inspiring. It attempts to re-create in the reader, hearer, or viewer the emotion of a moment as it was experienced by the artist. Of course, science evokes feelings too. But to do that is art's fundamental aim, to re-present life to us, including internal life, to enable us to share in the internal state of the artist, not just an idea—however important—or an argument. Science can distract us from this involvement, because it requires us to control our thought processes, which art sooner or later asks us to temporarily yield, long enough to have an experience that explanation and argument alone do not bring about.

Recently, I looked on while soprano Renée Fleming's brain was being scanned. Anyone can do it; it showed up as a link in my Twitter feed. She's part of a study of how the brain makes music. In one mood I'm fascinated and want to see the scan and all such results, like the scans relating to faith in earlier chapters. But when I'm listening to Fleming sing, I don't want to think about a brain process, much as I love thinking about the brain at other times. I want transcendence, beauty, pleasure, and if possible, awe. I want to be transported by the music co-created with her gifts. At that moment, the last thing I want in my brain is an image of hers.

Of course, a person can be a scientist and an artist both. Leonardo, Goethe, and Chekhov are examples. Many artists know a lot about science and try to depict it, to evoke a moment of discovery in a painting, or a long struggle with a scientific problem in a novel or play. Those can be instances of awe inspired by science, but they are not science itself. Scientists can have the eloquence of literary artists; we see that in the last passages of *The Origin of Species* ("There is grandeur in this view of life"), and in Einstein's essays ("Pure mathematics is . . . the poetry of logical ideas.").

But those passages are not the essence of these great scientists' contributions. Art, I think, has more in common with religion, as William James suggests when he writes about the similarity between poetry and mystical experience:

Single words, and conjunctions of words, effects of light on land and sea, odors and musical sounds, all bring it when the mind is tuned aright. Most of us can remember the strangely moving power of passages in certain poems read when we were young, irrational doorways as they were through which the mystery of fact, the wildness and the pang of life, stole into our hearts and thrilled them. The words have now perhaps become mere polished surfaces for us; but lyric poetry and music are alive and significant only in proportion as they fetch these vague vistas of a life continuous with our own, beckoning and inviting, yet ever eluding our pursuit. We are alive or dead to the eternal inner message of the arts according as we have kept or lost this mystical susceptibility.

Just as some people are tone-deaf to music, or insusceptible to poetry's magic, some atheists are insensitive to religion and spirituality. But no one who is musically tone-deaf goes around telling music lovers that they are imagining things and need to snap out of it.

Like all analogies, this one is inexact; the musically tone-deaf are a small minority. But suppose we consider people who shrug their shoulders at opera or Shakespeare's plays. They, too, don't try to talk the enthusiasts out of their passions. They just go about ignoring them and chalking it up to human variety, inexplicable tastes. They might think that a lot of money, including taxpayers' money, is wasted through direct and indirect subsidies of such minority egghead arts. But most don't make a career out of trying to get rid of those pursuits or even to eliminate the subsidies.

Personally, I think too much money is spent on sports, and in various ways I see harm done. I enjoy watching the World Series and the Super Bowl, so I do understand the general idea. But I'm baffled by the huge emotional and financial investment that billions of people around the world and around the year put into what seem to me mildly interesting, unproductive games. I'm not completely tone-deaf to sports; I just have much less of a feel for them than most others do. Those passions seem somewhat pointless and illogical to me.

But do I go around preaching against them? I teach students about the damage done to the brain by boxing and football, and I'm all for trying to limit the harms. But try to abolish football? Talk people out of it? Don't be ridiculous. People have passions that are different from mine—so much so that I have trouble understanding *why* they go to so much trouble. I might privately wish that they studied science or went to plays or at least ate healthier food at the ballpark. I worry about the distraction from studies, the violent behavior of some players and fans, the fruitless dreams of millions of young minds who prepare for sports careers that only a tiny fraction of them will have. But am I going to write books or make speeches proposing that people wise up and do things that are more logical or useful? I mean, really.

Atheists have many persuasive arguments, some of which I agree with. We still need more separation of church and state in most of the world, including the US. Abuses of nonconformists by religious authorities must be stopped. But a time may come when the question for a person who cares about individuality will be not *Do I have a right not to believe?* but *Do I have a right to faith?*

For generations, humanists have tried to find substitutes for religion—secular temples with at least some of the functions of religious ones; community support, common beliefs, optimism, hope, faith in the future. New religions have emerged in recent centuries—Mormonism and the Baha'i faith, for example—and won many millions of adherents. Secular humanism, which originated at the same time or earlier, has not generated the same kind of enthusiasm. Traditions can be new, but they have to have some flavor of the old. You can have weekly meetings, but what happens in them? It seems to me you would have to have a service.

The services would have to impress children, and you might want to have a school—something like the Ethical Culture schools, which are very noble in intent but whose students and families nationwide number in the thousands, not millions. You might want an official book of readings to choose from for a service, excerpts from the nontheist literatures and philosophies of the world. Science could play a role. You would need to raise money, do good works, and have meaningful marking of life-cycle events—birth, coming of age, marriage, and death, at least. You would need to support and sustain family life. Above all, you would need identity and community—mutual loyalty involving costly sacrifices.

Why haven't secular humanists yet been able to turn their movement into a secular religion that could attract and keep adherents? I don't think it's impossible that they will, but they haven't yet. Meanwhile, we have museums, zoos, and botanical gardens, adult education classes, scouts, sports leagues for kids and grown-ups, PTAs, political parties, book clubs, retirement communities, neighborhood pubs and bars, community pools and skating rinks, bridge clubs, volunteer groups at home and abroad, charities, martial-arts classes, encounter groups, gyms, twelve-step programs, and a thousand other ways of getting people together. But you can list as many as you like without finding anything that feeds the human hunger for commitment to something that really gives life larger meaning, as religion still does for many. Criticize it all you like. But eliminate it? I don't think so. Certainly the evidence doesn't justify that plan. "Would the world be better off without religion?" ask psychologists Scott Lilienfeld and Rachel Amirrati in a 2014 paper reviewing the evidence. They believe the question should continue to be debated, but "Contrary to the forceful assertions of some prominent atheist authors . . . the data consistently point to a negative association between religiosity and criminal behavior and a positive association between religiosity and prosocial behavior. Both relations are modest in magnitude and ambiguous with respect to causation. At the same time, they cannot be ignored. . . . As in all scientific debates, humility in the face of equivocal data should be the watchword."

Epilogue

Here's what we can conclude:

- Religion is far more varied than many observers admit, including extraordinary emotion, altered states of consciousness, logico-deductive systems, narratives, healing, communal attachment, ritual, spirituality, compassion, group identity, and, in general and always, the conviction of things unseen.
- Religious inclinations and capacities are built into the human brain—although not universally or uniformly among individuals—with increasingly known pathways and chemistry.
- Religious inclinations and capacities develop during childhood (again, not uniformly), partly as a result of genes and a maturational plan. Within any religion, devoutness is partly genetic. Exposure explains specific beliefs and practices, but indoctrination does not explain development or individual differences. Faith development is not the same as moral development, and their interaction is poorly understood. Would a world without faith be morally better, worse, or the same as the world we have now? Research will help with this question, but my current guess is, worse.
- Religion evolved by natural selection. It serves adaptive func-

tions, including managing fear and grief, assuaging existential loneliness, providing comfort through ritual, promoting altruism and cooperation, displaying commitment, and encouraging group defense. On balance in evolution, religion must have been adaptive or it would not be here.

• Religion coevolved with ethical behavior, but neither explains the other. We did not need supernatural instruction, but the evolution of moral systems was and is imperfect. Very bad things have come from religious commitments, but so have good things, including, probably, a lot of routine goodness.

• For most people, religion's functions cannot be replaced by science, or even, for many, by science, art, ethics, and community. Yet, in some countries with high levels of education and health, a third of people now lack any religious belief; the remainder are roughly divided between those who have conventional beliefs and those who say they are spiritual. This may be a stable equilibrium. Whether it is or not, the freedom to choose nonbelief should be sacrosanct. Forcing people to believe something is almost impossible, and forcing them to say or do things they don't believe in mocks both faith and freedom.

What do I think will happen next? The number of nonbelievers will grow, through cultural evolution. Populations adhering to conventional religions and supporting their institutions will continue to shrink, but the emigrants tend to become unconventionally spiritual. Most of them have faith; they believe in things unseen. Nones are unlikely to become a vast majority. There will be no end of faith. Religious inclinations are ingrained in human nature—evolved, developed, and partly encoded in genes that build circuits in the brain. And in every major religion, the most faithful have more children. So *genetic* evolution favors faith. The *cultural* evolution of nonbelief will continue, but it will run up against the intrinsic reproduction of believers, who add trends of their own in cultural evolution.

Predictions by intellectuals about the demise of religion and the end of faith have persisted since at least the eighteenth century. If the latest such predictions are right, they will be the first. The great majority of people in the world are religious, and they have more children than nonbelievers do. There is evidence that religious people are happier, more altruistic and cooperative (at least with co-religionists), and healthier than those without faith. In northern Europe, where declines in religion have been largest, most people still say they are either religious or spiritual—they believe there is more than just the material world—and many still follow conventional religions. Improved health and greater education lead to declines in religion but are accompanied by shrinking family size.

It remains to be seen how far the declines go. I see them leveling off as they meet the resistance of human nature—that is, the natures of at least a large minority of humans. I predict an equilibrium in which a substantial minority are conventionally religious, many are unconventionally religious or spiritual, and a substantial minority are Nones. People should follow their inclinations toward or away from faith, religious conventions and institutions, unconventional and personal spirituality. They should be allowed to believe what they want as long as they do not harm others, and if they do harm others, they should be punished for the harm, not the belief. I do not want to live in a world where people can be persecuted for their faith, whether particular or general, any more than I want to be chided for my lack of it.

The search for meaning need not be religious. Viktor Frankl, a psychiatrist who spent three years as a prisoner in Auschwitz, emerged believing that suffering must be given meaning, and he originated a method of psychotherapy based on finding meaning, which he thought the best and perhaps only way to adapt. He told the story, first set down by a German bishop, of a Jewish woman who a few years after World

War II had worn a bracelet with baby teeth set in gold. Questioned by a doctor, she explained, "This tooth here belonged to Esther, this one to Miriam," and so on. These teeth had been saved, one from each of her nine children, all murdered in Auschwitz. "How can you live with such a bracelet?" she was asked. "I am now," she said quietly, "in charge of an orphanage in Israel."

Buddhism, in a way, is about recognizing the inevitability of suffering and converting it into compassion. It is also perhaps the faith that demands the fewest hard-to-believe things. Two recent books illuminate the least hard-to-believe things and argue that they are compatible with science. David Barash's *Buddhist Biology* shows what a Darwinian view of life has in common with Buddhism: not-self, impermanence, connectedness, and engagement. He believes that the current popularity of Buddhism is due to what poet Friedrich Schiller and sociologist Max Weber called "the disenchantment of the world," and he sees some version of Buddhist practice as a possible antidote. Robert Wright's *Why Buddhism Is True* is a personal journey that shows how meditation can improve life, even for a self-confessed bad meditator. Both books explicitly reject all hard-to-believe aspects of Buddhism.

But the Dalai Lama embraces them. He visits an oracle who speaks to him in trance. He expects his monks to be masters of Buddhist texts even more than they are meditators, and he offers teachings to huge audiences that resemble rabbinical interpretative lectures. He believes in reincarnation, karmic progression, and the Buddha's miracles. But he talks about this differently to Western audiences than to his own followers. That is fine with me, and with (I think) Barash and Wright, although they don't follow him there, and they don't think that those parts of Buddhism, vital to true believers, are true. Barash (a self-described "Jew-Bu") cites Stephen Jay Gould's take on science and religion, which Gould called NOMA (non-overlapping magisteria), proposing POMA instead (productively overlapping magisteria).

I would go back to NOMA, with a different meaning: "neither one is magisterial." Science and faith are candles in a darkness that is vast compared to the light that either sheds. Art is a third. All include and convey awe, which we can imagine as the candlelight. Augustin Fuentes, in *The Creative Spark*—in part a defense of religion in the oldest and broadest sense—says that "religion, art, and science created the universe humans now perceive." The Dalai Lama has instructed his monks to embrace science. Jonathan Sacks, the former chief rabbi of Great Britain, has called it "the great partnership."

Religion's past attempts to snuff science out were a dangerous fool's errand and are coming to an end. Science's attempts to abolish religion are not much more than a century old, but they have intensified in the West. Meanwhile, conventional religions are in decline in advanced countries. But billions of people continue to have faith in them, and faith in its many forms will not go away. Nor will the growing numbers who consider themselves spiritual. I recently asked a young friend, who was devoutly Christian in her teens, what her faith is like a decade later. She does not go to church but says she is a believer. What does that mean? "I am God." Asked to clarify, she said she didn't mean it *that* way. She means God is in her, and she is part of God. She said it with a light in her eyes. I may not understand, but I, for one, am not going to try to talk her out of it.

Acknowledgments

The theological ethicist James Gustafson taught me to think of faith as originating in certain features of human nature, notably piety and thankfulness. My thankfulness began within Judaism, on the knee of my grandfather, Abraham Levin, and as I watched him sway in his prayer shawl and tefillin every morning. My parents, following his lead, saw to it that the local Orthodox synagogue became my second home; despite the handicaps of deafness and limited education, the first home they built was very Jewish. Together with the synagogue's rabbi, Bernard Berzon, the teachers, and even the scoutmaster there, my parents gave me a foundation that made my insider's understanding of religion possible.

I lost my faith at age 17, never to recover it, and there were many reasons, but teachers at Brooklyn College—Martin Lean in philosophy, Herbert Perluck in literature, and Dorothy Hammond and Gerald Henderson in anthropology—helped me build a new worldview. By the time I studied with Irven DeVore at Harvard, we were comparing notes on our past—his thumping and selling Bibles in East Texas, mine embracing the Torah in Brooklyn—as we tried to parse human origins and destiny in strictly evolutionary terms.

But a decade later when my children came, my (also nonbelieving) wife and I chose to pass on some traditions. Rabbi Arnold Goodman and others at the Ahavath Achim Conservative synagogue were tolerant of my odd relationship to Judaism and helped me revive and extend my childhood knowledge. Rabbi Emanuel Feldman, the distinguished leader of the Atlanta Orthodox community for almost forty years, bridged a huge gap of faith and practice to befriend me, and I have learned much from him over three decades.

During that time in Atlanta, Dr. Herbert and Hazel Karp invited us to share many Jewish festivals in their home. Drs. Shlomit and David Finkelstein did the same, and their more secular views—we were as likely to discuss Buddhism or quantum physics as Judaism—underscored for me the idea that religious practice does not require conventional faith. Rabbi David Blumenthal, founder of the Jewish Studies program at Emory, taught me much about passion and mysticism in religious life. Ursula Blumenthal's *salon* in their home was the locus of many important conversations. Dr. Leslie and Barbara Rubin and Dr. Boyd and Daphne Eaton helped me understand how highly intelligent people incorporate religion into their mostly secular lives.

Professor Reverend James M. Gustafson, a theological ethicist with a keen interest in science, became a friend and teacher of mine when he moved to Emory from the University of Chicago in 1988. He liked to say that I was religious despite my nonbelief because I was on a lifelong scientific quest to understand human nature. I did not object.

Also in 1988, I began teaching a course on Jewish anthropology, and I thank students of all faiths and no faith since for asking the right questions and forcing me to think more carefully about the answers. Meanwhile, I taught larger numbers of students about evolution, brain, and behavior; this helped me conceptualize the human spirit without supernatural hypotheses. I thank my colleagues in the Department of Anthropology, the Jewish Studies Program, and the Program in Neuroscience and Behavioral Biology at Emory University, and Presidents James Laney and Claire Sterk, for their open-minded support. Reverend Alison Williams, Professor Father Thomas Flynn, Reverend Joanna Adams, and Rabbi Herbert Friedman taught me much about how a religious leader engages with the world. Dr. James Fowler helped me think about how faith develops.

On one of my visits to Israel, my daughter Susanna took me to meet her Palestinian friends in Ramallah, East Jerusalem, and Amman. Their generous hospitality across a great gap of possible enmity will never be forgotten. One, Walid Husseini, befriended me too, and I am grateful for his insight into the bitter fate of his people.

The science and scholarship in the book rest on the teaching and advice of people far too numerous to mention, but in particular: Dora Venit advanced my understanding of Christianity's role in Western history, and Dr. Gerald Henderson laid the foundations of my knowledge of psychological anthropology. Drs. Richard and Judith Wurtman helped me understand neuropharmacology, and conversations with Drs. James Rilling, Jennifer Mascaro, and David Silbersweig greatly enhanced my grasp of brain-imaging research. Drs. Stefan Stein and Julian Gomez helped me interpret psychoanalysis in a modern context; Drs. Robert Paul, Bradd Shore, and Carol Worthman helped me put the mind in cross-cultural perspective; Drs. Robert McCauley and Darryl Neill improved my confidence that a psychology of religion is possible; and Dr. Jerome Kagan, at a critical early stage, taught me much of what I know about child development.

My writing life owes a great debt to Herbert Perluck, Charles McNair, and James Flannery, among others. My brother, Lawrence Konner, has been unfailingly supportive.

My agent for over three decades, Elaine Markson, believed in me early in my career. My late wife, the ethnographer Marjorie Shostak, was secular in origins and disposition, but she graciously supported my commitment to raising Jewish children, not to mention encouraging me for thirty years. Kathy Mote, our nanny and later my assistant, has been invaluable. Her devotion helped save our family during my wife's long illness and after her death.

My three children, Susanna, Adam, and Sarah, who were 18, 14, and 9 at my wife's passing, showed resilience and love that made it possible for me to face the future with new hopes and dreams. Susanna's husband, Doug Post, has been a devoted father to my grandchildren, and has reached across a religious gap to foster Jewish traditions for a new generation.

My life is now joined to that of Dr. Ann Cale Kruger, who has brightened it beyond measure. A believing Presbyterian, she has taught me much about the psychology of faith and about Christian belief and practice. Rabbi Alvin Sugarman co-officiated with Reverend Joanna Adams at our 2005 interfaith wedding; I am grateful for their tolerance and counsel. My Christian stepdaughter, Logan, and her Jewish wife, Leah, have deepened my understanding of tolerance and faith.

Conversations over many years with the late Reverend Robert Hamerton-Kelly and Dr. William Hurlbut enhanced my appreciation for religious minds in general and Christian ones in particular. During my 2011 six-week Fulbright-supported stay in Israel, Dr. Elliot Berry, professor of medicine at Hadassah Medical Center of the Hebrew University, provided a base and a fruitful intellectual collaboration. Long walks in the Jerusalem hills with Elliot taught me new things about the compatibility of religion and science.

In 2013, I had the privilege of teaching Tibetan Buddhist monks in Dharamsala, the seat of the Dalai Lama and Tibetan Buddhism today, about brain and behavior, under the auspices of the Emory-Tibet Science Initiative. Two anthropologists, Robert A. Paul and Carol Worthman, lifelong friends and colleagues, helped create and carry forward this initiative. The monks I taught also taught me—about Buddhist belief and practice, the paradox of nonexistence, the karmic cycle, and religion without God.

Over many years, an increasingly varied student body at Emory has educated me about the world's major religions outside of Judeo-Christian tradition. They have included Buddhist monks who come to

Atlanta to study with us; Yasmin Elhady, who helped me understand commitment to Islam and its compatibility with evolution; and Drs. Shveta Shah and Dinesh Raju, who, together with their families, welcomed my wife and me into their four-day Hindu wedding and into many years of friendship.

J. P. Mishra, a religious Hindu, was an exceptionally knowledgeable guide to Varanasi—its temples, cremations, and the meaning of its rites.

Professor Betsy Bryan helped me to understand the Ancient Egyptian "porch of drunkenness." Dr. Ryan Henner illuminated psychedelic agents and their potential therapeutic use in psychiatry. Carolyn Guérard Cale has enlightened me about a new generation's unconventional spirituality. Margaret Guérard Lachmayr has been very helpful to me in explaining the challenges of being a serious skeptic in a strongly religious environment.

I began work on this book on a sabbatical in 2013–14 supported jointly by the John Templeton Foundation and Emory University. For representation I thank Don Fehr of Trident, and for believing in the book and greatly improving it I thank John Glusman, my editor and the editor in chief at W. W. Norton. His assistant, Helen Thomaides, has been helpful throughout. Stephanie Hiebert is a gifted copy editor who guided me into saying things more clearly and backing up more carefully all the things I say. Others at Norton, an employee-owned publishing house, who have helped bring this book to completion and public awareness are Rebecca Homiski, Amy Medeiros, Mary Kanable, Beth Steidle, Sarahmay Wilkinson, and Caroline Saine. Tyler Fuller, a graduate student at Emory, read the manuscript and offered helpful comments.

None of these teachers, friends, and colleagues are, of course, in the slightest way responsible for my limitations on display in these pages. What is good here owes much to them; what is not is entirely mine.

Avondale Estates, Georgia, April 2019

Appendix: For Further Reading

Aside from the scriptures of all faiths, there are some classics that, like scriptures, are valuable despite their flaws. These include Edward Tylor's *Primitive Culture*, William James's *The Varieties of Religious Experience*, Sigmund Freud's *The Future of an Illusion*, Carl Jung's *Modern Man in Search of a Soul*, Mircea Eliade's *Shamanism: Archaic Techniques of Ecstasy*, and Robert Coles's *The Spiritual Lives of Children*.

For a sense of ethnology's great contribution to our grasp of the real varieties, William Lessa and Evon Vogt's *Reader in Comparative Religion* remains an indispensable collection. Scott Atran's *In Gods We Trust* is the best modern overview. Other anthropological approaches include Stewart Guthrie's *Faces in the Clouds* and Pascal Boyer's *Religion Explained*, Roy Rappaport's *Ritual and Religion in the Making of Humanity*, and Guy Swanson's *The Birth of the Gods*.

For cognitive approaches, I recommend Robert McCaulay's *Why Religion Is Natural and Science Is Not*, Todd Tremlin's *Minds and Gods*, and Justin Barrett's *Why Would Anyone Believe in God?* George Vaillant's *Spiritual Evolution: How We Are Wired for Faith, Hope, and Love* adds a needed emotional dimension to cognitive theories. Robert Fuller's *Spirituality in the Flesh: Bodily Sources of Religious Experience* delves still deeper into the body. And for the role of botanicals in the quest for a mystical, noncognitive kind of knowledge, I start with *Plants of the Gods*, by Richard Evans Schultes, Albert Hofmann, and Christian Rätsch.

Many recent books explore evolutionary angles. These include *The Creative Spark* by Augustin Fuentes, *Supernatural Selection* by Matt Rossano, *Darwin's Cathedral* by David Sloan Wilson, and *The Biological Evolution of Religious Mind and Behavior*, edited by Eckart Voland and Wulf Schiefenhövel. Stephen Jay Gould's *Rocks of Ages: Science and Religion in the Fullness of Life* is my favorite attempt at reconciliation. *The Good Book of Human Nature: An Evolutionary Reading of the Bible*, by Carel van Schaik and Kai Michel, is a sound and entertaining biobehavioral perspective. Karen Armstrong's *The Great Transformation: The Beginning of Our Religious Traditions* compares the deep history of major religions.

Of course, individual faiths—each of which has many faces—have been treated in a vast literature from within and without; I can name only some of my favorites.

For Hinduism, I like Wendy Doniger's translation of the Rig-Veda and Laurie Patton's of the Bhagavad Gita; helpful interpretation is offered in Doniger's *On Hinduism* and Diana Eck's small gem, *Darśan: Seeing the Divine Image in India*.

On Buddhism, *For the Benefit of All Beings: A Commentary on the Way of the Bodhisattva*, by Tenzin Gyatso, the fourteenth Dalai Lama, stays close to the ancient texts, especially in Tibetan Buddhism. *Buddhist Scriptures*, edited by Donald Lopez, is broader. Western admirers include David Barash in *Buddhist Biology* and Robert Wright in *Why Buddhism Is True*, although both skip the mystical paths that many Buddhists follow. Robert Paul's *The Tibetan Symbolic World* is an insightful psychodynamic and anthropological study.

A widely used translation of the Qur'an is by Talal Itani. *No God but God*, by Reza Aslan, is a readable, sympathetic account of Islam's history, while *The Shia Revival*, by Vali Nasr, presents the great Sunni-Shia division. Mustafa Umar's *Welcome to Islam: A Step by Step Guide for New Muslims* tells you what to do from day one. *Muslims of the World: Portraits and Stories of Hope, Survival, Loss, and Love*, by Sajjad Shah and Iman Mahoui, provides varied and vivid accounts of the lives of believers.

My favorite translation of both the Jewish and Christian Bibles remains the King James Version, despite its errors and biases. There are many others, and a few clicks of the fingertips will lead the reader to synoptic linear parallel translations that fit any and all tastes.

In the vast literature of and about Christianity, I am fond of James M. Gustafson's concise and elegant *A Sense of the Divine*; Elaine Pagels's *The Gnostic Gospels*; Sarah Coakley's feminist theology in *God, Sexuality, and the Self*; C. S. Lewis's *Mere Christianity*; and T. M. Luhrmann's stunning ethnography of evangelicals, *When God Talks Back*. Thomas Jefferson tried to extract the philosophy from the theology in *The Jefferson Bible: The Life and Morals of Jesus of Nazareth*. Reinhold Niebuhr's *The Nature and Destiny of Man* is a classic of liberal Christian theology.

My go-to Jewish Bible is the Jewish Publication Society's *Tanakh* in Hebrew and English. The Steinsaltz Talmud has brought the shelf of books that form the foundation of rabbinical Judaism properly into English for the first time. Emanuel Feldman's *On Judaism: Conversations on Being Jewish in Today's World* is a readable guide to modern Orthodox belief and practice. David Wolpe's *The Healer of Shattered Hearts: A Jewish View of God* is a more liberal but equally impassioned view of Jewish faith. Efroim Oshry's *Responsa from the Holocaust* reveals the commitments of faithful Jews trying to do the right thing in the middle of an all-too-real collective nightmare.

Among my favorite novels about faith, including its dark side, are Nathaniel Hawthorne's *The Scarlet Letter*, George Eliot's (Mary Anne Evans's) *Middlemarch*, Fyodor Dostoevsky's *The Brothers Karamazov*, William Faulkner's *As I Lay Dying*, Graham Greene's *The Power and the Glory*, Irène Némirovsky's *Suite Française*, James Baldwin's *Go Tell*

It on the Mountain, Chaim Grade's *The Yeshiva*, Yukio Mishima's *The Temple of Dawn*, Isaac Bashevis *Singer's Yentl the Yeshiva Boy*, John Updike's *In the Beauty of the Lilies*, and Zoë Heller's *The Believers*.

For nonbelief, the works I rely on are not the recent attacks on religion that I criticize in this book, but less tendentious classics like Bertrand Russell's *Why I Am Not a Christian* and *Mysticism and Logic*, A. J. Ayer's *The Meaning of Life* and *The Central Questions of Philosophy*, and Thomas Nagel's *The View from Nowhere*. Of twenty-first-century books about nonbelief, my favorite is Jennifer Michael Hecht's *Doubt: A History*. Good-humored, balanced, richly historical, and warmly human, it shows that doubt is as old and as distinguished as faith and concludes that while faith is durable, doubt is better.

Notes

Introduction

xiii **titles of certain popular books:** Sam Harris, *The End of Faith: Religion, Terror, and the Future of Reason* (New York: W. W. Norton, 2004); Richard Dawkins, *The God Delusion* (New York: Houghton Mifflin Harcourt, 2006); Daniel Dennett, *Breaking the Spell: Religion as a Natural Phenomenon* (New York: Penguin, 2007); Christopher Hitchens, *God Is Not Great: How Religion Poisons Everything* (New York: Twelve Books, 2007).

xvi **I'll just call them "the Quartet":** For a conference inspired by these writers and including three of them, see *Beyond Belief: Science, Reason, Religion & Survival* (symposium, Salk Institute, La Jolla, CA, November 5–7, 2006), Science Network, http://thesciencenetwork .org/programs/beyond-belief-science-religion-reason-and-survival.

xvi **Rabbi David Wolpe:** David Wolpe, "A Rabbi and Hitchens Walk into a Bar . . . ," *Slate*, December 16, 2011, http://www.slate.com/articles/news_ and_politics/fighting_words/2011/12/christopher_hitchens_death_ rabbi_david_wolpe_on_what_it_was_like_to_debate_hitchens_.html.

xvi **I am on an online list:** Oval Pike, "Celebrity Atheists: More Prominent Than You Think," accessed October 28, 2018, https://ovalpike.com/ celebrity-atheists-more-prominent-than-you-think.

xvii **"What Can Be Done with the College Chapels?":** Matt Ridley, "The Genetic Code Genius Failed to Kill Faith," *Spectator*, September 26, 2006, https://www.spectator.co.uk/2006/09/the-genetic-code-genius -failed-to-kill-faith. See also Ridley's biography: *Francis Crick: Discoverer of the Genetic Code* (New York: HarperCollins Ebooks), 2012, 124.

xviii **"The simple fables of the religions"**: Ridley, *Francis Crick*, 124.

xviii **"I should perhaps emphasize this point"**: Ridley, *Francis Crick*, 124.

xviii **"Atheists I know who proudly wear"**: "Neil deGrasse Tyson: Atheist or Agnostic?" YouTube, published by Big Think, April 25, 2012, http://www.youtube.com/watch?v=CzSMC5rWvos. For a superb conversation between Tyson and Dawkins in which the subject of religion barely comes up, see "The Poetry of Science: Richard Dawkins and Neil deGrasse Tyson," YouTube, published by Richard Dawkins Foundation for Reason & Science, October 20, 2010, https://www.youtube.com/watch?v=9RExQFZzHXQ.

xviii **"I'm not having it"**: Steven Weinberg, keynote address, *Beyond Belief* symposium, Session 1, MP4 video, about 0:27:30, http://s3.amazonaws.com/thesciencenetwork/GoogleVideos%2FBB-1.mp4.

xviii **"If not religion, what?"**: Steven Weinberg, at *Beyond Belief* symposium, Session 2, MP4 video, about 1:07:50, http://s3.amazonaws.com/thesciencenetwork/GoogleVideos%2FBB-2.mp4.

xix **"I won't miss her at all"**: Richard Dawkins, presentation at *Beyond Belief* symposium, Session 3, MP4 video, about 0:30:20, http://s3.amazonaws.com/thesciencenetwork/GoogleVideos%2FBB-3.mp4.

xix **Western Europe has experienced**: Gabe Bullard, "The World's Newest Major Religion: No Religion," *National Geographic*, April 22, 2016, https://news.nationalgeographic.com/2016/04/160422-atheism-agnostic-secular-nones-rising-religion.

xix **population growth among the religious**: Pew Research Center, "The Future of World Religions: Population Growth Projections, 2010–2050," April 2, 2015, http://www.pewforum.org/2015/04/02/religious-projections-2010-2050/#projected-growth-map.

xx **"We are, by our very nature"**: Wulf Schiefenhövel, "Explaining the Inexplicable: Traditional and Syncretistic Religiosity in Melanesia," in *The Biological Evolution of Religious Mind and Behavior*, ed. Eckart Voland and Wulf Schiefenhövel (Berlin: Springer, 2009), 143.

xxi **"There are six billion people"**: Francisco Ayala, at *Beyond Belief* symposium, Session 3, about 47:00.

xxiii **"the credibility of the Bible rises"**: Joan Roughgarden, at *Beyond Belief* symposium, Session 3, about 17:40.

xxiii **"it's not irrational for someone"**: Joan Roughgarden, at *Beyond Belief* symposium, Session 3, about 18:06 and 18:41.

xxiv **The Qur'an seems to condone violence:** Javed Ahmad Ghamidi, "The Islamic Law of Jihad," *Renaissance Monthly Journal*, June 1, 2002, http://www.javedahmadghamidi.com/renaissance/view/the-islamic -law-of-jihad-part-1–2. Like almost all Muslim theologians, Ghamidi insists that these verses, if understood in context, do not offer blanket approval of violence.

Chapter 1: Encounters

3 **"Nothing nothings itself":** This statement, *Das nichts selbst nichtet* in German, is also translated as "Nothing itself nothings," and is criticized along with many other such "pseudo-statements" in Rudolph Carnap's "The Elimination of Metaphysics through Logical Analysis of Language," a foundational text of analytic philosophy. Carnap cites it from Heidegger's *Was ist Metaphysik?* ("What is Metaphysics?"). See the translation of Carnap's paper—originally published as "Überwindung der Metaphysik durch logische Analyse der Sprache," *Erkentniss* 2 (1932): 60–81—by Arthur Pap, https://philpapers.org/archive/TEO .pdf, p. 69.

4 **"If the being of phenomena":** Jean-Paul Sartre, *Being and Nothingness: A Phenomenological Essay on Ontology*, trans. Hazel P. Barnes (New York: Washington Square Press, 1956), 8–9.

4 **"Phenomenology as the science":** Donn Welton, *The Essential Husserl: Basic Writings in Transcendental Phenomenology* (Bloomington: University of Indiana, 1999), 333.

4 **"To make itself understandable":** Martin Heidegger, *Contributions to Philosophy (of the Event)*, trans. Richard Rojcewicz and Daniela Vallega-Neu (Bloomington: University of Indiana Press, 1999), 344.

4 **"Only a god can save us":** M. P. Alter and J. D. Caputo, trans., "Only a God Can Save Us: Der Spiegel's Interview with Martin Heidegger," *Philosophy Today* 20, no. 4 (Winter 1976): 267–85, reprinted in Richard Wolin, *The Heidegger Controversy: A Critical Reader* (Cambridge, MA: MIT Press, 1998), 91–116.

8 **Mill's father taught him:** John Stuart Mill, *The Autobiography of John Stuart Mill* (1873; repr., London: Penguin, 1989), 52.

8 **Bertrand Russell, in his 1927 essay:** Bertrand Russell, "Why I Am Not a Christian," reprinted in *Bertrand Russell on God and Religion*, ed. Al Seckel (Buffalo, NY: Prometheus Books, 1986), 59.

8 **"If there can be anything"**: Russell, "Why I Am Not a Christian," 60.

9 **Third, anthropology would help:** Jared Diamond's book *Guns, Germs, and Steel* expressed this outlook well, although, as he understood, materialist anthropologists had been pursuing it for generations. Jared M. Diamond, *Guns, Germs, and Steel: The Fates of Human Societies* (New York: W. W. Norton, 1997). See also Lawrence A. Kuznar and Stephen K. Sanderson, eds., *Studying Societies and Cultures: Marvin Harris's Cultural Materialism and Its Legacy* (Boulder, CO: Paradigm, 2007).

9 **"The one thing that science"**: Steven Weinberg, keynote address, at *Beyond Belief: Science, Reason, Religion & Survival* (symposium, Salk Institute, La Jolla, CA, November 5–7, 2006), Science Network, Session 1, MP4 video, about 25:40, http://s3.amazonaws.com/thesciencenetwork/GoogleVideos%2FBB-1.mp4.

Chapter 2: Varieties

15 **"the feelings, acts and experiences"**: William James, *The Varieties of Religious Experience: A Study of Human Nature, Being the Gifford Lectures on Natural Religion Delivered at Edinburgh in 1901–1902*, in *Writings 1902–1910*, ed. Bruce Kucklick (New York: Library of America, 1902), 36.

15 **"theologies, philosophies, orthodoxies"**: Peter Steinfels, "Beliefs: After 100 Years, William James's 'Varieties,' Maybe Not Flawless, Resonates Nonetheless," *New York Times*, March 2, 2002, http://www.nytimes.com/2002/03/09/nyregion/beliefs-after-100-years-william-james-s-varieties-maybe-not-flawless-resonates.html.

15 **"Let us imagine that we think"**: Charles Taylor, *The Varieties of Religious Life Today: William James Revisited* (Cambridge, MA: Harvard University Press, 2003), 23–24.

16 **"The world of our present consciousness"**: James, *Varieties of Religious Experience*, 463.

16 **"I can, of course"**: James, *Varieties of Religious Experience*, 463.

17 **"an impartial science of religions"**: James, *Varieties of Religious Experience*, 456.

18 **"The *subconscious self* is nowadays"**: James, *Varieties of Religious Experience*, 457–58.

19 **"since the relation may be"**: James, *Varieties of Religious Experience*, 36.

Notes

19 **"allies it to the feeling of dependence"**: James, *Varieties of Religious Experience*, 32–33.

19 **"Modern transcendental idealism"**: James, *Varieties of Religious Experience*, 36.

20 **"Through the transparent darkness"**: This and the following quotes come from Ralph Waldo Emerson, "Divinity School Address" in *Nature: Addresses and Lectures* (1849), republished online at Ralph Waldo Emerson, accessed September 3, 2018, http://www.emersoncentral.com/divaddr.htm. James's comments on Emerson are from James, *Varieties of Religious Experience*, 38–40.

21 **"What is finally indisputable"**: James M. Gustafson, *A Sense of the Divine: The Natural Environment from a Theocentric Perspective* (Cleveland, OH: Pilgrim Press, 1994), 44.

22 **"Awe—the sense that"**: Emanuel Feldman, email message to the author, approximately 2014.

22 **"A religious life . . . does tend"**: James, *Varieties of Religious Experience*, 15.

22 **"the pattern-setters . . . individuals"**: James, *Varieties of Religious Experience*, 15.

22 **"Few of us are not in some way"**: James, *Varieties of Religious Experience*, 30.

23 **"God is more real to me"**: James, *Varieties of Religious Experience*, 70–71.

24 **"a composite photograph of universal saintliness"**: James, *Varieties of Religious Experience*, 249–51.

24 **"Francis of Assisi kisses his lepers"**: James, *Varieties of Religious Experience*, 261.

24 **"Hindu fakirs, Buddhist monks, and"**: James, *Varieties of Religious Experience*, 291.

24 As for **"cosmic or mystic consciousness"**: James, *Varieties of Religious Experience*, 361–62. James is, in part, quoting Swami Vivekananda's book *Raja Yoga*; he cites it as published in English in 1896. For an online copy, accessed September 3, 2018, see http://shardsofconsciousness.com/user/sites/shardsofconsciousness.com/files/ebooks/RajaYoga_Vivekananda.pdf.

25 **"The Science of the Sufis"**: James, *Varieties of Religious Experience*, 363.

25 **Al-Ghazali recounts the discipline:** James, *Varieties of Religious Experience*, 363–66. He cites A. Schmölders, *Essai sur les écoles philosophiques chez les Arabes* (Paris: Firmin Didot, 1842), 54–68, abridged.

25 **Some Sufis whirl in ceremonial dress:** Annemarie Schimmel, *Mystical Dimensions of Islam* (Chapel Hill: University of North Carolina Press, 1975). Schimmel confirms the general framework of Islamic mysticism as described by James. For a video of Sufis whirling, see "The Sufi Whirling Dervishes of Istanbul," YouTube, published by 4transform, August 22, 2007, https://www.youtube.com/watch?v=L_Cf-ZxDfZA.

25 **"keep more sane and true":** James, *Varieties of Religious Experience*, 463.

26 **"The future of psychology":** These quotations are from Peter Gay, *Freud: A Life for Our Time* (New York: W. W. Norton, 1988), 211–12.

27 **"the earth, which quakes":** Sigmund Freud, *The Future of an Illusion*, trans. James Strachey (1927; repr. New York: W. W. Norton, 1961), 15–16.

27 **"Impersonal forces and destinies":** Freud, *Future of an Illusion*, 16–17.

28 **"Life in this world serves":** Freud, *Future of an Illusion*, 18–19.

28 **"pious America laid claim":** Freud, *Future of an Illusion*, 19.

28 **"we are met with three answers":** Freud, *Future of an Illusion*, 26–27.

29 **"They are full of contradictions":** Freud, *Future of an Illusion*, 27.

29 **"desperate efforts" to "evade the problem":** Freud, *Future of an Illusion*, 28.

29 **"the philosophy of 'As if' ":** Freud, *Future of an Illusion*, 28.

29 **"the admission that something is absurd":** Freud, *Future of an Illusion*, 29.

30 **"We may expect that people will":** Freud, *Future of an Illusion*, 28–29.

30 **Religion is "the universal obsessional neurosis":** Freud, *Future of an Illusion*, 43.

30 **"devout believers are safeguarded":** Freud, *Future of an Illusion*, 44.

30 **" 'Man has imperative needs' ":** Freud, *Future of an Illusion*, 35.

30 **"Men cannot remain children for ever":** Freud, *Future of an Illusion*, 49.

30 **"the voice of the intellect":** Freud, *Future of an Illusion*, 53.

31 **"Have you learned nothing from history?":** Freud, *Future of an Illusion*, 46.

31 **"to deprive people of all stimulants":** Freud, *Future of an Illusion*, 49.

31 **"Psychology has profited greatly":** Carl Jung, *Modern Man in Search of a Soul*, trans. W. S. Dell and Cary F. Baynes (New York: Harcourt Brace Jovanovich, 1933), 41.

32 **"This is a regrettable error"**: Jung, *Modern Man*, 41.
32 **"the way to a normally disillusioned life"**: Jung, *Modern Man*, 46.
32 **"that the elements of the psyche"**: Jung, *Modern Man*, 58.
32 **"hygienic ... a goal towards which"**: Jung, *Modern Man*, 112.
32 **"are suffering from no clinically definable neurosis"**: Jung, *Modern Man*, 61.
33 **"the matter-of-fact and the commonplace"**: Jung, *Modern Man*, 65–66.
33 **"Truth to tell, I have"**: Jung, *Modern Man*, 66.
33 **"To the psychologist there is nothing"**: Jung, *Modern Man*, 73.
33 **"a positive value to all religions"**: Jung, *Modern Man*, 119.
33 **"that man has, everywhere and always"**: Jung, *Modern Man*, 122–23.

Chapter 3: Elementary Forms

35 **Consider the scene:** What follows is my own participant-observer account. For a vivid and authentic film, see John Marshall, *N/um Tchai: The Ceremonial Dance of the !Kung Bushmen*, !Kung Series (Watertown, MA: Documentary Educational Resources, 1969), http://www.der.org/films/num-tchai.html. Films of /Gwi and !Ko Bushman trance dances by Irenäus Eibl-Eibesfeldt may be found in the Human Ethology Film Archive, accessed November 10, 2018, http://www.humanetho.de/en/EIWF2.html (search on "Trancetanz").

37 **three experts on this ritual:** Lorna Marshall, "The Medicine Dance of the !Kung Bushmen," *Africa* 39 (1981): 347–81; Richard Lee, "The Sociology of !Kung Bushman Trance Performances," in *Trance and Possession States*, ed. R. Prince (Montreal: Bucke Memorial Society, 1968), 35–54; Richard Katz, *Boiling Energy: Community Healing among the Kalahari !Kung* (Cambridge, MA: Harvard University Press, 1982).

41 **"A missionary heard a Chiriquane woman":** Edward B. Tylor, *Primitive Culture: Researches into the Development of Mythology, Philosophy, Religion, Art, and Custom*, vol. 2 (London: John Murray, 1871), 6. Available on Google Books at https://books.google.com/books?id=eW11O76PNK4C&pg =PA183&dq=%22in+tasmania,+a+native%22+tylor&hl=en&sa=X&ved =oahUKEwizt6y_8cneAhWrGDQIHTd7ANUQ6AEILjAB#v=onep age&q=the%20cases%20in%20which%20disease%20possession&f=false.

41 **"a portion of the wide doctrine":** Tylor, *Primitive Culture*, 7.
41 **"As it seems that the first conception":** Tylor, *Primitive Culture*, 15.
41 **San hunter-gatherers believed:** Lorna J. Marshall, *Nyae Nyae !Kung:*

Beliefs and Rites (Cambridge, MA: Harvard University Press, 1999); Megan Biesele, *Women Like Meat: The Folklore and Foraging Ideology of the Kalahari Ju/'hoan* (Johannesburg, South Africa: Witwatersrand University Press, 1993); Megan Biesele, *Ju/'hoan Folktales: Transcriptions and English Translations: A Literacy Primer by and for Youth and Adults of the Ju/'hoan Community* (Bloomington, IN: Trafford, 2009).

41 **"All argument is against it"**: Tylor, *Primitive Culture*, 21.

42 **"Zulu Dante"**: Tylor, *Primitive Culture*, 46.

42 **"St. Patrick's Purgatory"**: Tylor, *Primitive Culture*, 50.

42 **"the bright dwelling"**: Tylor, *Primitive Culture*, 63.

42 **Recent observations confirm**: Brian Lehmann, "The Living Dead," *National Geographic*, April 2016, https://www.brianlehmann.com/national-geographic-the-living-dead.

42 **For the Basuto, "shades wander about"**: Tylor, *Primitive Culture*, 73.

42 **"I would rather follow the plough"**: Homer, *The Odyssey of Homer*, trans. Richmond Lattimore (New York: Harper & Row, 1967), xx.

42 **"Patagonians lived in terror"**: Tylor, *Primitive Culture*, 102.

42 **"The cases in which disease-possession"**: Tylor, *Primitive Culture*, 119.

43 **"devotional calculating machine"**: Tylor, *Primitive Culture*, 337.

43 **"As prayer is a request made"**: Tylor, *Primitive Culture*, 340.

43 **"In Tasmania, a native has been heard"**: Tylor, *Primitive Culture*, 183.

43 **"for there seems no human thought"**: Tylor, *Primitive Culture*, 409.

44 **"The criticism . . . loses much"**: Robert Redfield, introduction to *Magic, Science, and Religion and Other Essays*, by Bronislaw Malinowski (1948; repr., Garden City, NY: Doubleday, 1954).

Chapter 4: The God Map

46 **"set Dr. Persinger's theories"**: *Horizon*, "God on the Brain—Transcript," BBC, September 14, 2014, http://www.bbc.co.uk/science/horizon/2003/godonbraintrans.shtml.

47 **"I was a failure"**: Richard Dawkins, at *Beyond Belief: Science, Reason, Religion & Survival* (symposium, Salk Institute, La Jolla, CA, November 5–7, 2006), Session 4, about 1:09:35 and 1:23:40, http://thesciencenetwork.org/programs/beyond-belief-science-religion-reason-and-survival/session-4-1.

47 **"Well, so what?"**: V. S. Ramachandran, at *Beyond Belief* symposium, Session 4, about 54:00.

48 **"Scientific theories are organically conditioned":** William James, *The Varieties of Religious Experience: A Study of Human Nature, Being the Gifford Lectures on Natural Religion Delivered at Edinburgh in 1901– 1902*, in *Writings 1902–1910*, ed. Bruce Kucklick (New York: Library of America, 1902), 21–22.

48 **"The air was filled with a big noise":** Fyodor Dostoyevsky, cited in O. Devinsky and G. Lai, "Spirituality and Religion in Epilepsy," *Epilepsy & Behavior* 12 (2008): 638.

48 **In a study of 11 patients:** B. Å. Hansen and E. Brodtkorb, "Partial Epilepsy with 'Ecstatic' Seizures," *Epilepsy & Behavior* 4 (2003): 669–70.

49 **A bus driver was depressed:** K. Dewhurst and A. W. Beard, "Sudden Religious Conversions in Temporal Lobe Epilepsy," *Epilepsy & Behavior* 4 (2003): 79. First published 1970.

50 **In 2012, Tracy Butler in their lab:** T. Butler et al., "Neuroimaging of Frontal-Limbic Dysfunction in Schizophrenia and Epilepsy-Related Psychosis: Toward a Convergent Neurobiology," *Epilepsy & Behavior* 23, no. 2 (2012): 113–22.

50 **buzz from "the God helmet":** L. S. St. Pierre and M. A. Persinger, "Experimental Facilitation of the Sensed Presence Is Predicted by the Specific Patterns of the Applied Magnetic Fields, Not by Suggestibility: Re-analyses of 19 Experiments," *International Journal of Neuroscience* 116, no. 9 (2006): 1080.

50 **But one double-blind study:** P. Granqvist et al., "Sensed Presence and Mystical Experiences Are Predicted by Suggestibility, Not by the Application of Transcranial Weak Complex Magnetic Fields," *Neuroscience Letters* 379, no. 1 (2005): 1–6.

50 **The dispute continues:** M. A. Persinger and S. A. Koren, "A Response to Granqvist et al. 'Sensed Presence and Mystical Experiences Are Predicted by Suggestibility, Not by the Application of Transcranial Weak Magnetic Fields,'" *Neuroscience Letters* 380, no. 3 (2005): 346–47 (author reply, 348–50); St. Pierre and Persinger, "Experimental Facilitation of the Sensed Presence."

50 **"Experimental neuroscience must appreciate":** U. Schjoedt, "The Religious Brain: A General Introduction to the Experimental Neuroscience of Religion," *Method & Theory in the Study of Religion* 21, no. 3 (2009): 313.

51 **Schjoedt interprets the deactivation:** U. Schjødt et al., "Rewarding Prayers," *Neuroscience Letters* 443, no. 3 (2008): 165–68; U. Schjoedt et al., "The Power of Charisma—Perceived Charisma Inhibits the Frontal Executive Network of Believers in Intercessory Prayer," *Social Cognitive and Affective Neuroscience* 6, no. 1 (2011): 119–27.

51 **"fantastic visual hallucinations":** John Smythies, at *Beyond Belief* symposium, Session 4, 1:02:25 and following. See also A. L. Halberstadt and M. A. Geyer, "Multiple Receptors Contribute to the Behavioral Effects of Indoleamine Hallucinogens," *Neuropharmacology* 61, no. 3 (2011): 364–81.

52 **"One study ... took a group":** Smythies's account here is a useful simplification. For details, see Jacqueline Borg et al., "The Serotonin System and Spiritual Experiences," *American Journal of Psychiatry* 160, no. 11 (2003): 1965–69.

52 **In Italy, Cosimo Urgesi and:** C. Urgesi et al., "The Spiritual Brain: Selective Cortical Lesions Modulate Human Self-Transcendence," *Neuron* 65, no. 3 (2010): 309–19.

53 **In two studies in Missouri:** B. Johnstone et al., "Right Parietal Lobe-Related 'Selflessness' as the Neuropsychological Basis of Spiritual Transcendence," *International Journal for the Psychology of Religion* 22, no. 4 (2012): 267–84.

53 **They suggest that selflessness ranges:** Johnstone et al., "Right Parietal Lobe-Related 'Selflessness,'" 280.

53 **Paul Butler's group in Boston:** P. M. Butler, P. McNamara, and R. Durso, "Deficits in the Automatic Activation of Religious Concepts in Patients with Parkinson's Disease," *Journal of the International Neuropsychological Society* 16, no. 2 (2010): 252–61; P. M. Butler, P. McNamara, and R. Durso, "Side of Onset in Parkinson's Disease and Alterations in Religiosity: Novel Behavioral Phenotypes," *Behavioural Neurology* 24, no. 2 (2011): 133–41.

54 **In the next study, the researchers:** Butler, McNamara, and Durso, "Side of Onset in Parkinson's Disease," 134.

55 **A study led by Erik Asp:** E. Asp, K. Ramchandran, and D. Tranel, "Authoritarianism, Religious Fundamentalism, and the Human Prefrontal Cortex," *Neuropsychology* 26, no. 4 (2012): 414–21; see also A. Damasio, *Descartes' Error: Emotion, Reason, and the Human Brain* (New York: G. P. Putnam's Sons, 1994).

Notes

55 **The husband of one saw her:** Asp, Ramchandran, and Tranel, "Authoritarianism," 418. See also E. Asp and D. Tranel, "False Tagging Theory: Toward a Unitary Account of Prefrontal Cortex Function," in *Principles of Frontal Lobe Function*, ed. D. T. Stuss and R. T. Knight (New York: Oxford University Press, 2013), 390.

55 **Tony, a 42-year-old surgeon:** O. Sacks, *Musicophilia: Tales of Music and the Brain* (New York: Knopf, 2007), 4.

56 **it was the future I saw":** Sacks, *Musicophilia*, 30.

56 **"hallucinations in the sane":** Sacks, *Musicophilia*, 61.

57 **Two scientists in Montreal:** M. Beauregard and V. Paquette, "Neural Correlates of a Mystical Experience in Carmelite Nuns," *Neuroscience Letters* 405, no. 3 (2006): 186–90.

58 **Eugene d'Aquili and Andrew Newberg:** A. B. Newberg and E. G. d'Aquili, "The Neuropsychology of Religious and Spiritual Experience," *Journal of Consciousness Studies* 7, no. 11–12 (2000): 251–66.

58 **Flow is energetic:** This state was beautifully defined by Mihaly Csikszentmihalyi in his book *Flow: The Psychology of Optimal Experience* (New York: Harper & Row, 1990).

58 **my Bushman trance-dance experience:** For other examples of dance-induced states, see William McNeill, *Keeping Together in Time: Dance and Drill in Human History* (Cambridge, MA: Harvard University, 1995).

59 **David Silbersweig collaborated:** D. R. Vago and D. A. Silbersweig, "Self-Awareness, Self-Regulation, and Self-Transcendence (S-ART): A Framework for Understanding the Neurobiological Mechanisms of Mindfulness," *Frontiers in Human Neuroscience* 6 (2012): 296.

59 **In an elegant brain-imaging experiment:** J. S. Mascaro et al., "Compassion Meditation Enhances Empathic Accuracy and Related Neural Activity," *Social Cognitive and Affective Neuroscience* 8, no. 1 (2013): 48–55.

60 **When someone in either group said yes:** S. Harris et al., "The Neural Correlates of Religious and Nonreligious Belief," *PLoS One* 4, no. 10 (2009): e0007272, p. 6.

60 **"an internally oriented neural stream":** M. J. Hove et al., "Brain Network Reconfiguration and Perceptual Decoupling during an Absorptive State of Consciousness," *Cerebral Cortex* 26, no. 7 (2016): 3116.

61 including **"greater functional connectivity"**: F. Hoeft et al., "Functional Brain Basis of Hypnotizability," *Archives of General Psychiatry* 69, no. 10 (2012): 1064–72.

Chapter 5: Harvesting Faith

65 **In one set of experiments:** C. S. Pomerleau and O. F. Pomerleau, "Euphoriant Effects of Nicotine in Smokers," *Psychopharmacology* 108 (1992): 460–65.

65 **and it is correlated with psychosis:** W. A. van Gastel et al., "Cigarette Smoking and Cannabis Use Are Equally Strongly Associated with Psychotic-like Experiences: A Cross-Sectional Study in 1929 Young Adults," *Psychological Medicine* 43, no. 11 (2013): 2393–401.

65 **nicotine has been found in mummies' hair:** J. Echeverría and H. M. Niemeyer, "Nicotine in the Hair of Mummies from San Pedro de Atacama (Northern Chile)," *Journal of Archaeological Science* 40, no. 10 (2013): 3561–68; S. Tushingham et al., "Hunter-Gatherer Tobacco Smoking: Earliest Evidence from the Pacific Northwest Coast of North America," *Journal of Archaeological Science* 40, no. 2 (2013): 1397–407.

65 **Among the Algonquins, "smoking was indulged in":** Ralph Linton, *Use of Tobacco among the North American Indians* (Chicago: Field Museum of Natural History, 1924), 23.

66 **Smoking together, the parties invoked:** J. N. B. Hewitt, quoted in Linton, *Use of Tobacco*, 26.

66 **"All these peoples":** Joseph Epes Brown, *The Sacred Pipe: Black Elk's Account of the Seven Rites of the Oglala Sioux* (Norman: University of Oklahoma Press, 1953), Kindle ed., chap. 1, para. 5. See also Raymond A. Bucko, *The Lakota Ritual of the Sweat Lodge: History and Contemporary Practice* (Lincoln: University of Nebraska Press, 1998).

66 **Shaman healers among the Warao:** Johannes Wilbert, "Tobacco and Shamanistic Ecstasy among the Warao Indians of Venezuela," in *Flesh of the Gods: The Ritual Use of Hallucinogens*, ed. P. T. Furst (1972; repr., Prospect Heights, IL: Waveland Press, 1990), 62–63.

66 **"acuteness of vision, night vision":** Johannes Wilbert, *Tobacco and Shamanism in South America* (New Haven, CT: Yale University Press, 1993), 194–96.

Notes

67 **"The jaguar-man takes . . . nicotine":** Wilbert, *Tobacco and Shamanism in South America*, 198.

67 **Among the Mapuche of Chile:** Wilbert, *Tobacco and Shamanism in South America*, 121.

67 **but their shamans *snuffed* tobacco:** Joseph C. Winter, "Traditional Uses of Tobacco by Native Americans," in *Tobacco Use by Native North Americans: Sacred Smoke and Silent Killer*, ed. J. C. Winter (Norman: University of Oklahoma Press, 2001), 9–58.

68 **Kava root broth, drunk for centuries:** Tyler Fuller, a student of theology and public health, writes, "I can attest to this. I lived in Fiji for 2.5 years as a peace corps volunteer and drank my share of Kava. In Vanuatu they forgo steeping Kava root in water and grind it to drink the concentrated juices, it is said to be much stronger and fast acting than kava root that is steeped in water to make a broth." Tyler Fuller, email message to the author, August 28, 2018.

71 **"in mock ecstasies among the thickets":** Euripides, *The Bacchae*, in *Euripides III*, ed. David Grene and Richmond Lattimore (New York: Modern Library/Random House, 1959), 367–68.

71 **"the loosing of cares":** Euripides, *Bacchae*, 373.

71 **"To rich and poor he gives":** Euripides, *Bacchae*, 373–75, 391.

71 **"The gods have many shapes":** Euripides, *Bacchae*, 424.

71 **Wherever grains or grapes were sown:** Patrick E. McGovern, *Uncorking the Past: The Quest for Wine, Beer, and Other Alcoholic Beverages* (Berkeley: University of California Press, 2009). It is becoming increasingly routine to analyze archeological specimens for traces of wine and beer, among other mind-altering substances.

72 **"We are talking about a festival":** Alan Boyle, "Sex and Booze Figured in Egyptian Rites: Archaeologists Find Evidence for Ancient Version of 'Girls Gone Wild,'" NBCNews.com, October 30, 2006, http://www.nbcnews.com/id/15475319/ns/technology_and_science-science/t/sex-booze-figured-egyptian-rites/#.W8O5ovlReMI.

72 **"They sail men and women together":** Herodotus, *The History of Herodotus*, vol. 1, trans. G. C. Macaulay (London: MacMillan, 1890), Project Gutenberg EBook, http://www.gutenberg.org/files/2707/2707-h/2707-h.htm#link22H_4_0001.

73 **During the thousand years between:** Dan Stanislawski, "Dionysus Westward: Early Religion and the Economic Geography of Wine,"

Notes

Geography Review 65, no. 4 (1975): 427–44. This superb, extensively referenced article is the main source of the account that follows.

73 **"activist and explosive fervor":** Stanislawski, "Dionysus Westward," 428.

73 **"The ancient cults of fertility":** Stanislawski, "Dionysus Westward," 435–36.

74 **"The sway of alcohol over mankind":** William James, *The Varieties of Religious Experience: A Study of Human Nature, Being the Gifford Lectures on Natural Religion Delivered at Edinburgh in 1901–1902*, in *Writings 1902–1910*, ed. Bruce Kucklick (New York: Library of America, 1902), 348–49.

74 **"If all the goblet's bliss were o'er":** Anacreon, *Odes of Anacreon*, trans. Thomas Moore, in *The Poetical Works of Thomas Moore*, ed. Charles Kent (London: G. Routledge, 1883), 21 ("Ode LXXVIII"), Google Books, https://books.google.com/books?id=M5M-AAAAIAAJ&pg=PA21&dq =if+all+the+goblet%27s+bliss+were+o%27er&hl=en&sa=X&ved=0ah UKEwjjyYT96InfAhVvS98KHUfTBkMQ6AEIKjAA#v=snippet&q= %22if%20all%20the%20goblet's%20bliss%22&f=false.

75 **Hashish and marijuana have long been:** R. Mechoulam and L. A. Parker, "The Endocannabinoid System and the Brain," *Annual Review of Psychology* 64 (2013): 22.

75 **"the drug that takes away the mind":** Mechoulam and Parker, "Endocannabinoid System," 22.

75 **Hashish was popular:** Richard Schultes, Albert Hofmann, and Christian Rätsch, *Plants of the Gods: Their Sacred, Healing, and Hallucinogenic Powers*, rev. and exp. edition (Rochester, VT: Healing Arts Press, 1998), 101. This classic by two leading scientists in the field of psychoactive plants is updated here by Rätsch.

75 **Buddha himself was said to have lived:** He later left asceticism in favor of "the Middle Way."

76 **The brain's own cannabis:** Mechoulam and Parker, "Endocannabinoid System," 26.

76 **phantasms can be unpleasant:** D. C. D'Souza et al., "The Psychotomimetic Effects of Intravenous Delta-9-Tetrahydrocannabinol in Healthy Individuals: Implications for Psychosis," *Neuropsychopharmacology* 29, no. 8 (2004): 1558–72.

76 **THC, the active ingredient:** Δ9-THC, delta-9-tetrahydrocannabinol.

76 **But our natural cannabinoids:** B. M. Fonseca et al., "Endogenous Can-

nabinoids Revisited: A Biochemistry Perspective," *Prostaglandins & Other Lipid Mediators* 102–3 (2013): 13–30.

76 **Cannabis indirectly stimulates:** P. D. Morrison and R. M. Murray, "From Real-World Events to Psychosis: The Emerging Neuropharmacology of Delusions," *Schizophrenia Bulletin* 35, no. 4 (2009): 668–74.

76 **"fly agaric":** A mushroom is the fruiting body of a fungus. "Agaric" just means a fungus that yields a mushroom; this one used to be crumbled into a saucer of milk to catch flies, and an old idea holds that a fly entering someone's head could cause madness.

77 **"The Tremyugan shaman begins":** Mircea Eliade, *Shamanism: Archaic Techniques of Ecstasy* (1951; repr., Princeton, NJ: Princeton University Press, 2004), 220.

77 **"the technique is markedly different":** Eliade, *Shamanism*, 220–21.

77 **"Ecstasy through intoxication":** Eliade, *Shamanism*, 221.

78 **"He had snatched me":** Quoted by Schultes, Hofmann, and Rätsch, *Plants of the Gods*, 85.

79 **In studies by Roland Griffiths:** R. R. Griffiths et al., "Psilocybin Can Occasion Mystical-Type Experiences Having Substantial and Sustained Personal Meaning and Spiritual Significance," *Psychopharmacology* 187 (2006): 268–83.

79 **"Two of the eight volunteers":** Griffiths et al., "Psilocybin Can Occasion," 279.

80 **The positive changes persisted:** R. Griffiths et al., "Mystical-Type Experiences Occasioned by Psilocybin Mediate the Attribution of Personal Meaning and Spiritual Significance 14 Months Later," *Journal of Psychopharmacology* 22, no. 6 (2008): 621–32.

80 **They had predictable dose-response reactions:** R. R. Griffiths et al., "Psilocybin Occasioned Mystical-Type Experiences: Immediate and Persisting Dose-Related Effects," *Psychopharmacology* 218, no. 4 (2011): 649–65.

80 **"There is a world beyond ours":** Schultes, Hofmann, and Rätsch, *Plants of the Gods*, 156.

81 **"Woman who thunders am I":** Schultes, Hofmann, and Rätsch, *Plants of the Gods*, 159.

81 **"I take the 'little one who springs up'":** Schultes, Hofmann, and Rätsch, *Plants of the Gods*, 163.

81 **"Few sensory experiences can match":** Glenn H. Shepard, "A Sensory

Ecology of Medicinal Plant Therapy in Two Amazonian Societies,"
American Anthropologist 106, no. 2 (2004): 257.

82 **"You're sitting in the hammock"**: Fernando Payaguaje, quoted in
Steven F. White, "Shamanic Ayahuasca Narratives and Production of
Neo-Indigenista Literature," *Latin American Indian Literatures Journal*
17, no. 2 (2001): 113–14.

82 **"Songs are a shaman's most"**: Graham Townsley, "Song Paths: The
Ways and Means of Yaminahua Shamanic Knowledge," *L'Homme* 33,
no. 126 (1993): 457.

83 **"Painted cliff people . . ."**: Townsley, "Song Paths," 464.

83 **The Huichol put peyote "above wine"**: Peter T. Furst, "To Find Our
Life: Peyote among the Huichol Indians of Mexico," in *Flesh of the
Gods: The Ritual Use of Hallucinogens*, ed. Peter T. Furst (1972; repr.,
Prospect Heights, IL: Waveland Press, 1990), 136.

83 **"powers of creation"**: Furst, "To Find Our Life," 138.

83 **"The night was passed in singing"**: Furst, "To Find Our Life," 180–81.

84 **"These names are said to emerge"**: Furst, "To Find Our Life," 180–81.

84 **"Nothing but flowers here . . ."**: Furst, "To Find Our Life," 184.

Chapter 6: Convergences

85 **a.k.a., the Good Friday Experiment:** Walter N. Pahnke, "Drugs and
Mysticism: An Analysis of the Relationship between Psychedelic
Drugs and the Mystical Consciousness" (PhD diss., Harvard University, 1963); Walter N. Pahnke, "Drugs and Mysticism," *International
Journal of Parapsychology* 8, no. 2 (1966): 295–313, http://www.erowid
.org/entheogens/journals/entheogens_journal3.shtml.

85 **But in a long-term follow-up:** Rick Doblin, "Pahnke's 'Good Friday
Experiment': A Long-Term Follow-up and Methodological Critique," *Journal of Transpersonal Psychology* 23, no. 1 (1991): 1–28.

86 **"experimental subjects wrote that"**: Doblin, "Pahnke's 'Good Friday
Experiment,'" 12.

87 **"I saw a light coming out of the sky"**: This and the following quotes
are from Doblin, "Pahnke's 'Good Friday Experiment,'" 14–21.

89 **A recent study used the shamans' potion:** Rachel Harris and Lee Gurel,
"A Study of Ayahuasca Use in North America," *Journal of Psychoactive
Drugs* 44, no. 3 (2012): 209–15.

90 **"A shaman or leader was present"**: Harris and Gurel, "Study of Ayahuasca Use," 211–12.

90 **"emotional triggers":** This and the following quotes are from Harris and Gurel, "Study of Ayahuasca Use," 212–13.

91 **"I have tasted the sweet drink of life . . .":** Wendy Doniger O'Flaherty, *The Rig Veda, an Anthology: One Hundred and Eight Hymns, Selected, Translated and Annotated* (Hammondsworth, England: Penguin, 1981), mandala 8, hymn 48.

92 **perhaps hemp's original home:** H. E. Jiang et al., "A New Insight into *Cannabis sativa* (Cannabaceae) Utilization from 2500-Year-Old Yanghai Tombs, Xinjiang, China," *Journal of Ethnopharmacology* 108, no. 3 (2006): 414–22.

92 **The popular Shinto religion:** William P. Fairchild, "Shamanism in Japan," *Folklore Studies* 21 (1962): 1–122.

93 **enabling "unrestrained cognition":** R. L. Carhart-Harris et al., "Neural Correlates of the Psychedelic State as Determined by fMRI Studies with Psilocybin," *Proceedings of the National Academy of Sciences of the USA* 109, no. 6 (2012): 2138–43; "Dr. Robin Carhart-Harris— Psilocybin and the Psychedelic State," Vimeo, accessed December 7, 2018, http://vimeo.com/44412867.

93 **The psilocybin effects may resemble:** R. L. Carhart-Harris et al., "Functional Connectivity Measures after Psilocybin Inform a Novel Hypothesis of Early Psychosis," *Schizophrenia Bulletin* 39, no. 6 (2013): 1343–51.

94 **an internal network active when:** This network includes the medial prefrontal cortex, the posterior cingulate cortex, and the inferior parietal cortex.

94 **"It was quite difficult at times":** Carhart-Harris et al., "Functional Connectivity Measures," 1350.

94 **Only one of seven personality traits:** Jacqueline Borg et al., "The Serotonin System and Spiritual Experiences," *American Journal of Psychiatry* 160, no. 11 (2003): 1967.

94 **"endorse extrasensory perception and ideation":** Borg et al., "Serotonin System," 1967.

95 **One split-brain patient's right hemisphere:** V. S. Ramachandran, "Split Brain with One Half Atheist and One Half Theist" (excerpt from a lecture at *Beyond Belief: Science, Reason, Religion & Survival* [symposium, Salk Institute, La Jolla, CA, November 5–7, 2006]), YouTube, published by wimsweden, June 3, 2010, https://www.youtube.com/watch?v=PFJPtVRlI64.

Chapter 7: Good to Think?

97 **"There is no such entity as 'religion'"**: Scott Atran, *In Gods We Trust: The Evolutionary Landscape of Religion* (New York: Oxford University Press, 2002), 15.

97 **"*passionate communal displays*"**: Atran, *In Gods We Trust*, 13.

98 **Stewart Guthrie's *Faces in the Clouds*:** Stewart Elliott Guthrie, *Faces in the Clouds: A New Theory of Religion* (New York: Oxford University Press, 1993).

98 **An explicitly cognitive anthropologist:** Pascal Boyer, *Religion Explained: The Evolutionary Origins of Religious Thought* (New York: Basic Books, 2001).

98 **His "framework for a cognitive neuroscience":** Pascal Boyer, "Religious Thought and Behaviour as By-Products of Brain Function," *Trends in Cognitive Sciences* 7, no. 3 (2003): 122.

99 **gods and spirits seem real:** For further support and explanation, see also Martin Brüne, "On Shared Psychological Mechanisms of Religiousness and Delusional Beliefs," in *The Biological Evolution of Religious Mind and Behavior*, ed. Eckart Voland and Wulf Schiefenhövel (Berlin: Springer, 2009), 217–28.

99 **"by-product of the normal operation":** Boyer, "Religious Thought and Behaviour," 123.

100 **"People are universally equipped":** J. L. Barrett, "Review of Pascal Boyer's *The Naturalness of Religious Ideas: A Cognitive Theory of Religion*," *Journal for the Scientific Study of Religion* 35, no. 4 (1996): 449.

100 **"Whether or not this text foreshadows":** Barrett, "Review of Pascal Boyer's," 449.

100 **In one story, God saves:** J. L. Barrett and F. C. Keil, "Conceptualizing a Nonnatural Entity: Anthropomorphism in God Concepts," *Cognitive Psychology* 31 (1996): 224.

100 **Barrett's group did parallel work:** Justin L. Barrett, "Cognitive Constraints on Hindu Concepts of the Divine," *Journal for the Scientific Study of Religion* 37, no. 4 (1998): 608–19.

101 **Todd Tremlin's *Minds and Gods*:** Todd Tremlin, *Minds and Gods: The Cognitive Foundations of Religion* (Oxford: Oxford University Press, 2005).

101 **"ADD and ToMM are not":** Tremlin, *Minds and Gods*, 134.

101 **Philosopher and cognitive scientist Robert McCauley:** Robert N.

McCauley, *Why Religion Is Natural and Science Is Not* (New York: Oxford University Press, 2011).

101 **Together with comparative religion scholar:** E. Thomas Lawson and Robert N. McCauley, *Rethinking Religion: Connecting Cognition and Culture* (Cambridge: Cambridge University Press, 1993); Robert N. McCauley and E. Thomas Lawson, *Bringing Ritual to Mind: Psychological Foundations of Cultural Forms* (New York: Cambridge University Press, 2002).

101 **"The sciences do not provide full":** R. N. McCauley, "A Cognitive Science of Religion Will Be Difficult, Expensive, Complicated, Radically Counter-intuitive, and Possible: A Response to Martin and Wiebe," *Journal of the American Academy of Religion* 80, no. 3 (2012): 605–10.

101 **"maturationally natural cognition":** McCauley, *Why Religion Is Natural*, 147.

102 **"From an evolutionary standpoint":** Atran, *In Gods We Trust*, ix.

102 **"infant-mother paradigm":** Atran, *In Gods We Trust*, 72.

102 **"agent-detection module":** Atran, *In Gods We Trust*, 267.

102 **"a near universal association of mountains":** Atran, *In Gods We Trust*, 100.

102 **"primary emotions" identified by Darwin:** Atran, *In Gods We Trust*, 11.

102 **biologically prepared mental and behavioral capacities:** M. Konner, *The Tangled Wing: Biological Constraints on the Human Spirit*, 2nd ed. (New York: Times Books, 2002); M. Konner, *The Evolution of Childhood: Relationships, Emotion, Mind* (Cambridge, MA: Belknap Press of Harvard University Press, 2010).

102 **Like the cognitive theorists:** Some readers may be familiar with the metaphor of the "spandrel," which is a name for a certain architectural feature that is not structurally necessary, put forth in a widely read paper: Stephen Jay Gould and Richard C. Lewontin, "The Spandrels of San Marco and the Panglossian Paradigm: A Critique of the Adaptationist Programme," *Proceedings of the Royal Society of London. Series B, Biological Sciences* 205 (1979): 581–98. Countercritiques have argued that the architectural facts were wrong and that the "adaptationist program" was a straw man.

102 **Others of comparable sophistication:** Rüdiger Vaas, "Gods, Gains, and Genes: On the Natural Origin of Religiosity by Means of Bio-cultural Selection," in *Biological Evolution of Religious Mind and Behavior*, ed. Eckart Voland and Wulf Schiefenhövel (Berlin: Springer, 2009), 25–49.

102 **Even more difficult to rule out:** Stephen Jay Gould and Elisabeth S. Vrba, "Exaptation—a Missing Term in the Science of Form," *Paleobiology* 8, no. 1 (1982): 4–15.

103 **"does not provide a comprehensive theory":** McCauley, *Why Religion Is Natural*, 148.

103 **Consider what are called dissociations:** S. J. Lynn et al., "Dissociation and Dissociative Disorders: Challenging Conventional Wisdom," *Current Directions in Psychological Science* 21, no. 1 (2012): 48–53; C. J. Dalenberg et al., "Evaluation of the Evidence for the Trauma and Fantasy Models of Dissociation," *Psychological Bulletin* 138, no. 3 (2012): 550–88; S. J. Lynn et al., "The Trauma Model of Dissociation: Inconvenient Truths and Stubborn Fictions. Comment on Dalenberg et al. (2012)," *Psychological Bulletin* 140, no. 3 (2014): 896–910; C. J. Dalenberg et al., "Reality versus Fantasy: Reply to Lynn et al. (2014)," *Psychological Bulletin* 140, no. 3 (2014): 911–20.

104 **Dissociative identity disorder was a diagnostic fad:** J. Paris, "The Rise and Fall of Dissociative Identity Disorder," *Journal of Nervous and Mental Disease* 200, no. 12 (2012): 1076–79.

104 **"normative dissociations":** Lisa D. Butler, "Normative Dissociation," *Psychiatric Clinics of North America* 29, no. 1 (2006): 46.

104 **She argues that complete absorption:** Butler, "Normative Dissociation," 59.

104 **The state we are in when a task:** Mihaly Csikszentmihalyi, *Flow: The Psychology of Optimal Experience* (New York: Harper & Row, 1990).

Chapter 8: The Voice of the Child

106 **"It is child abuse to label a child":** These quotes are from Richard Dawkins, presentation at *Beyond Belief: Science, Reason, Religion & Survival* (symposium, Salk Institute, La Jolla, CA, November 5–7, 2006), Science Network, Session 7, MP4 video, about 41:40, http://thesciencenetwork.org/programs/beyond-belief-science-religion-reason-and-survival/session-7-1.

107 **"Children, I'll argue, have a human right":** Nicholas Humphrey, "What Shall We Tell the Children? The Oxford Amnesty Lecture, February 1997," *Social Research* 65, no. 4 (1998): 777–805.

108 **Even the small Jewish minority:** Michael Beizer, "Congress of Jewish Religious Communities and Organizations in Russia," trans. I. Michael Aronson, *YIVO Encyclopedia of the Jews of Eastern*

Europe, accessed August 20, 2018, http://www.yivoencyclopedia.org/article.aspx/Congress_of_Jewish_Religious_Communities_and_Organizations_in_Russia.

108 **In China, after sixty-five years:** Pew Research Center, "The Global Religious Landscape," December 2012, http://www.pewforum.org/global-religious-landscape.aspx.

109 **But the fact that religiousness:** Eugene C. Roehlkepartain et al., eds. *Handbook of Spiritual Development in Childhood and Adolescence* (Thousand Oaks, CA: SAGE, 2006); C. M. Barry et al., "Religiosity and Spirituality during the Transition to Adulthood," *International Journal of Behavioral Development* 34, no. 4 (2010): 311–24.

109 **Faith trajectories in adulthood:** James W. Fowler, *Stages of Faith: The Psychology of Human Development and the Quest for Meaning* (San Francisco: Harper San Francisco, 1995); James W. Fowler and Robin W. Lovin, eds., *Trajectories of Faith: Life Stories of Malcolm X, Anne Hutchinson, Blaise Pascal, Ludwig Wittgenstein, & Dietrich Bonhoeffer* (Nashville, TN: Abingdon, 1980).

109 **generativity, integration:** These terms come from Erik H. Erikson, "Identity and the Life Cycle," *Psychological Issues* 1, no. 1 (1959): 1–171, and are also consistent with the perspectives on the second half of life taken by Carl Jung and discussed in Chapter 2.

110 **From studies of 72 pairs of twins:** Thomas J. Bouchard Jr. et al., "Intrinsic and Extrinsic Religiousness: Genetic and Environmental Influences and Personality Correlates," *Twin Research* 2, no. 2 (1999): 88–98, https://www.ncbi.nlm.nih.gov/pubmed/10480743.

110 **twice as heritable as giving or risk taking:** David Cesarini et al., "Genetic Variation in Preferences for Giving and Risk Taking," *Quarterly Journal of Economics* 124, no. 2 (2009): 809–42.

111 **But it is fair to say that height:** Karri Silventoinen et al., "Heritability of Adult Body Height—A Comparative Study of Twin Cohorts in Eight Countries," *Twin Research* 6, no. 5 (2003): 399–408.

111 **For example, ultra-Orthodox Jewish teens:** *Trembling before G-d*, directed by Sandi Simcha Dubowski (Simcha Leib Productions, 2001), documentary, 94 min. See also Hella Winston, *Unchosen: The Hidden Lives of Hasidic Rebels* (Boston: Beacon Press, 2005).

112 **Matt Bradshaw and Christopher Ellison:** Matt Bradshaw and Christopher G. Ellison, "Do Genetic Factors Influence Religious Life?

Findings from a Behavior Genetic Analysis of Twin Siblings," *Journal for the Scientific Study of Religion* 47, no. 4 (2008): 529–44.

112 **"Genetic influences are sizable":** Bradshaw and Ellison, "Do Genetic Factors Influence Religions Life?" 537.

112 **Tanya Button and her colleagues:** T. M. Button et al., "The Etiology of Stability and Change in Religious Values and Religious Attendance," *Behavior Genetics* 41, no. 2 (2011): 201–10.

112 **How important is it to you . . .:** Button et al., "Etiology of Stability and Change," 203.

113 **Other developmental studies:** C. Kandler and R. Riemann, "Genetic and Environmental Sources of Individual Religiousness: The Roles of Individual Personality Traits and Perceived Environmental Religiousness," *Behavior Genetics* 43, no. 4 (2013): 297–313.

113 **One impressive application:** V. Saroglou, "Religiousness as a Cultural Adaptation of Basic Traits: A Five-Factor Model Perspective," *Personality and Social Psychology Review* 14 (2010): 108–25.

113 **"Agreeableness and Conscientiousness were reliable":** Saroglou, "Religiousness as a Cultural Adaptation," 115.

113 **personality predicts future religiousness:** M. E. McCullough, J. A. Tsang, and S. Brion, "Personality Traits in Adolescence as Predictors of Religiousness in Early Adulthood: Findings from the Terman Longitudinal Study," *Personality and Social Psychology Bulletin* 29, no. 8 (2003): 980–91; P. Wink et al., "Religiousness, Spiritual Seeking, and Personality: Findings from a Longitudinal Study," *Journal of Personality* 75, no. 5 (2007): 1051–70.

114 **These values are predicted:** V. Saroglou, V. Delpierre, and R. Dernelle, "Values and Religiosity: A Meta-analysis," *Personality and Individual Differences* 37, no. 4 (2004): 721–34.

114 **"Religiousness itself may reflect":** Kandler and Riemann, "Genetic and Environmental Sources," 310.

114 **Ralph Piedmont pioneered a scale:** Ralph L. Piedmont, "Does Spirituality Represent the Sixth Factor of Personality? Spiritual Transcendence and the Five-Factor Model," *Journal of Personality* 67, no. 6 (1999): 988.

114 **Piedmont asked people how strongly:** As quoted in Pavel Říčan et al., "Spirituality of American and Czech Students—A Cross-Cultural Comparison," *Studia Psychologica* 52, no. 3 (2010): 243–51.

114 **Piedmont and Mark Leach tested this idea:** R. L. Piedmont and M. M. Leach, "Cross-Cultural Generalizability of the Spiritual Transcendence Scale in India: Spirituality as a Universal Aspect of Human Experience," *American Behavioral Scientist* 45, no. 12 (2002): 1888–1901.

114 **"Spirituality represents the raw":** Piedmont and Leach, "Cross-Cultural Generalizability," 1898–99.

115 **Prague Spirituality Questionnaire:** Pavel Rican and Pavlina Janosova, "Spirituality as a Basic Aspect of Personality: A Cross-Cultural Verification of Piedmont's Model," *International Journal for the Psychology of Religion* 20, no. 1 (2010): 2–13.

115 **"the extremely secularized Czech youth":** Rican and Janosova, "Spirituality as a Basic Aspect of Personality," 2.

115 **"a universal human phenomenon":** Rican and Janosova, "Spirituality as a Basic Aspect of Personality," 3.

115 **Another study, looking at variants:** J. Y. Sasaki et al., "Religion Priming Differentially Increases Prosocial Behavior among Variants of the Dopamine D4 Receptor (DRD4) Gene," *Social Cognitive and Affective Neuroscience* 8, no. 2 (2013): 209–15.

116 **But if genes consistently contribute:** R. Rowthorn, "Religion, Fertility and Genes: A Dual Inheritance Model," *Proceedings of the Royal Society of London. Series B, Biological Sciences* 278, no. 1717 (2011): 2519–27.

116 **Ideas about gods and spirits exist:** Guy E. Swanson, *The Birth of the Gods: The Origin of Primitive Beliefs* (Ann Arbor: University of Michigan Press, 1964); William Lessa and Evan Z. Vogt, eds., *Reader in Comparative Religion: An Anthropological Approach*, 4th ed. (New York: Harper & Row, 1979).

116 **Classic interview studies:** Robert Coles, *The Spiritual Life of Children* (Boston: Houghton Mifflin, 1990), 19–20.

117 **"The sky watches us":** Coles, *Spiritual Life of Children*, 25.

117 **"They want the land":** Coles, *Spiritual Life of Children*, 27.

117 **But Hopi religious indoctrination:** Dorothy Eggan, "The General Problem of Hopi Adjustment," *American Anthropologist* 45 (1943): 357–73; Esther Goldfrank, "Socialization, Personality, and the Structure of Pueblo Society," *American Anthropologist* 47 (1945): 516–39; David Aberle, "The Psychosocial Analysis of a Hopi Life-History," in *Personalities and Cultures: Readings in Psychological Anthropology*, ed. Robert Hunt (Garden City, NY: Natural History Press, 1967), 79–138.

118 **"a We'e'e Kachina in a blue mask":** Goldfrank, "Socialization, Personality, and the Structure," 514.

118 **"The children tremble":** Goldfrank, "Socialization, Personality, and the Structure," 517–18.

118 **"to save their lives":** Goldfrank, "Socialization, Personality, and the Structure," 529.

118 **"I now know it was best":** Goldfrank, "Socialization, Personality, and the Structure," 530.

119 **In James Fowler's pioneering model:** J. W. Fowler, "Strength for the Journey: Early Childhood Development in Selfhood and Faith," in *Faith Development in Early Childhood*, ed. D. A. Blazer (Kansas City, MO: Sheed & Ward, 1989), 1–36; J. W. Fowler, "Stages in Faith Consciousness," *New Directions for Child Development*, no. 52 (Summer 1991): 27–45; J. W. Fowler and M. L. Dell, "Stages of Faith and Identity: Birth to Teens," *Child and Adolescent Psychiatric Clinics of North America* 13, no. 1 (2004): 17–33; J. W. Fowler and M. L. Dell, "Stages of Faith from Infancy through Adolescence: Reflections on Three Decades of Faith Development Theory," in *The Handbook of Spiritual Development in Childhood and Adolescence*, ed. E. C. Roehlkepartain et al. (Thousand Oaks, CA: SAGE, 2006), 34–45.

119 **These models develop the claims:** Fowler, "Strength for the Journey," 1989.

119 **Current models are better:** K. S. Rosengren, C. N. Johnson, and P. L. Harris, eds., *Imagining the Impossible: Magical, Scientific, and Religious Thinking in Children* (New York: Cambridge University Press, 2000); Roehlkepartain et al., *Handbook of Spiritual Development*; R. A. Richert, C. J. Boyatzis, and P. E. King, "Introduction to the British Journal of Developmental Psychology Special Issue on Religion, Culture, and Development," *British Journal of Developmental Psychology* 35, no. 1 (2017): 1–3, https://doi.org/10.1111/bjdp.12179.

119 **Patricia Ebstyne King and Chris Boyatzis:** P. E. King and C. J. Boyatzis, "Religious and Spiritual Development," in *Handbook of Child Psychology and Developmental Science*, ed. Richard M. Lerner and Michael E. Lamb, vol. 3, *Socioemotional Processes* (Hoboken, NJ: Wiley, 2015), 975–1021.

120 **"The wind winds. The glass hits":** M. Mead, "An Investigation of the Thought of Primitive Children, with Special Reference to Animism," *Journal of the Royal Anthropological Institute* 62 (1932): 185–86.

120 **"The Manus child is less ... animistic":** Mead, "Investigation of the Thought," 186.

120 **Cristine Legare, in a study:** C. H. Legare and S. A. Gelman, "Bewitchment, Biology, or Both: The Co-existence of Natural and Supernatural Explanatory Frameworks across Development," *Cognitive Science* 32, no. 4 (2008): 607–42, https://doi.org/10.1080/03640210802066766.

120 **"Contrary to traditional accounts":** C. H. Legare et al., "The Coexistence of Natural and Supernatural Explanations across Cultures and Development," *Child Development* 83, no. 3 (2012): 779, https://doi.org/10.1111/j.1467-8624.2012.01743.x.

120 **"Coexistence reasoning ... is pervasive":** J. T. A. Busch, R. E. Watson-Jones, and C. H. Legare, "The Coexistence of Natural and Supernatural Explanations within and across Domains and Development," *British Journal of Developmental Psychology* 35, no. 1 (2017): 4, https://doi.org/10.1111/bjdp.12164.

120 **King and Boyatzis credit Fowler's:** King and Boyatzis, "Religious and Spiritual Development," 982.

121 **Twenty-first-century psychodynamic approaches:** P. Granqvist, M. Mikulincer, and P. R. Shaver, "Religion as Attachment: Normative Processes and Individual Differences," *Personality and Social Psychology Review* 14, no. 1 (2010): 49–59, https://doi.org/10.1177/1088868309348618.

121 **One study compared 30:** R. Cassibba et al., "Attachment and God Representations among Lay Catholics, Priests, and Religious: A Matched Comparison Study Based on the Adult Attachment Interview," *Developmental Psychology* 44, no. 6 (2008): 1753–63, https://doi.org/10.1037/a0013772.

121 **Interpersonal attachment styles:** P. Granqvist et al., "Experimental Findings on God as an Attachment Figure: Normative Processes and Moderating Effects of Internal Working Models," *Journal of Personality and Social Psychology* 103, no. 5 (2012): 804–18, https://doi.org/10.1037/a0029344.

121 **Research on 181 university students:** P. Granqvist and B. Hagekull, "Religiousness and Perceived Childhood Attachment: Profiling Socialized Correspondence and Emotional Compensation," *Journal for the Scientific Study of Religion* 38, no. 2 (1999): 254–73.

121 **And in 119 Christian:** C. N. Kimball et al., "Attachment to God: A Qualitative Exploration of Emerging Adults' Spiritual Relationship with God," *Journal of Psychology and Theology* 41, no. 3: 175.

121 **Other studies suggest that relationships:** K. Laurin, K. Schumann, and J. G. Holmes, "A Relationship with God? Connecting with the Divine to Assuage Fears of Interpersonal Rejection," *Social Psychological and Personality Science* 5, no. 7 (2014): 777–85, https://doi.org/10 .1177/1948550614531800.

121 **People with autism spectrum disorders:** H. Schaap-Jonker et al., "Autism Spectrum Disorders and the Image of God as a Core Aspect of Religiousness," *International Journal for the Psychology of Religion* 23, no. 2 (2013): 145–60, https://doi.org/10.1080/10508619.2012.688005.

121 **People with disorganized attachment:** P. Granqvist, B. Hagekull, and T. Ivarsson, "Disorganized Attachment Promotes Mystical Experiences via a Propensity for Alterations in Consciousness (Absorption)," *International Journal for the Psychology of Religion* 22, no. 3 (2012): 180– 97, https://doi.org/10.1080/10508619.2012.670012.

122 **Richard Dawkins recalls "trying gently":** Richard Dawkins, *Unweaving the Rainbow: Science, Delusion, and the Appetite for Wonder* (Boston: Houghton Mifflin, 1998), 141–42.

123 **But, really intriguingly:** N. M. Prentice, M. Manosevitz, and L. Hubbs, "Imaginary Figures of Early Childhood: Santa Claus, Easter Bunny, and the Tooth Fairy," *American Journal of Orthopsychiatry* 48, no. 4 (1978): 618–28.

123 **and many express sadness when:** R. Cluley, "The Organization of Santa: Fetishism, Ambivalence and Narcissism," *Organization* 18, no. 6 (2011): 779–94.

123 **"I can still feel the excitement":** Ann Cale Kruger, Educational Psychology Division, College of Education, Georgia State University, conversation with the author, August 27, 2017, quote reconfirmed by Kruger March 13, 2019.

124 **A study of 140 Jewish American children:** N. M. Prentice and D. A. Gordon, "Santa Claus and the Tooth Fairy for the Jewish Child and Parent," *Journal of Genetic Psychology* 148, no. 2 (1987): 139–51.

124 **A 2015 study of 47 children:** A. Shtulman and R. I. Yoo, "Children's Understanding of Physical Possibility Constrains Their Belief in Santa Claus," *Cognitive Development* 34 (2015): 51–62.

124 **"God concepts must be":** J. L. Barrett, "Why Santa Claus Is Not a God," *Journal of Cognition and Culture* 8, no. 1 (2008): 150, https://doi .org/10.1163/156770908x289251.

124 **Contrary to some assumptions:** J. M. Pierucci et al., "Fantasy Orientation Constructs and Related Executive Function Development in Preschool: Developmental Benefits to Executive Functions by Being a Fantasy-Oriented Child," *International Journal of Behavioral Development* 38, no. 1 (2014): 62–69.

125 **and a capacity for emotion regulation:** A. T. Gilpin, M. M. Brown, and J. M. Pierucci, "Relations between Fantasy Orientation and Emotion Regulation in Preschool," *Early Education and Development* 26, no. 7 (2015): 920–32.

125 **Such children are less shy:** M. Taylor et al., "The Assessment of Elaborated Role-Play in Young Children: Invisible Friends, Personified Objects, and Pretend Identities," *Social Development* 22, no. 1 (2013): 75–93.

125 **But between 15 and 25 percent:** M. Gimenez-Dasi, F. Pons, and P. K. Bender, "Imaginary Companions, Theory of Mind and Emotion Understanding in Young Children," *European Early Childhood Education Research Journal* 24, no. 2 (2016): 186–97.

125 **ICs are associated with theory of mind:** Gimenez-Dasi et al., "Imaginary Companions."

125 **and predict emotion understanding later:** M. Taylor et al., "The Characteristics and Correlates of Fantasy in School-Age Children: Imaginary Companions, Impersonation, and Social Understanding," *Developmental Psychology* 40, no. 6 (2004): 1173–87.

125 **children with ICs are more likely:** P. E. Davis, E. Meins, and C. Fernyhough, "Children with Imaginary Companions Focus on Mental Characteristics When Describing Their Real-Life Friends," *Infant and Child Development* 23, no. 6 (2014): 622–33.

125 **For some children, ICs:** K. Majors, "Children's Perceptions of Their Imaginary Companions and the Purposes They Serve: An Exploratory Study in the United Kingdom," *Childhood—A Global Journal of Child Research* 20, no. 4 (2013): 550–65.

125 **Tanya Luhrmann studied evangelicals:** T. M. Luhrmann, *When God Talks Back: Understanding the American Evangelical Relationship with God* (New York: Knopf, 2012).

125 **Yet children have to deal with death:** E. H. Cassem, "The Person Confronting Death," in *The Harvard Guide to Modern Psychiatry*, ed. A. M. J. Nicholi (Cambridge, MA: Harvard University Press, 1999), 699–731; M. Stambrook and K. C. H. Parker, "The Develop-

ment of the Concept of Death in Childhood: A Review of the Literature," *Merrill-Palmer Quarterly* 33, no. 2 (1987): 133–57.

126 **In a 2017 study comparing children:** R. E. Watson-Jones et al., "Does the Body Survive Death? Cultural Variation in Beliefs about Life Everlasting," *Cognitive Science* 41 (2017): 455–76.

126 **In rural Madagascar:** R. Astuti and P. L. Harris, "Understanding Mortality and the Life of the Ancestors in Rural Madagascar," *Cognitive Science* 32, no. 4 (2008): 713–40.

126 **In a touching and sensitive study:** Bonnie Hewlett, "Vulnerable Lives: The Experience of Death and Loss among the Aka and Ngandu Adolescents of the Central African Republic," in *Hunter-Gatherer Childhoods: Evolutionary, Developmental & Cultural Perspectives*, ed. Barry S. Hewlett and Michael E. Lamb (New Brunswick, NJ: Aldine Transaction): 322–42.

126 **All adolescents in both cultures:** King and Boyatzis, "Religious and Spiritual Development"; Marie Good and Teena Willoughby, "Adolescence as a Sensitive Period for Spiritual Development," *Child Development Perspectives* 2, no. 1 (2008): 32–37.

127 **Genes play a role, but cultural factors:** L. Steinberg and A. S. Morris, "Adolescent Development," *Journal of Cognitive Education and Psychology* 2, no. 1 (2009): 55–87; D. Reiss, *The Relationship Code: Deciphering Genetic and Social Influences on Adolescent Development* (Cambridge, MA: Harvard University Press, 2000).

127 **Rites of passage, often around puberty:** A. Schlegel and H. I. Barry, *Adolescence: An Anthropological Inquiry* (New York: Free Press, 1991).

127 **"The neophyte is at once prepared":** Mircea Eliade, *Rites and Symbols of Initiation: The Mysteries of Birth and Rebirth*, 3rd ed. (Thompson, CT: Spring Publications, 2017), Kindle ed., loc. 635–38.

128 **Among the San, girls have:** Marjorie Shostak, *Nisa: The Life and Words of a !Kung Woman* (Cambridge, MA: Harvard University Press, 1982).

128 **Among the Baka, hunter-gatherers:** Kathleen Higgens, "Ritual and Symbol in Baka Life History," *Anthropology and Humanism Quarterly* 10, no. 4 (1985): 100–106.

128 **The Native American vision quest:** Robert H. Lowie, *Indians of the Plains* (New York: American Museum of Natural History, 1954).

129 **Formal instruction is usually included:** A. C. Kruger and M. Tomasello, "Cultural Learning and Learning Culture," in *Handbook of Education and Human Development: New Models of Learning, Teach-*

ing, and Schooling, ed. D. Olson and N. Torrance (Oxford: Basil Blackwell, 1996), 369–87.

130 **Traditional initiation harnesses these forces:** W. A. Collins and L. Steinberg, "Adolescent Development in Interpersonal Context," in *Handbook of Child Psychology*, ed. W. Damon and R. M. Lerner, vol. 3, *Social, Emotional, and Personality Development*, by N. Eisenberg, W. Damon, and R. M. Lerner (Hoboken, NJ: Wiley, 2006), 1003–67.

130 **"Instead of participating":** Mircea Eliade, foreword to *Rites and Symbols of Initiation*, by Michael Meade, loc. 104–9.

130 **A longitudinal study of 3,000:** S. D. Li, "Familial Religiosity, Family Processes, and Juvenile Delinquency in a National Sample of Early Adolescents," *Journal of Early Adolescence* 34, no. 4 (2014): 436–62, https://doi.org/10.1177/0272431613495445.

131 **In a 2017 study of 1,300:** D. B. Lee and E. W. Neblett, "Religious Development in African American Adolescents: Growth Patterns That Offer Protection," *Child Development*, Epub ahead of print, July 14, 2017, https://doi.org/10.1111/cdev.12896.

131 **In one, looking at 220 youngsters:** G. S. Longo, B. C. Bray, and J. Kim-Spoon, "Profiles of Adolescent Religiousness Using Latent Profile Analysis: Implications for Psychopathology," *British Journal of Developmental Psychology* 35, no. 1 (2017): 91–105, https://doi.org/10.1111/bjdp.12183.

131 **In addition, different types:** C. J. Holmes and J. Kim-Spoon, "Positive and Negative Associations between Adolescents' Religiousness and Health Behaviors via Self-Regulation," *Religion, Brain & Behavior* 6, no. 3 (2016): 188–206, https://doi.org/10.1080/2153599x.2015.1029513.

131 **connection always trumps authenticity:** For this felicitous phrase I thank Irene Lyon, who cites family therapist Gabor Maté: "The Need for Authenticity—Gabor Maté," YouTube, published by AronGoch, November 30, 2016, https://www.youtube.com/watch?v=pUGGNPAK6uw. My daughter Sarah Konner called my attention to this.

131 **"reciprocating spirituality":** King and Boyatzis, "Religious and Spiritual Development."

Chapter 9: Awe Evolving

134 **"When the chimpanzees approach":** "Waterfall Displays," published by Jane Goodall Institute, January 6, 2011, https://www.youtube.com/watch?v=jjQCZClpaaY.

135 **"although [fruiting] vines":** J. D. Pruetz and T. C. LaDuke, "Brief Communication: Reaction to Fire by Savanna Chimpanzees (*Pan troglodytes verus*) at Fongoli, Senegal: Conceptualization of 'Fire Behavior' and the Case for a Chimpanzee Model," *American Journal of Physical Anthropology* 141, no. 4 (2010): 647–48.

135 **"Chimps everywhere have":** Jill Pruetz, quoted in "'Fire-Dancing' Chimps Shed Light on Man's Evolution, Say Scientists," *Daily Mail*, January 16, 2010, http://www.dailymail.co.uk/sciencetech/article-1243693/Fire-dancing-chimps-shed-light-mans-evolution.html#ixzz2uj5XGb7H.

136 **"Animals engage in a struggle":** Ehsan Masood, "Islam's Evolutionary Legacy," *Guardian*, March 1, 2009, https://www.theguardian.com/commentisfree/belief/2009/feb/27/islam-religion-evolution-science.

136 **"Origin of man now proved":** Darwin Online, accessed January 2, 2019, http://darwin-online.org.uk/content/frameset?viewtype=side&itemID=CUL-DAR125.-&pageseq=63, loc. 84e.

136 **"Psychology will be securely based on":** Charles Darwin, *The Origin of Species by Means of Natural Selection, or the Preservation of Favored Races in the Struggle for Life* (1859; repr., New York: New American Library, 1958), 415.

136 **"from the war of nature":** Darwin, *Origin of Species*, 416.

137 **"What a book a Devil's chaplain might write":** Charles Darwin to J. D. Hooker, July 13, 1856, Darwin Correspondence Project, https://www.darwinproject.ac.uk/letter/DCP-LETT-1924.xml.

137 **"I feel most strongly that":** Charles Darwin to Asa Gray, May 22, 1860, Darwin Correspondence Project, https://www.darwinproject.ac.uk/letter/DCP-LETT-1924.xml.

137 **"consisting of love, complete submission":** Charles Darwin, *The Descent of Man, and Selection in Relation to Sex* (1871; repr., Princeton, NJ: Princeton University Press, 1981), 68.

138 **These spirits' dangerous powers:** Wulf Schiefenhövel, "Explaining the Inexplicable: Traditional and Syncretistic Religiosity in Melanesia," in *The Biological Evolution of Religious Mind and Behavior*, ed. Eckart Voland and Wulf Schiefenhövel (Berlin: Springer, 2009).

139 **Many Nones find things:** A. Storr, *Solitude: A Return to the Self* (New York: Free Press, 1988). This brief on the value of solitude is not just about Nones.

139 **"they experience part of their mind":** T. M. Luhrmann, *When God*

Talks Back: Understanding the American Evangelical Relationship with God (New York: Knopf, 2012), xxi.

139 **"absorption hypothesis":** T. M. Luhrmann, H. Nusbaum, and R. Thisted, "The Absorption Hypothesis: Learning to Hear God in Evangelical Christianity," *American Anthropologist* 112, no. 1 (2010): 66–78, https://doi.org/10.1111/j.1548-1433.2009.01197.x.

139 **"God is an observant Jew":** Rabbi Emanuel Feldman, Beth Jacob Synagogue, Atlanta, email message to the author, December 25, 2018.

140 **Mystically inclined Jews:** G. Scholem, *Kabbalah* (New York: Dorset Press, 1987).

140 **"Where I go, You":** H. M. Rabinowicz, *Hasidism: The Movement and Its Masters* (Northvale, NJ: Jason Aronson, 1988), 65.

140 *I and Thou:* Martin Buber, *I and Thou* (New York: Charles Scribner's Sons, 1958).

141 **But most are also:** This has been shown for the imaginary companions of childhood (see Chapter 8).

141 **The "Watch me, Mommy!" need:** Ann Cale Kruger, "Communion and Culture," in *Mimesis and Science: Empirical Research on Imitation and the Mimetic Theory of Culture and Religion*, ed. S. Garrels (East Lansing: Michigan State University Press, 2011), 111–28.

142 **In the Mbuti:** Colin M. Turnbull, *The Forest People: A Study of the Pygmies of the Congo* (New York: Simon & Schuster, 1962).

142 **When the Sirionó:** Allan R. Holmberg, *Nomads of the Long Bow: The Siriono of Eastern Bolivia* (Garden City, NY: Natural History Press, 1969).

142 **Megan Biesele's book:** Megan Biesele, *Women Like Meat: The Folklore and Foraging Ideology of the Kalahari Ju/'hoan* (Johannesburg, South Africa: Witwatersrand University Press, 1993).

142 **In two other hunter-gatherer groups:** Kristen Hawkes, "Showing Off: Tests of an Hypothesis about Men's Foraging Goals," *Ethology & Sociobiology* 12, no. 1 (1991): 29–54; K. Hawkes, J. F. O'Connell, and N. G. Jones, "Hunting Income Patterns among the Hadza: Big Game, Common Goods, Foraging Goals, and the Evolution of the Human Diet," *Philosophical Transactions of the Royal Society of London. Series B. Biological Sciences* 334 (1991): 243–51.

142 **Even many non-hunter-gatherer cultures:** David D. Gilmore, *Manhood in the Making: Cultural Concepts of Masculinity* (New Haven, CT: Yale University Press, 1990).

Notes

142 **how the hunt has been celebrated:** Matt Cartmill, *A View to Death in the Morning: Hunting and Nature through History* (Cambridge, MA: Harvard University Press, 1993).

142 **Even a primitive species like** *Homo naledi***:** Lee R. Berger et al., "*Homo naledi*, a New Species of the Genus *Homo* from the Dinaledi Chamber, South Africa," *eLIFE Journal*, September 10, 2015, https://doi.org/10 .7554/eLife.09560. Like the later Neanderthals, *Homo naledi* were not human ancestors, but a parallel branch.

142 **Neanderthals probably had systematic rituals:** Johannes Maringer, *The Gods of Prehistoric Man* (New York: Knopf, 1960); Francois Bordes, *The Old Stone Age* (New York: McGraw-Hill, 1968).

142 **and deliberate burials:** Richard Klein, *The Human Career*, 2nd ed. (Chicago: University of Chicago Press, 1999).

142 **At La Ferrassie in France:** Ralph S. Solecki, *Shanidar, the First Flower People* (New York: Knopf, 1971).

143 **Biological and cultural evolution:** S. McBrearty and A. S. Brooks, "The Revolution That Wasn't: A New Interpretation of the Origin of Modern Human Behavior," *Journal of Human Evolution* 39, no. 5 (2000): 453–563.

143 **fine bone and ivory flutes:** Nicholas J. Conard, Maria Malina, and Susanne C. Münzel, "New Flutes Document the Earliest Musical Tradition in Southwestern Germany," *Nature* 460, no. 7256 (2009): 737–40.

143 **The Cave of Altamira:** Henri Breuil, *Four Hundred Centuries of Cave Art*, trans. Mary E. Boyle (Montignac, [France]: Centre d'études et de documentation préhistoriques, 1952).

143 **Chauvet in southern France:** Jean-Marie Chauvet, Eliette Brunel Deschamps, and Christian Hillaire, *Dawn of Art: The Chauvet Cave, the Oldest Known Paintings in the World* (New York: Harry N. Abrams, 1996).

143 **"Caves are special places":** Holley Moyes, ed., *Sacred Darkness: A Global Perspective on the Ritual Use of Caves* (Boulder: University Press of Colorado, 2012).

143 **perhaps a pubertal initiation rite:** John E. Pfeiffer, *The Emergence of Culture* (New York: Harper & Row, 1982).

144 **Inaccessibility may have had:** Ann Sieveking, *The Cave Artists* (London: Thames and Hudson, 1979).

144 **Starting with the oldest:** H. C. Peoples, P. Duda, and F. W. Marlowe, "Hunter-Gatherers and the Origins of Religion," *Human Nature* 27, no. 3 (2016): 261–82, https://doi.org/10.1007/s12110-016-9260-0.

144 **The belief that high gods:** Guy E. Swanson, *The Birth of the Gods: The Origin of Primitive Beliefs* (Ann Arbor: University of Michigan Press, 1964).

145 **high population density made hierarchy possible:** D. Wengrow and D. Graeber, "Farewell to the 'Childhood of Man': Ritual, Seasonality, and the Origins of Inequality," *Journal of the Royal Anthropological Institute* 21, no. 3 (2015): 597–619, https://doi.org/10.1111/1467-9655.12247.

145 **"one of the most important":** O. Dietrich et al., "The Role of Cult and Feasting in the Emergence of Neolithic Communities. New Evidence from Gobekli Tepe, South-Eastern Turkey," *Antiquity* 86, no. 333 (2012): 674.

145 **While there was some agriculture:** C. Lang et al., "Gazelle Behaviour and Human Presence at Early Neolithic Gobekli Tepe, South-East Anatolia," *World Archaeology* 45, no. 3 (2013): 410–29, https://doi.org/10.1080/00438243.2013.820648.

145 **"explosion of images":** Dietrich et al., "Role of Cult and Feasting," 684.

145 **One widely discussed model:** A. Norenzayan, *Big Gods: How Religion Transformed Cooperation and Conflict* (Princeton, NJ: Princeton University Press, 2013); "Book Symposium: *Big Gods* by Ara Norenzayan," *Religion, Brain & Behavior* 5, no. 4 (2015), 266–342, https://doi.org/10.1080/2153599X.2014.928351 (multiple commentaries and reply by the author); A. Norenzayan et al., "The Cultural Evolution of Prosocial Religions," *Behavioral and Brain Sciences*, 39 (2016), https://doi.org/10.1017/s0140525x14001356 (with commentaries and reply).

146 **"1. Watched people are nice people":** Norenzayan, *Big Gods*, xiii.

146 **Scholars of religion often find:** M. Stausberg, "Big Gods in Review: Introducing Ara Norenzayan and His Critics," *Religion* 44, no. 4 (2014): 592–608, https://doi.org/10.1080/0048721x.2014.954353.

147 **"the lived experience of religion":** A. Fuentes, "Hyper-cooperation Is Deep in Our Evolutionary History and Individual Perception of Belief Matters," *Religion, Brain & Behavior* 5, no. 4 (2015): 288.

147 **"the gods of cosmopolitan Greek":** H. L. Lenfesty and J. P. Schloss, "Big Gods and the Greater Good," *Religion, Brain & Behavior* 5, no. 4 (2015): 305, https://doi.org/10.1080/2153599x.2014.928357.

147 **Richard Sosis and his colleagues:** R. R. Sosis and J. Bulbulia, "The Behavioral Ecology of Religion: The Benefits and Costs of One Evolutionary Approach," *Religion* 41, no. 3 (2011): 341–62, https://doi.org/10.1080/0048721x.2011.604514.

147 **Sosis compared the longevity:** R. Sosis, "Religion and Intragroup Cooperation: Preliminary Results of a Comparative Analysis of Utopian
Communities," *Cross-Cultural Research* 34, no. 1 (2000): 70–87; R. Sosis
and E. R. Bressler, "Cooperation and Commune Longevity: A Test of
the Costly Signaling Theory of Religion," *Cross-Cultural Research* 37,
no. 2 (2003): 211–39, https://doi.org/10.1177/1069397103037002003.

147 **Snake-handling religions:** Dennis Covington, *Salvation on Sand Mountain: Snake Handling and Redemption in Southern Appalachia* (Boston:
Addison-Wesley, 1994).

147 **Making pilgrimages to Mecca:** A. Zahavi, *The Handicap Principle: A
Missing Piece of Darwin's Puzzle* (New York: Oxford University Press,
1999); J. Bulbulia and R. Sosis, "Signalling Theory and the Evolution
of Religious Cooperation," *Religion* 41, no. 3 (2011): 363–88, https://doi
.org/10.1080/0048721x.2011.604508.

148 **Eleanor Power, in a 2017 study:** E. A. Power, "Discerning Devotion:
Testing the Signaling Theory of Religion," *Evolution and Human
Behavior* 38, no. 1 (2017): 82–91, https://doi.org/10.1016/j.evolhumbehav
.2016.07.003.

148 **Religion is a complex adaptive system:** R. Sosis and J. Kiper, "Why
Religion Is Better Conceived as a Complex System than a Norm-
Enforcing Institution," *Behavioral and Brain Sciences* 37, no. 3 (2014):
275–76, https://doi.org/10.1017/s0140525x13003038.

148 **Some, like historian of religion Karen Armstrong:** K. Armstrong, *Fields
of Blood: Religion and the History of Violence* (New York: Knopf, 2014).

148 **Rituals, including dance and music:** R. Rappaport, *Ritual and Religion
in the Making of Humanity* (Cambridge: Cambridge University Press,
1999); C. S. Alcorta and R. Sosis, "Why Ritual Works: A Rejection of
the By-Product Hypothesis," *Behavioral and Brain Sciences* 29, no. 6
(2006), 613–14, https://doi.org/10.1017/s0140525x06009344.

148 **Better-functioning groups:** D. S. Wilson, *Darwin's Cathedral: Evolution, Religion, and the Nature of Society* (Chicago: University of Chicago, 2003); P. Richerson et al., "Cultural Group Selection Plays an
Essential Role in Explaining Human Cooperation: A Sketch of the
Evidence," *Behavioral and Brain Sciences* 39 (2016), https://doi.org/10
.1017/s0140525x1400106x.

149 **One recent theory gives raiding and war:** S. Bowles, "Did Warfare
among Ancestral Hunter-Gatherers Affect the Evolution of Human

Social Behaviors?" *Science* 324, no. 5932 (2009): 1293–98, https://doi .org/10.1126/science.1168112; S. Bowles and H. Gintis, *The Cooperative Species: Human Reciprocity and Its Evolution* (Princeton, NJ: Princeton University Press, 2011).

149 **Some fossil evidence supports this:** M. M. Lahr, "Inter-group Violence among Early Holocene Hunter-Gatherers of West Turkana, Kenya," *Nature* 529, no. 7586 (2016), 394–98, https://doi.org/10.1038/ nature16477.

149 **but recent hunter-gatherers do not:** D. P. Fry and P. Soderberg, "Lethal Aggression in Mobile Forager Bands and Implications for the Origins of War," *Science* 341, no. 6143 (2013): 270–73, https://doi.org/10.1126/ science.1235675.

149 **We know intergroup violence grew:** R. B. Ferguson, "The Prehistory of War and Peace in Europe and the Near East," in War, Peace and Human Nature: The Convergence of Evolutionary and Cultural Views, ed. D. P. Fry (New York: Oxford University Press, 2013), 191– 240; P. M. Lambert, "The Archaeology of War—a North American Perspective," *Journal of Archaeological Research* 10, no. 3 (2002): 207– 41.

149 **The good news is that:** S. Pinker, *The Better Angels of Our Nature: Why Violence Has Declined* (New York: Viking, 2011).

150 **Karen Armstrong says no:** Armstrong, *Fields of Blood*.

150 **Group differences—far from always practical:** M. Konner, "The Weather of Violence: Metaphors and Models, Predictions and Surprises," *CTX Journal*, 5, no. 3 (2015): 53–63, https://www.melvinkonner .com/wp-content/uploads/2010/07/Konner-Weather-of-Violence-CTX -Vol5No3-2015-reduced-no-cover.pdf; M. Konner, "Sacred Violence, Mimetic Rivalry, and War," in *Mimesis and Science*, ed. S. Garrels (East Lansing: Michigan State University Press, 2011); M. Konner, "Human Nature, Ethnic Violence, and War," in *The Psychology of Resolving Global Conflicts: From War to Peace*, ed. M. Fitzduff and C. E. Stout, vol. 1, *Nature vs. Nurture* (Westport, CT: Praeger Security International, 2006), 1–39, http://www.melvinkonner.com/wp-content/uploads/2009/02/ Konner—Hum-Nat-Ethn-Viol-War—Fitzduff-volume-06.pdf.

150 **Bias against out-groups:** M. M. McDonald, C. D. Navarrete, and M. Van Vugt, "Evolution and the Psychology of Intergroup Conflict: The Male Warrior Hypothesis," *Philosophical Transactions of the Royal Society of*

London. Series B, Biological Sciences 367, no. 1589 (2012): 670–79, https://doi.org/10.1098/rstb.2011.0301; M. Konner, *Women after All: Sex, Evolution, and the End of Male Supremacy* (New York: W. W. Norton, 2015).

150 **We know that in all:** See Konner, *Women after All*, chaps. 6–7, for detailed explanation and references.

150 **Culture and genes evolve:** W. H. Durham, *Coevolution: Genes, Culture, and Human Diversity* (Stanford, CA: Stanford University Press, 1991).

150 **Culture can (as conventionally assumed):** J. Marks, *Tales of the Ex-apes: How We Think about Human Evolution* (Berkeley: University of California Press, 2015).

150 **or it can amplify genetic evolution:** Durham, *Coevolution*; C. Lumsden and E. O. Wilson, *Genes, Mind, and Culture: The Coevolutionary Process* (Cambridge, MA: Harvard University Press, 1981).

151 **Salem camp meetings:** Bradd Shore, "Spiritual Work, Memory Work: Revival and Recollection at Salem Camp Meeting," *Ethos* 36, no. 1 (2008): 98–119.

151 **"gossiping, catching up":** Shore, *Spiritual Work*, 106.

152 **"camp meeting is both":** Shore, *Spiritual Work*, 107.

152 **"inform narrative expression:** Shore, *Spiritual Work*, 114–15.

Chapter 10: Goodness!

153 **a model of courage, disproving:** Hitchens is not the only one. P. Granqvist and J. Moström, "There Are Plenty of Atheists in Foxholes—in Sweden," *Archive for the Psychology of Religion/Archiv für Religionspsychologie* 36, no. 2 (2014): 199–213, https://doi.org/10.1163/15736121-12341285.

153 **His essay was called "Thank Goodness!":** At this writing the article is freely available at several places on the World Wide Web, including here: Daniel C. Dennett, "Thank Goodness!" *Edge*, November 2, 2006, http://www.edge.org/conversation/thank-goodness.

155 **Start with a study:** F. A. Curlin et al., "Religious Characteristics of U.S. Physicians: A National Survey," *Journal of General Internal Medicine* 20, no. 7 (2005): 629–34, https://doi.org/10.1111/j.1525-1497.2005.0119.x.

156 **A 2017 study, based on 2,097:** K. A. Robinson et al., "Religious and Spiritual Beliefs of Physicians," *Journal of Religion & Health* 56, no. 1 (2017): 205–25.

157 **A study of 339 oncology nurses:** M. J. Balboni et al., "Nurse and Physician Barriers to Spiritual Care Provision at the End of Life," *Journal*

of Pain and Symptom Management 48, no. 3 (2014): 400–410, https://doi
.org/10.1016/j.jpainsymman.2013.09.020.

157 **A 2012 study of 324 Polish physicians:** J. Pawlikowski, J. J. Sak, and K.
Marczewski, "Physicians' Religiosity and Attitudes towards Patients,"
Annals of Agricultural and Environmental Medicine 19, no. 3 (2012): 503–7.

157 **An ambitious 2014 study:** D. C. Malloy et al., "Religiosity and Ethical
Ideology of Physicians: A Cross-Cultural Study," *Journal of Religion
and Health* 53, no. 1 (2014): 244–54.

157 **A very large international collaborative study:** A. Kørup et al., "The
International NERSH Data Pool—a Methodological Description of
a Data Pool of Religious and Spiritual Values of Health Professionals
from Six Continents," *Religions* 8, no. 2 (2017): 24, https://doi.org/10.3390/
rel8020024. Most of the data have been collected and are being analyzed.

157 **One study points to:** Gabriele Prati, Luca Pietrantoni, and Elvira
Cicognani, "Coping Strategies and Collective Efficacy as Mediators
between Stress Appraisal and Quality of Life among Rescue Workers," *International Journal of Stress Management* 18, no. 2 (2011): 181–95.

157 **A 2016 meta-analysis combined:** A. F. Shariff et al., "Religious
Priming: A Meta-analysis with a Focus on Prosociality," *Personality
and Social Psychology Review* 20, no. 1 (2016): 27, https://doi.org/10
.1177/1088868314568811.

158 **Another 2016 meta-analysis:** Y. Hartberg, M. Cox, and S. Villamayor-
Tomas, "Supernatural Monitoring and Sanctioning in Community-
Based Resource Management," *Religion, Brain & Behavior* 6, no. 2
(2016): 95, https://doi.org/10.1080/2153599x.2014.959547

158 **A series of six cross-cultural studies:** Y. Bai et al., "Awe, the Dimin-
ished Self, and Collective Engagement: Universals and Cultural Variations in the Small Self," *Journal of Personality and Social Psychology*
113, no. 2 (2017): 185, https://doi.org/10.1037/pspa0000087.

158 **"women, on a religious day":** F. Pazhoohi, M. Pinho, and J. Arantes,
"Effect of Religious Day on Prosocial Behavior: A Field Study," *International Journal for the Psychology of Religion* 27, no. 2 (2017): 116,
https://doi.org/10.1080/10508619.2017.1301742.

158 **Another experiment, with shopkeepers:** E. P. Duhaime, "Is the Call
to Prayer a Call to Cooperate? A Field Experiment on the Impact of
Religious Salience on Prosocial Behavior," *Judgment and Decision Making* 10, no. 6 (2015): 593–96.

158 **Observers of extreme rituals:** P. Mitkidis et al., "The Effects of Extreme Rituals on Moral Behavior: The Performers-Observers Gap Hypothesis," *Journal of Economic Psychology* 59 (2017): 1–7, https://doi.org/10 .1016/j.joep.2016.12.007.

159 **In a milder challenge:** M. Lang et al., "Music as a Sacred Cue? Effects of Religious Music on Moral Behavior," *Frontiers in Psychology*, June 7, 2016, https://doi.org/10.3389/fpsyg.2016.00814.

160 **A 2017 study found:** M. A. Bruce et al., "Church Attendance, Allostatic Load and Mortality in Middle Aged Adults," *PLoS One* 12, no. 5 (2017).

160 **The Black Women's Health Study:** T. J. VanderWeele et al., "Attendance at Religious Services, Prayer, Religious Coping, and Religious/ Spiritual Identity as Predictors of All-Cause Mortality in the Black Women's Health Study," *American Journal of Epidemiology* 185, no. 7 (2017): 515–22, https://doi.org/10.1093/aje/kww179.

160 **The Nurses Health Study:** S. S. Li et al., "Association of Religious Service Attendance with Mortality among Women," *JAMA Internal Medicine* 176, no. 6 (2016): 777–85, https://doi.org/10.1001/jamainternmed.2016.1615.

160 **A 2015 meta-analysis:** H. S. L. Jim et al., "Religion, Spirituality, and Physical Health in Cancer Patients: A Meta-analysis," *Cancer* 121, no. 21 (2015): 3760–68, https://doi.org/10.1002/cncr.29353.

160 **Almost 37,000 patients in Tokyo:** D. Kobayashi et al., "The Relationship between Religiosity and Cardiovascular Risk Factors in Japan: A Large-Scale Cohort Study," *Journal of the American Society of Hypertension* 9, no. 7 (2015): 553–62, https://doi.org/10.1016/j.jash.2015.04.003.

161 **On Crete, in a rural town:** D. Anyfantakis et al., "Impact of Religiosity/ Spirituality on Biological and Preclinical Markers Related to Cardiovascular Disease. Results from the SPILI III Study," *Hormones: International Journal of Endocrinology and Metabolism* 12, no. 3 (2013): 386–96.

161 **In Thailand, 48 women:** P. C. Lundberg and S. Thrakul, "Religion and Self-Management of Thai Buddhist and Muslim Women with Type 2 Diabetes," *Journal of Clinical Nursing* 22, no. 13–14 (2013): 1907–16.

161 **In Saudi Arabia, 310 dialysis patients:** F. Al Zaben et al., "Religious Involvement and Health in Dialysis Patients in Saudi Arabia," *Journal of Religion & Health* 54, no. 2 (2015): 713, https://doi.org/10.1007/ s10943-014-9962-8.

161 **5,442 Canadians were followed:** A. T. Banerjee et al., "The Relationship between Religious Service Attendance and Coronary Heart Disease and

Related Risk Factors in Saskatchewan, Canada," *Journal of Religion & Health* 53, no. 1 (2014): 141–56, https://doi.org/10.1007/s10943-012-9609-6.

161 **After a recent catastrophic earthquake:** P. Stratta et al., "Spirituality and Religiosity in the Aftermath of a Natural Catastrophe in Italy," *Journal of Religion & Health* 52, no. 3 (2013): 1029–37, https://doi.org/10 .1007/s10943-012-9591-z.

162 **792 Hindus in rural northern India:** S. S. Khan et al., "Efficacy and Well-Being in Rural North India: The Role of Social Identification with a Large-Scale Community Identity, *European Journal of Social Psychology* 44, no. 7 (2014): 787–98, https://doi.org/10.1002/ejsp.2060.

162 **81 young African American women:** D. C. Cooper, J. F. Thayer, and S. R. Waldstein, "Coping with Racism: The Impact of Prayer on Cardiovascular Reactivity and Post-stress Recovery in African American Women," *Annals of Behavioral Medicine* 47, no. 2 (2014): 218–30, https://doi.org/10.1007/s12160-013-9540-4.

162 **In Denmark, one of the least:** H. F. Pedersen et al., "Religious Coping and Quality of Life among Severely Ill Lung Patients in a Secular Society," *International Journal for the Psychology of Religion* 23, no. 3 (2013): 188–203, https://doi.org/10.1080/10508619.2012.728068.

162 **And in Hungary, in 2002:** T. B. Konkolÿ et al., "Relationship between Religiosity and Health: Evidence from a Post-communist Country," *International Journal of Behavioral Medicine* 20, no. 4 (2013): 477–86, https://doi.org/10.1007/s12529-012-9258-x.

163 **Jesse Graham and Jonathan Haidt:** J. Graham and J. Haidt, "Beyond Beliefs: Religions Bind Individuals into Moral Communities," *Personality and Social Psychology Review* 14, no. 1 (2010): 140–50, https://doi .org/10.1177/1088868309353415.

163 **A 2017 study by Becky Read-Wahidi:** M. R. Read-Wahidi and J. A. DeCaro, "Guadalupan Devotion as a Moderator of Psychosocial Stress among Mexican Immigrants in the Rural Southern United States," *Medical Anthropology Quarterly* 31, no. 4 (2017): 572–91.

Chapter 11: If Not Religion, What?

165 **"the world needs to wake up":** Steven Weinberg, keynote address, *Beyond Belief* symposium, Session 1, MP4 video, about 0:28:00, http:// s3.amazonaws.com/thesciencenetwork/GoogleVideos%2FBB-1.mp4.

165 **"one of the staunchest atheists on the planet":** Richard Dawkins, presenta-

tion at *Beyond Belief* symposium, Session 3, MP4 video, about 0:28:40, http://s3.amazonaws.com/thesciencenetwork/GoogleVideos%2FBB-3.mp4.

165 **"If not religion, what?":** Steven Weinberg, at *Beyond Belief* symposium, Session 2, MP4 video, about 1:07:40, http://s3.amazonaws.com/thesciencenetwork/GoogleVideos%2FBB-2.mp4.

166 **"crazy old aunt":** Weinberg, at *Beyond Belief* symposium, Session 2, about 1:07:50.

166 **"Richard Dawkins declared":** Dawkins, presentation at *Beyond Belief* symposium, Session 3, about 0:30:20.

166 **"We would miss the music":** Dawkins, presentation at *Beyond Belief* symposium, Session 3, about 0:31:00.

167 **"Where there is devotional music":** Michael Marissen, "Bach Was Far More Religious Than You Might Think," *New York Times*, March 18, 2018, https://www.nytimes.com/2018/03/30/arts/music/bach-religion-music.html.

167 **The title, he says, "is from Keats":** Richard Dawkins, *Unweaving the Rainbow: Science, Delusion, and the Appetite for Wonder* (Boston: Houghton Mifflin, 1998), x.

167 **"There was an awful rainbow":** Dawkins, *Unweaving the Rainbow*, 39.

167 **"Light from the sun enters":** Dawkins, *Unweaving the Rainbow*, 48.

168 **"I think that if Wordsworth":** Dawkins, *Unweaving the Rainbow*, 47.

168 **"At his very best Akenside is":** E. Gosse, *A History of Eighteenth Century Literature (1660–1780)* (London: Macmillan, 1891), 312.

168 **"There shall be love between":** Walt Whitman, "The Preface to the 1855 Edition of *Leaves of Grass*," Modern American Poetry, accessed December 26, 2018, http://www.english.illinois.edu/maps/poets/s_z/whitman/preface.htm.

168 **"When I heard the learn'd astronomer":** Walt Whitman, *Leaves of Grass: Poems of Walt Whitman*, selected by Lawrence Clark Powell (New York: Thomas Y. Crowell, 1964).

169 **"The most beautiful thing":** Albert Einstein, "Reflections," in *Living Philosophies: The Reflections of Some Eminent Men and Women of Our Time*, ed. Clifton Fadiman (New York, Simon & Schuster, 1931), 6.

170 **soprano Renée Fleming's brain:** "Renée Fleming's Brain Scan: Understanding Music and the Mind," YouTube, published by the Kennedy Center, June 8, 2017, https://www.youtube.com/watch?v=1d-PlEAQMBY.

171 **"There is grandeur in this view of life":** Charles Darwin, *The Origin of Species by Means of Natural Selection, or the Preservation of Favored*

Races in the Struggle for Life (1859; repr., New York: New American Library, 1958), 416.

171 **"Pure mathematics is . . . the poetry":** From an obituary that Einstein wrote in the *New York Times* about mathematician Emmy Noether, quoted in Rose Simone, "The Poetry of Logical Ideas," Perimeter Institute for Theoretical Physics, accessed October 2, 2017, https://www.perimeterinstitute.ca/poetry-logical-ideas.

171 **"Single words, and conjunctions":** William James, *The Varieties of Religious Experience: A Study of Human Nature, Being the Gifford Lectures on Natural Religion Delivered at Edinburgh in 1901–1902, in Writings 1902–1910*, ed. Bruce Kucklick (New York: Library of America, 1902), 345.

174 **"Contrary to the forceful assertions":** Scott O. Lilienfeld and Rachel Amirrati, "Would the World Be Better Off Without Religion? A Skeptic's Guide to the Debate." *Skeptical Inquirer* 38, no. 4 (July/August 2014), https://www.csicop.org/si/show/would_the_world_be_better_off_without_religion_a_skeptics_guide_to_the_deba.

Epilogue

176 **And in every major religion:** Michael Blume, "The Reproductive Benefits of Religious Affiliation," in *The Biological Evolution of Religious Mind and Behavior*, ed. Eckart Voland and Wulf Schiefenhövel (Berlin: Springer, 2009), 117–26; Pew Research Center, "The Future of World Religions: Population Growth Projections, 2010–2050," April 2, 2015, http://www.pewforum.org/2015/04/02/religious-projections-2010–2050/#projected-growth-map.

177 **Viktor Frankl, a psychiatrist:** Viktor E. Frankl, *Man's Search for Meaning* (New York: Simon & Schuster, 1984).

178 **Questioned by a doctor:** Viktor E. Frankl, *Man's Search for Ultimate Meaning* (Cambridge, MA: Perseus, 2000), 142.

178 **"the disenchantment of the world":** David Barash, *Buddhist Biology: Ancient Eastern Wisdom Meets Modern Western Science* (New York: Oxford University Press, 2014), 25.

179 **"religion, art, and science created":** Augustin Fuentes, *The Creative Spark: How Imagination Made Humans Exceptional* (New York: Dutton/Penguin Random House, 2017), 189.

179 **"the great partnership":** Jonathan Sacks, *The Great Partnership: God, Science and the Search for Meaning* (London: Hodder & Stoughton, 2011).

Index

Index

Index

Index

Index

Index

Index

Index

Index

Index

Index

transcranial magnetic stimulation (TMS), 50

transmigration, 41

Tremlin, Todd, *Minds and Gods*, 101

Tremyugan shaman, 77

Trobriand Islands, 44

trust, 51

and trance, 38

Tu B'shvat, 69

Turanian tribes of North Asia, 42

Turkey, Göbekli Tepe, 145

twins, research on, 109

Tylor, Edward, 43, 141, 144

Primitive Culture, 40

unbelievers, xi

United States, "Nones" as trend in religious life, xiii

University of Cambridge, 144

Urgesi, Cosimo, 52

Vago, David, 59

values, 113–14

Vanuatu, 120

Vedas, 12

Vesalius, 5

violence, atheists on religion and, 150

Virgin of Guadalupe, 164

virtue, 21

Vishnu, 100

volunteerism, 116

Wakan-Tanka (Great Spirit), 66

war, causes, 150

Warao of Venezuela, 66

Weber, Max, 178

Weinberg, Steven, xviii–xix, 9, 165, 166

Western Europe, decline in religion, xix

Whitman, Walt, 168–69

Wilson, E.O., 21

wine, 74, 91

wish fulfillment, and false belief, 30

witchcraft, 138

Wittgenstein, Ludwig, 3

Wolpe, David, xvi

Wordsworth, William, 168

Wright, Robert, *Why Buddhism Is True*, 178

writings, vs. methods, 5

yoga, 24

Yoruba, 41

Zeus, 11